# Law in the United States, 2nd Edition

*Law in the United States, 2nd Edition*, is a concise presentation of the salient elements of the American legal system designed mainly for jurists of civil law backgrounds. It focuses on those attributes of American law that are likely to be least familiar to jurists from other legal traditions such as American common law, the federal structure of the U.S. legal system, and the American constitutional tradition. The use of comparative law technique permits foreign jurists to appreciate the American legal system in comparison with legal systems with which they are already familiar. Chapters of the second edition also cover such topics as American civil justice, criminal law, jury trial, choice of laws and international jurisdiction, the American legal profession, and the influence of American law in the global legal order.

Arthur T. von Mehren (1922–2006) was Professor of Law Emeritus at Harvard Law School. He represented the United States for thirty-eight years in the Hague Conference of Private International Law. He wrote 210 publications in English, French, Spanish, Italian, German, and Japanese. They include the groundbreaking *Civil Law System*, his pioneering two books and nine articles on Japanese law, his highly original *Law of Multistate Problems*, his foundational monographs on contract formation and form, his articles on jurisdiction, and his award-winning Hague lectures.

Peter L. Murray is the Robert Braucher Visiting Professor of Law from Practice at Harvard Law School. He served as the Faculty Director of the Harvard Legal Aid Bureau and continues to serve as Director of the Winter Trial Advocacy Workshop. He is the author of *Basic Trial Advocacy*, an advocacy training treatise; a co-author of Green, Nesson, and Murray's *Problems, Cases, & Materials on Evidence*; a co-author of Murray & Stürner, *German Civil Justice*; and an author and co-author of many legal articles. He has worked extensively in comparative law with particular reference to civil procedure in Germany and Europe.

# Law in the United States

## SECOND EDITION

### Arthur T. von Mehren

Harvard Law School

### Peter L. Murray

Harvard Law School

CAMBRIDGE UNIVERSITY PRESS

CAMBRIDGE UNIVERSITY PRESS
Cambridge, New York, Melbourne, Madrid, Cape Town, Singapore, São Paulo

Cambridge University Press
32 Avenue of the Americas, New York, NY 10013-2473, USA

www.cambridge.org
Information on this title: www.cambridge.org/9780521852067

First published 2007

Printed in the United States of America

*A catalog record for this publication is available from the British Library.*

*Library of Congress Cataloging in Publication Data*
von Mehren, Arthur Taylor.
Law in the United States / Arthur T. von Mehren, Peter L. Murray. – 2nd ed.
p. cm.
Includes bibliographical references and index.
ISBN-13: 978-0-521-85206-7 (hardback) – ISBN-10: 0-521-85206-4 (hardback)
ISBN-13: 978-0-521-61753-6 (pbk.) – ISBN-10: 0-521-61753-7 (pbk.)
1. Law – United States.   2. Comparative law.   I. Murray, Peter L.   II. Title.
KF385.V66   2007
349.73–dc22        2006028592

ISBN   978-0-521-85206-7 hardback
ISBN   978-0-521-61753-6 paperback

*To Arthur Taylor von Mehren*
*Scholar, Teacher, and Builder of International Bridges*
*1922–2006*

# Contents

Contents

Contents

Contents

# Preface

The first edition of this book was an outgrowth of a series of lectures that were given by Professor von Mehren in the fall of 1983 and the spring of 1984 at the University of Ghent, Belgium. Professor von Mehren explained the focus of the book in the Preface to the first edition in the following terms:

> A principal focus of my legal scholarship during the last four decades or so has been to compare the Civil Law (especially as expressed in the legal systems of France and Germany) with the Common Law. Only the last three chapters of *Law in the United States: A General and Comparative View* are fully and explicitly comparative. However, the book as a whole rests on a comparative foundation: The topics selected for discussion are those that seemed to me most basic for a foreign jurist's understanding of the American legal scene. The treatment given each subject seeks to be sensitive to how a jurist not trained in American law – or, more generally, in the Common Law – can most easily find his way in the complex of legal orders that collectively comprise law in the United States.
>
> The book is designed to introduce but to be more than introductory. The matters discussed are of fundamental importance and, on occasion, of considerable difficulty; my effort and hope are not only to impart essential information but also to give basic understanding.

In the nearly two decades since *Law in the United States* first appeared in 1987, jurists from around the world have found its systemic analysis and comparative approach helpful to reaching an understanding of the American legal system. Teachers of introductory courses on American law have used the work as a core text in their courses. The book's comparative orientation, which makes use of foreign jurists' preexisting knowledge of their own legal systems, has brought a richness to the dialogue that a purely descriptive approach would seem to lack.

The undersigned first used *Law in the United States* as a teaching text in a course on Introduction to American Law given at the University of Freiburg, Germany, in 1998. Although the first edition was allowed to go out of print by around 2000, it has continued as the core text in a number of long and short courses on the American legal system taught at Harvard Law School, the University of Freiburg, and the University of St. Gallen Master of European and International Business Law program in the years since. Over the years, supplementary materials have been created to cover areas of American law not treated in the first edition.

Although there had been discussions with Professor von Mehren about a second edition for some years, it took John Berger of the Cambridge University Press to get the project off the ground. His suggestion in 2003 that it was high time for a new edition of Professor von Mehren's small classic resulted in the collaboration for this volume.

The second edition retains virtually all of the contents of the first edition, although updated and somewhat rearranged to facilitate use of the work as a course text. This rearrangement reflects the junior author's preferences from nearly ten years of teaching in this area. As was the case with the first edition, the chapters are configured to be more or less freestanding, so that colleagues can freely select and rearrange the material to suit their own pedagogical approaches. Chapters 2 (American Common Law), 6 (American Civil Justice), 9 (Choice of Law, International Civil Jurisdiction, and Recognition of Judgments in the United States), and 10 (The American Legal Profession) contain considerable additional material new to the second edition. Chapters 7 (American Criminal Justice), 8 (American Trial by Jury), and 11 (The United States and the Global Legal Community) are entirely new.

Although all the new and updated material in the second edition was discussed with Professor von Mehren, the original plan that he would carefully review and contribute to all of the new and revised material was frustrated by his untimely death on January 6, 2006. Thus, only Chapters 1 and 2 bear the imprint of his recent editing. For the remaining new material in the second edition, the undersigned bears the responsibility and, for any errors, the sole blame.

During the last thirteen years of his productive life as Joseph Story Professor of Law Emeritus at Harvard Law School, Professor von Mehren was assisted by a succession of gifted young German law academics, the Joseph Story Research Fellows. Following Professor von Mehren's death, the last phases of preparation of the manuscript for the second edition were greatly aided by the helpful assistance of Dr. Eckart Gottschalk, the last Story Fellow, who carefully read each chapter and contributed helpful comments and suggestions.

Professor von Mehren's extraordinary career as international legal scholar and teacher has been of immense meaning and influence on many levels in the United States and abroad. This second edition is dedicated to his memory.

Peter L. Murray
Cambridge, Massachusetts
July 2006

# The Sources of American Law

A CONSIDERATION OF THE SOURCES OF LAW IN A LEGAL order must deal with a variety of different, although related, matters. Historical roots and derivations need explanation. The system's formal allocation of authority over the creation and adaptation of legal rules and principles deserves attention, as do the manner in which legal rules are presented and the processes of analysis through which they are applied. Finally, those structural features somewhat particular to the legal system that may affect significantly its general style and operational modes should be discussed.

## A. HISTORICAL ROOTS

Historically speaking, American private law's source is the English common law. The reception on the North American continent of the common law is considered in Chapter 2, The American common law. A few words can be said here respecting certain structural features of the common law thus received that have particular importance for American law's general style and modes of operation.

The common law makes extensive use of juries in the administration of civil as well as criminal justice. The jury, which always deliberates separately from the judge, is basically responsible for deciding disputed issues of fact. Widespread use of juries carries with it a number of consequences, some of which are mentioned later in this chapter or considered in greater detail in Chapters 6 and 8. These include concentration of the trial at first instance into a single episode, the development of a sophisticated and complex body of exclusionary rules of evidence, and giving community feelings and views greater weight in the administration of justice than is the case where professionals alone bear responsibility.

Another ramification of jury trial is the unacceptability of the civil law principle of *double degré de juridiction*. In a jury-trial system, there is no opportunity to redo the case at the first level of appellate review. On the one hand, considerations of cost and feasibility stand in the way of constituting a jury for each appeal in which factual issues might be raised; on the other, allowing appellate courts, sitting without juries, to decide contested factual issues would drastically reduce the significance of jury trial. Accordingly, American appellate review is limited to questions of law, including whether the evidence presented at first instance was sufficient to justify a reasonable trier of fact making particular findings.

Another characteristic of the common law derives from the emergence, alongside the traditional common law courts, of a separate judicial hierarchy, the courts of equity. These courts developed and administered a body of rules and principles – the law of equity – that supplemented the common law. By the fourteenth and fifteenth centuries, the King's courts had become in many matters rigid and narrow in their approach. Over the years, the kinds of issues needing adjudication had expanded beyond the traditional jurisdiction of these courts to include matters ill suited to their jury trial processes and the common law doctrines they applied. Reform could have been accomplished by reshaping the common law, but this approach would have required creative judicial activity in a degree and at a rate that was perhaps then unacceptable. The needed changes could also have been undertaken by the legislature; however, the society of the time was not accustomed to such extensive legislative intervention. Allowing a new body of rules and principles to emerge from the work of a different judicial hierarchy provided a solution that avoided these difficulties and was compatible with the judicial process's central position in the legal order.

An uneasy truce between common law and equity was maintained by the principle that equity would act only where the remedy at law was inadequate. For example, the law courts did not grant specific performance of contracts. Equity would order specific performance but only if money damages – the remedy at law – could not put the obligee in a position substantially equivalent to that which he or she would have enjoyed had the contract been performed. Unlike the courts of law, equity was prepared to recognize a distinction between legal and equitable interests and entitlements; the law of trusts, developed by the courts of equity, rests on this distinction.

Although the equity courts, like the common law courts, operated without any abstract code of legal principles, either substantive or procedural, the equity courts frequently cited and purported to apply more or less abstract "maxims" of equity as guides to decision making. However, most of these maxims, such as "equity will not leave undone that which ought to have been done," were couched at such a level of generality that they could be and frequently were cited to support almost any conceivable equitable argument or disposition.

The courts of equity not only administered a special body of rule and principle, they also differed institutionally from the common law courts. For example, equity did not use juries. As a consequence, trials in equity could – and did – proceed as a series of episodes, whereas the trial at law was a single, continuous event. The absence of the jury also affected the law of evidence; in particular, exclusionary rules had in equity courts much less importance than at law.

The existence of parallel and overlapping judicial hierarchies always creates complications for a legal system. By the nineteenth century in both England and the United States, these complications had become considerable; furthermore, law reform no longer depended on the existence of separate courts of equity. American courts of law and equity alike had demonstrated a creative capacity; moreover, legislation now provided an effective means of law reform. The New York Constitution of 1846 abolished the court of chancery; the New York Code of Civil Procedure (1848), drafted by David Dudley Field, merged law and equity. By 1900, the movement thus begun had been emulated by many sister states.

The disappearance of separate courts of equity did not, however, do away with the law of equity. That body of rule and principle still complements the body of rule and principle deriving from the work of the common law courts. Moreover, the historical distinction between proceedings at law and in equity continues to have procedural consequences. In particular, the right to trial by jury, guaranteed by the U.S. Constitution and by the constitutions of several states (e.g., Constitution of Massachusetts, Articles XII and XV), does not attach to matters that historically were within the equity jurisdiction.

The emergence in England of a separate hierarchy of courts of equity did not foreshadow a general proliferation of judicial hierarchies. In particular, neither in England nor in the United States did a separate system of administrative courts emerge; matters falling within what the French call the *droit administratif* and the Germans *Verwaltungsrecht* are handled by the regular courts.

## B. ALLOCATION OF AUTHORITY TO CREATE AND ADAPT LEGAL RULES AND PRINCIPLES

With the Declaration of Independence in 1776, the former colonies fully controlled the allocation of authority over the creation and adaptation of their public and private laws. Colonial history and the form taken by the struggle to obtain independence led to the new states breaking with English tradition by adopting written state constitutions, such as the Constitution of Massachusetts adopted in 1780. These state constitutions constitute the ultimate source of state law; they formally allocate the authority to make and adapt law.

The importance of the Constitution of the United States (1789) as a source of American law and the special role played by the U.S. Supreme Court are discussed in Chapter 5. In this chapter, the allocation of lawmaking and adapting authority is discussed in general terms with special attention given to the work of the courts.

American state constitutional arrangements provide for legislatures; subject to such limitations as flow from the state or federal constitution, these have ultimate formal authority to make and to change law. With rapid and pervasive changes in economic, political, and social circumstances, such as those occurring late in the nineteenth century and throughout the twentieth century, legislatively formulated rules and principles have assumed ever-increasing importance. This is particularly true of public law. Although the American colonies inherited and applied a common law of crimes for a time after the Revolution, it is safe to say that by the end of the nineteenth century all American public law had its formal source in legislation.

The product of American legislatures is not, of course, to be compared to a European code, but rather to more usual legislative products. It is worth remarking that, on occasion, the denominations carried by American legislative products can be misleading. For example, the Federal Internal Revenue Code – a highly complex, very detailed, and extremely specific corpus of rules – is the polar opposite to a continental code with its generalized, structured, and systematized statement of rules and principles.

This increase in the importance of the legislature's role ultimately brought about a decline in the relative importance of the role of courts in creating and adapting the law. However, the new constitutions did not seek to limit – let alone eliminate – the creative role of courts. Subject to legislative preemption, judicial decisions remained a source of law. Moreover, the advent of written constitutions was to give judicial decisions ultimate primacy over legislation with respect to issues regulated by constitutional provisions.

Another source of law – one whose importance has increased dramatically in the course of the twentieth century – is executive and administrative action. Administrative regulations and decisions shape many areas of contemporary law. Although in theory they could in large part be set aside or revised by legislation or by judicial decision, administrative regulations and decisions today constitute an extremely important source of law.

Starting during the twentieth century, American courts have asserted a kind of legislative competence to promulgate court rules governing procedure and other matters relating to the courts and even the practice of law in general. The exercise of this authority has occasionally brought the courts into conflict with the legislature, as was the case with the promulgation of the Federal Rules of Evidence in the early 1970s. Despite concerns about the scope and democratic legitimacy of court rulemaking, court rules are now an important source of procedural law at the federal level and in many states and also govern regulation of the bar in some states.

In discussing sources of law, it is traditional to consider the role of custom. Here, the American and western European situations are similar. For example, trade practices and usages play a significant role in commercial life and can be of great importance in interpreting contracts. However, if "source" is understood in a more formal sense, custom has relatively little contemporary importance.

## 1. The Judicial Decision

Because the forms and techniques of legislation and administrative decisions in the United States are, on the one hand, fairly readily understandable by a jurist with a civil law background and, on the other, the judicial decision is in common law systems a source of law of central importance, a discussion of these sources appropriately gives more attention to the judicial decision than to legislation or executive action.

Some general observations serve to set the stage. In the common law, a court's opinion gives a far more explicit and complete explanation of the court's reasoning than is true in French or German law. The opinion is written by one judge and bears his or her name. Other judges are free to concur or dissent in separate, reasoned, and signed opinions. Unlike continental European courts, American courts do not face the outside world as a single authority that always speaks with only one unanimous and anonymous voice.

In view of the role of the judicial decision as a source of law, the existence of an extensive system of reporters, both official and unofficial, does not surprise. Following the English tradition, from the earliest days of statehood, each state court of last resort has published its decisions in bound volumes available for purchase by lawyers and the public. The unofficial – but important – National Reporter System has covered state court decisions (principally appellate) from at least 1887 to the present.

This vast body of decisional material had to be organized so that the relevant decisions could be located with reasonable dispatch and certainty. Because comprehensive codes did not exist at earlier periods and are still today by no means the rule, the full corpus of decisional law cannot be made available by annotating codes as is typical in civil law systems. Instead, an elaborate system for analyzing and digesting cases was devised. The American Digest System, created near the end of the nineteenth century, covers reports of appellate cases from 1658 onward. By using key numbers, decisions that deal with a given issue are brought together. Access to the decisional law is also possible through words and phrases that typically occur in decisions dealing with the type of problem that has arisen. A further selection among the decisions thus located can be made in terms of date and jurisdiction.

Modern computer technology today makes the search for authority much more rapid and less subject to error and omission than in the past. The digest system described previously can be searched by computer. Furthermore, entire decisions are now entered into databases that one can consult by asking for material containing key words or by presenting a selected pattern of words.

In view of the principle of *stare decisis*, discussed herein, a jurist must know whether decisions have been overruled or otherwise limited. *Shepard's Citations* and other online services permit a lawyer to check quickly on a decision's status. Here again, the computer now simplifies the lawyer's task.

What effect does an American judicial decision have? The first effect is one recognized by all legal systems. Subject only to the possibilities for revision or reversal provided by the legal order, an end is put to the controversy before the court. This quietus may be temporary – for example, dismissal of the action as prematurely brought – or permanent – judgment for the plaintiff or the defendant on the merits. In all events, the court is, at a minimum, obliged to decide an issue that disposes of the controversy at least temporarily. As in civil law systems, courts are not to refuse to decide because the relevant law is obscure or nonexistent.

The second effect of an American decision is somewhat particular to common law systems; the decision creates a precedent that will control the disposition of later cases in which the same issue or issues arise. The principle of precedent, or *stare decisis*, combines two propositions.

The first is a principle of hierarchy: The lower court is under a duty to accept the position held on any given issue by its hierarchical superior. Because the decided case is, in its own right, a source of law, the fact that the lower court thinks the decision wrong does not justify its ignoring the precedent. In civil law systems, where codes are a formal source of law but decisions are not, lower courts have at least in theory the freedom to depart from previous decisions of hierarchically superior courts. Of course, as a practical matter in the great majority of cases, lower courts in all systems accept the positions taken by their hierarchical superiors. The latter ultimately have the last word if review is sought; the lower court's taking of a different view usually simply makes the administration of justice more expensive.

The second proposition that flows from the principle of *stare decisis* is that a court is bound by its *own* previous decisions. Unlike the hierarchical principle, this proposition is not a logical entailment of the view that judicial decisions are a source of law. However, practical considerations argue strongly for this view, especially where there is no code to give the law structure and coherence. Considerations of equality of treatment, predictability, and economy of effort all support the proposition that a court should, in principle, follow its previous decisions. To the extent that these considerations are sociologically based, of course they operate in civil law systems as well; the highest courts in these systems exhibit a strong tendency to follow their previous decisions. However, the civil law view that the judicial decision is not, in principle, a source of law means that prior decisions do not enjoy the same standing as in the common law.

Not all common law jurisdictions take the same position respecting the extent to which a court is bound to its own previous decision. Furthermore, not only are broad cyclical patterns to be observed, but also any given court may change its attitude toward *stare decisis* from era to era. Most, perhaps all, courts of last resort in the United States have felt and still feel a considerable sense of freedom; they remain more willing to overrule their previous decisions than British courts of last resort.

These different views respecting the requirements of *stare decisis* obviously cannot be explained as logical entailments of the proposition that judicial decisions are a formal source of law. Nothing in the concept of source requires that only one creative effort be permitted with respect to any given issue. The differences that have emerged are rather to be explained in intellectual, political, and sociological terms.

In the first place, the American federal system – by placing control over most private-law matters in the states of the union – makes it likely that for many issues, more than one solution will emerge. Because of the numerous channels of communication among jurists in the several states and because so much of legal education is national rather than local, a comparative dimension is present in American law that historically has no true counterpart in English law. This comparative dimension facilitates persuasive criticism of the results reached in previous decisions.

Also of importance is the American experience in adapting a received law to a new society and a new environment. In carrying out that task, jurists constantly had to face the relationship between social and economic circumstance and decisional law.

The effectiveness and capacity for decisive action that the British parliamentary system possesses are also of significance here. A court of last resort in Great Britain can have rather greater confidence than its American counterpart that the rule it announces in a decision will be rectified by legislation if the society so desires.

Even were American legislatures more likely to correct judicial decisions respecting ordinary legal issues than the foregoing analysis suggests, the legislatures have no power to change – even prospectively – court resolutions of constitutional issues through the ordinary legislative process. Here, the judicial decision enjoys primacy over legislation as a source of law. Accordingly, at least in this area, the strict English view of *stare decisis* had in the United States far more important consequences than in Great Britain, where the rule established by any judicial decision can be changed by Parliament. Of course, a distinction can be drawn between the constitutional and nonconstitutional cases for purposes of *stare decisis*; indeed, to some extent, American courts make this distinction. However, a spillover effect from the position considered appropriate for constitutional decisions to other decisions is natural and perhaps inevitable.

Use of a principle of *stare decisis*, even one that is not as rigid and absolute as the English principle once was – and, at least as formally stated, largely still is – entails a particular way of analyzing judicial decisions; reasonable limits to the decision's *stare decisis* effects are set by making a distinction between what in the decision is essential and what is incidental. The line drawn is usually between holding and dictum. The holding is limited to the point or points on which the court rested – or, in a stricter version, had to rest – its disposition of the case. The rest of what was said is dictum and does not fall within the scope of the principle of *stare decisis*. A dictum has a degree of persuasiveness, but a court is free to disregard its own dicta, and the principle of hierarchy does not require a lower court to accept the dicta of its hierarchical superior.

Views can and do differ on just what constitutes a holding, both as a matter of general theory and with respect to a particular decision. Because in deciding cases courts necessarily combine propositions of law and propositions of fact, what the court actually holds is normally open to discussion. By emphasizing or de-emphasizing the factual elements in the decisional equation, the holding can be contracted or expanded.

Where the principle of *stare decisis* is recognized, a distinction such as that between holding and dictum is unavoidable if the courts are to retain some freedom for change and development. However, the distinction also rests on prudential considerations and on the view that courts can wisely decide only the case or controversy presented to them. The reluctance of courts in common law systems to give advisory opinions is similarly based; to decide wisely, courts need the discipline that flows the effort to relate abstract propositions to precise factual situations.

John Marshall (1755–1833), the greatest Chief Justice that the U.S. Supreme Court has ever had, in discussing *Marbury v. Madison* in the later case of *Cohens v. Virginia*, 19 U.S. (6 Wheat.) 364, 399–400 (1821), made the point clearly and effectively:

> It is a maxim not to be disregarded, that general expressions, in every opinion, are to be taken in connection with the case in which those expressions are used. If they go beyond the case, they may be respected, but ought not to control the judgment in a subsequent suit when the very point is presented for decision. The reason of this maxim is obvious. The question actually before the Court is investigated with care, and considered in its full extent. Other principles which may serve to illustrate it are considered in their relation to the case decided, but their possible bearing on all other cases is seldom completely investigated.

The complexities that the principle of *stare decisis* brings with it are not limited to the problem of distinguishing holding from dictum. What, for example, is the precedential status of a holding that rests on more than one ground where not all of the grounds reach to the matter now up for decision? Courts have taken various positions on this question; today, it is of less importance than in the past because rather looser views of precedent are now held quite generally.

One further issue that arises where judicial decisions are a source of law deserves brief consideration: Does the overruling of a prior decision have retroactive effect? The answer, as far as previously decided cases are concerned, is plainly no; the principle and policy of *res judicata* prevail. But what is the situation with respect to transactions, not yet litigated, but entered into before the overruling occurred? At one time the answer, although based on a formal and debatable proposition, was thought to be clear: Because courts declare – rather than make – law, the law had always been the same and no issue of retroactivity arises.

In an era that explicitly recognizes judicial decisions as a source of law, this explanation will not do. The problem is now seen to involve practical considerations. For reasons that relate to differences between the judicial and legislative processes, the latter's general rule of nonretroactivity is usually not applied when an overruling occurs. One must, therefore, assume the risk of a change of decisional law with retroactive effects, even though had the change been made by legislation, only prospective effects would have attached. In some situations, a Supreme Court will declare that an overruling has only prospective effects. In other cases, the court will refrain from overruling a precedent but declare that, in future litigation, the precedent will no longer be applied. Although by no means commonplace, these practices are increasingly encountered, especially in criminal cases raising constitutional issues. The development is one of the signs that contemporary American courts are giving greater emphasis to their law-making function even at some possible expense to their responsibility for dispute-resolution functions.

## 2. Legislation

Except with respect to constitutional issues, from the birth of American law at the end of the eighteenth century, legislation has enjoyed primacy as a source of law in theory, if not always in practice. With the increasing complexity of economic and social life, the amount and importance of legislation have increased; this is especially true of federal legislation.

Because the United States is a federal system, its legislative hierarchy is relatively complex. Article VI of the U.S. Constitution provides:

> This Constitution, and the Laws of the United States which shall be made in Pursuance thereof; and all Treaties made, or which shall be made, under the Authority of the United States, shall be the supreme Law of the Land; and the Judges in every States shall be bound thereby, any Thing in the Constitution or Laws of any State to the Contrary notwithstanding.

Within the area of federal authority, treaties and federal statutes are authoritative with the later in date controlling in the event of conflict. The next level of federal authority is that of executive orders and administrative rules and regulations. (In some matters, however, the executive branch exercises authority independently of legislative permission or sanction.)

As the Tenth Amendment (1791) to the U.S. Constitution makes explicit,

> The powers not delegated to the United States by the Constitution, nor prohibited by it to the States, are reserved to the States respectively, or to the people.

Within each state, the hierarchy of authority parallels that described previously for the federal government: state constitution, statutes, administrative rules and regulations, and – on the municipal level – ordinances, rules, and regulations all provide authoritative rules and principles here appropriate.

Because at least until modern times the growing point of the common law was in the courts rather than the legislature, the common law held a conception of legislation very different from that found in the civil law. In *Heydon's Case* (1548), 3 Coke 7a, 7b Eng. Rep. 637 (K.B. 1584), Lord Coke assumed that the body of law that rested on judicial decisions was a complete and coherent system. Therefore, a statute was to be construed to suppress only the particular mischief it was intended to cure. In consequence, statutes were not seen as containing germinating principles or as providing a basis for reasoning by analogy.

In the nineteenth century, American courts accepted this view of statutes and construed legislation strictly and narrowly. The proposition that "statutes in derogation of the common law are to be strictly construed" found its way into judicial opinions construing legislative provisions. The twentieth century saw a relaxation of this view. For example, the Restatement of the Law Second, Contracts 2d (1979), bases several of its propositions on reasoning by analogy from provisions contained in the Uniform Commercial Code.

The doctrine of precedent also applies to judicial decisions interpreting statutes. Indeed, early in this century, it was often said that *stare decisis* operates more strictly where statutory interpretation is in issue because legislative silence in effect confirms the judicial interpretation. Today, the competing view is urged by many jurists that *stare decisis* as applied to decisions interpreting statutes does not differ fundamentally from *stare decisis* where case law is in question. The civil law takes, of course, a third and diametrically opposed view; a court is not bound by previous judicial interpretations of legislation even if the interpretation emanates from a hierarchically superior court. Here again, we see the consequence of the differences in the positions that courts have traditionally occupied in these two legal traditions – differences that entail the common law's acceptance of the judicial decision as a formal source of law.

In civil law systems the most important form taken by legislation in the area of private law is the code. In conception and style, these codes are emanations of the legal science that developed over the centuries in continental European universities. Codes exhibit the qualities of comprehensiveness, high-level generality, and internal coherence. Although in the common law, statutes are seen as remedies for particular mischiefs, a civil law code provides comprehensive and systematic solutions that are to be found not only in explicit code provisions but also by drawing analogies or by reasoning *a contrario* from code provisions. Either explicitly or implicitly, codes thus provide – at least in a strictly formal sense – solutions to all the issues that can arise with regard to the sector of economic or social life to which their provisions are directed.

The codification ideal has at times attracted American jurists. A movement for codification emerged in the United States around the middle of the nineteenth century largely due to the efforts of David Dudley Field (1805–1894), a distinguished New York lawyer. On his initiative, two commissions were established in 1847 in New York, one to reform civil and criminal procedure, the other to codify the substantive law. Largely through Field's efforts, the practice commission had by 1848 prepared a Code of Civil Procedure. This Code went into effect in 1849. By 1850, the commission presented complete codes of civil and criminal procedure. The former, which revised and substantially extended the scope of the Code of 1849, was never enacted; the latter was ultimately adopted in 1882. The substantive-law commission, which also reported in 1850, had made far less progress; indeed, a majority of that commission doubted not only the feasibility but also the wisdom of codification of the substantive law. The natural consequence was the commission's abolition. In 1857, Field was able to secure the appointment of a new commission to codify "the whole body of the law." By 1865, this commission had added to the complete codes of civil and criminal procedure, presented in 1850, codes of penal law, civil law, and political law. The legislature passed the civil code in 1879, but the governor vetoed the measure at the instigation of the New York bar. All subsequent efforts to enact the civil code likewise failed. The controversy was finally ended in 1883 for New York by James C. Carter's – Field's arch opponent – paper on "The Proposed Codification of Our Common Law." This paper, perhaps an American analogue to Savigny's *Vom Beruf unserer Zeit für Gesetzgebung und Rechtswissenschaft*, originally published in 1814 and in English translation in 1831, was read on December 13, 1883, at a meeting of the Committee of the Association of the Bar of the City of New York, appointed "to urge the rejection of the proposed [Field] Civil Code" and unanimously approved.[1]

Of Field's codes, the civil procedure code had the widest influence. Ultimately, it was adopted by some thirty states. Sixteen states adopted the penal code and the code of criminal procedure. Five states, including California, adopted and retained Field's civil code. Do these adoptions indicate that by the end of the nineteenth century the codification ideal had taken root in at least some states of the United States?

Consideration of the fate of Field's civil code in California suggests a negative answer. In 1884, Professor Pomeroy published in California an article in which he argued that the code's provisions were to be regarded as declaratory of common law and of equitable rules and doctrines except where a clear intent to depart from these was discernible. He based his position on the proposition that, because the code did not provide explicit answers for many questions, it should not constitute the primary source of

---

[1]  J. Carter, *The Proposed Codification of the Common Law* (N.Y., 1884), p. 3.

the law of private rights. The unspoken premise is that the code is not an organic and coherent whole and, accordingly, does not provide a starting point for legal reasoning. Therefore, it is to be disregarded except where it gives specific answers. Essentially, Professor Pomeroy viewed the California civil code as the common law viewed an ordinary statute.

Some jurists were prepared to take the opposite point of view and treat the code as a fresh start to be developed on the basis of analogical reasoning. However, Pomeroy's position prevailed. The code came to be looked upon as a compilation and systematization of common law rules and principles with some revisions and improvements. Many states of the United States have today so-called codes; however, these codes are for the most part viewed as Pomeroy viewed the civil code of California.

As our third millennium begins, much of American state and federal legislation is arranged in "codes," such as "The United States Code Annotated." These codes are for the most part merely convenient, sometimes unofficial, groupings of legislation according to subject matter. They do not pretend to the status or function of civil law codifications.

Probably the most recent effort to reach a codification of an area of law that would be comparable to a civil law code is the Uniform Commercial Code. This project commenced in the 1930s and culminated in the 1960s with the adoption of most articles by all American jurisdictions. The sponsoring organization was a partnership of the American Law Institute and the National Conference of Commissioners on Uniform State Laws. The Uniform Commercial Code was conceived of as a codification of American commercial law in the areas of sales, commercial paper, payments, letters of credit, transfers of investment securities, and secured transactions in personal property at a level of system and abstract coherence that would go beyond ordinary American legislation. One of the chief authors of this project, Professor Karl Llewellan, was, in part, a product of a civil law legal education. The goal of systematic abstraction was achieved in varying degrees in the codes provisions. For the most part, however, one does not find the systematic and organic structure and the relatively high degree of generalization typical of codes in civil law systems. One must conclude, therefore, that only modest movement has occurred in contemporary American juridical thinking in the direction of viewing "codes" as fresh starts rather than mere compilations, systematizations, and declarations of judicially established propositions.

## 3. Court Rules

An important source of American civil and criminal procedural law that is virtually unknown in the civil law world is court rule making. Although traditionally court law-making activity was confined to judicial decisions, since the early twentieth century, American courts have increasingly turned to the promulgation of generalized legislation-like rules to govern court procedure and related matters. The authority for this quasilegislative activity has come in some cases from enabling acts adopted by legislatures and in other cases from the court's own conception of its authority as an independent branch of government to regulate its own activities.

The Federal Rules of Civil Procedure, adopted in the late 1930s, were the first comprehensive attempt at judicial legislation of this kind. The Rules were developed by an Advisory Committee consisting of eminent judges, lawyers, and legal academics and were considered and promulgated by the U.S. Supreme Court to govern civil procedure in the various U.S. District Courts under its overall oversight. Sanctioned by federal enabling legislation, the success of the Federal Rules of Civil Procedure led many states to adopt the court-rules model for procedural law.

The civil rules were followed by Federal Rules of Criminal Procedure, Federal Rules of Appellate Procedure, and Federal Rules of Evidence, all products of similar processes. The last led to a kind of confrontation with the U.S. Congress, which feared that the creation of rules governing the admissibility and adequacy of proof and the obligations of persons to provide evidence would not only determine case outcomes but could also affect out-of-court behavior of ordinary citizens. When the Court, acting without the support of specific enabling legislation, promulgated the new evidence rules in 1973, Congress passed legislation suspending their effectiveness and ultimately enacted a set of rules of its own, granting the Court the authority to amend and supplement the legislatively enacted rules through a process that would allow Congress the opportunity to act to block changes that it did not approve.

In recent years, court rule-making activities have been extended in some states to all aspects of the operations of the civil and criminal justice systems and even to the regulation of the legal profession in general. In states such as Massachusetts and Maine, where the tradition of judicial independence is particularly strong, all aspects of licensing and regulation of the legal profession are now governed by rules promulgated by state supreme courts. These rules are generally published along with judicial decisions and are made available to practitioners in printed pamphlets and online.

## 4. Secondary Sources

There is one route over which the style of thought and presentation embodied in civil law codes has achieved a significant degree of acceptance by American jurists. The American federal system, with its diversity of private law, has given impetus to what can be considered an unofficial form of codification, the Restatements of the Law sponsored by the American Law Institute (ALI). Restatements have only persuasive authority but they importantly influence the administration of justice.

The ALI is a private organization that brings together judges, practitioners, and scholars. Concern with the uncertainty and complexity of American common law led to the Institute's creation in 1923 by a group of distinguished judges, lawyers, and legal academics. Its task was to produce systematic and concise statements of the rules and principles derived from a study of the myriad reported American decisions. "Restatements" present the area of law in question in a comprehensive, generalized, and systematic form; the dispositive propositions advanced are printed in "black letter" sections, which can be compared with the articles of a civil law code. Deference is paid to the common law tradition by supplying for each black-letter section comments, illustrations, and a reporter's note.

The institute appoints a reporter to draft each restatement as well as a group of advisers with whom he or she consults. Their product is reviewed within the institute by the members of the project's advisory committee and the council of the institute. Once this process, which often takes a decade or more, has been completed, the restatement is promulgated by the institute at an annual meeting.

The first restatement to be finished was the Restatement of the Law of Contracts, promulgated in May 1932. It was followed by other restatements dealing with such subjects as Agency, Conflict of Laws, Foreign Relations Law, Judgments, Property, Restitution, Security, Torts, and Trusts. After World War II, the institute undertook the task of reexamining and revising the existing restatements. Among the revisions that have been promulgated are Restatements of the Law Second for Agency, Conflict of Laws, Contracts, Property (Landlord and Tenant), Torts, and Trusts.

The restatements have been influential not only for the specific solutions they provide but also due to their general style of legal thinking and analysis. Their presentation of areas of law in comprehensive, generalized, and systematic terms has encouraged thinking along these lines on the part of judges, lawyers, and scholars.

One further source, also secondary in character, of American law deserves brief consideration: American legal scholarship. For reasons that relate to the characteristics of the common law tradition as well as the emphasis on discussion and on facts in American law teaching, comprehensive treatises are much less common than in civil law countries. Moreover, American treatises give much more attention than their continental European analogues to discrete factual situations and detailed analysis of decisional law.

Outstanding comprehensive treatises were produced in the twentieth century by such well-known scholars as Arthur Corbin, Austin Scott, Henry Wigmore, and Samuel Williston. However, the energy of American legal scholarship, which is considerable, has in large measure gone into monographs, law review articles, and course (or case) books. Here again is seen the common law's penchant for dealing with specific matters rather than with generalized problems and situations.

As a secondary source of law, American legal scholarship has been and remains significantly more important for the work of American courts than is English legal scholarship for English courts. Early in the history of American law, the writings of such great nineteenth-century text writers as Kent and Story were influential not only for practitioners but also for judges. By the end of the nineteenth century, there existed in the United States a strong desire to achieve structure, system, and unity for a private law that was now continental in its economic and social aspects but remained parochial because the several states controlled its substance and administration. One way of overcoming parochialism was seen to be the creation of a national legal scholarship that could unify and rationalize American private law. Scholarship thus assumed a role somewhat comparable to that which it had played on the continent of Europe before the great nineteenth-century codifications.

Contemporary American legal scholarship finds a major outlet in law reviews published at the nation's law schools and other institutions of scholarship. Many legal journals are published at law schools and edited by select boards of student editors, whose energy and attention to detail in selecting and editing articles by academics and practitioners contributes much to American legal scholarship.

## C. FINDING AMERICAN LAW

Finding the legal principle that is applicable to resolve a particular question of American law can be a difficult and daunting task. The division of law-making authority between the American states and the federal government, and between the states themselves, gives rise to a choice of law issues of considerable complexity in all but the simplest of cases. Which law will apply, state or federal? And if state law applies, which state's law? American choice of law doctrine is discussed in Chapter 9.

Once it has been determined which jurisdiction's law will apply, if the question is one within the ambit of the common law, the practitioner must search out the relevant reported judicial decisions that will furnish the answer to the question posed. The volume and variety of legal material in print and online mean that a researcher has many routes that can be followed in search of an answer to a legal question.

Assume, for instance, that a lawyer wishes to determine whether his client, who has been subjected to a distasteful and alarming experience, can recover from other involved parties for the negligent infliction of emotional distress. How will the lawyer determine whether the law to be applied supports such a claim?

The first question is usually which law will apply to the issue in question. Although ordinary torts are usually subject to state law, under certain conditions, such as those involving unlawful discrimination, federal law can provide an additional or even preemptive remedy. Sometimes the conflicts rules of several jurisdictions may be relevant.

Once the potentially concerned jurisdictions have been ascertained, the lawyer must review their law, including their legislation. All state statutes of general application are collected and published, usually in "codes" with indices and often annotations to cases applying or interpreting the legislative provisions. These "codes" are not like civil law codes but rather are mere collections of relevant statutory material by subject matter, without attempt at comprehensiveness or logical abstract consistency. Reference to these indices, or online word searching using key words such as "emotional distress," should lead to any legislative provisions that might touch on the question to be answered.

Even cases that are governed by legislation may also be governed in part by case law. Thus, the lawyer needs to find the relevant cases or "cases in point." These are the reported cases that have a high factual similarity with the facts under consideration or that discuss the principles likely to be involved. Most of the time, it is well to precede case searching by "reading around" the subject matter of the question in a treatise or law review article. This secondary literature can provide the conceptual organization and systematic analysis that can help refine the question and relate it to existing case law. Secondary literature also frequently contains citations to key cases in the area that can serve as handles for further case searching. If a Restatement covers the relevant area of law, it may furnish a good starting point for case-law research.

Once research in secondary authority has given the lawyer an idea of the logical parameters of the question and which facts are likely to be of significance, the lawyer will turn to the traditional tools of case research. Various kinds of indexing systems, the most well known of which is the West Key Number system, correlate words and concepts associated with words to a hierarchical series of numbers. Consulting the index will yield "key numbers" that are likely associated with the question under consideration. Most American jurisdictions have case-law digests that are organized by these key numbers. There are also regional and even national digests that catalog cases from several and all American jurisdictions, respectively. Under each key number are collected citations and usually brief summaries (known as "squibs") of cases that address the legal issue associated with the key number. By reading the squibs collected under the relevant key numbers, a lawyer can get a sense of which actual cases might be helpful on the issue posed.

The next step is to read the relevant case reports themselves. These can be found using the citation provided or, as is increasingly possible, by a direct link online. A decision's significance for a particular issue or question can only be determined by reading the reported decision itself.

Online searching has traditionally relied on patterns of words associated with the key point to be addressed. Cases in which these patterns of words appeared would be electronically summoned from a massive electronic database. Depending on the accuracy of the words chosen and the susceptibility of the question to be identified with these words, traditional word searching could be seriously overinclusive or underinclusive of the cases that count. In recent years, increasing sophistication of electronic search engines and better organization of electronic databases have resulted in more accurate and less wasteful electronic research.

Once the lawyer has found one or more precedent cases that seem to be on point and from which an answer to the question at bar can be inferred, it is important to determine whether these cases are still authoritative precedent. Various case-checking services, the best known of which is Shepard's Citator, permit a lawyer to look up a case citation to see if the case has ever been expressly reversed or overruled by a higher or later court.

After the lawyer has collected those cases that appear to be the closest to the fact situation under consideration, the lawyer must then determine which cases provide the answer. It is unlikely that there will be a case that is identical to the case under consideration. The question becomes: What are the differences and which differences count? In this analysis, similarity of the relevant facts is important. Are the facts that count similar or are they in some significant way different? Is the case "on point" or can it be distinguished? The process of common law analysis is discussed in greater detail in Chapter 2.

2

# American Common Law

## A. THE TWO WESTERN LEGAL TRADITIONS

The law and legal system of what is now the United States of America form, especially so far as private law is concerned, a part of the common law. With its beginnings in England, the common law constitutes one of the two great legal traditions of the Western world, the other being the civil law, rooted in continental Europe.

These two traditions hold much in common. Both are products of western civilization and share its cultural and ethical heritage. However, important differences existed – and still exist, though to a lesser degree – between the two traditions. One difference respects the manner in which the authoritative starting points for legal reasoning are set out: In the civil law, these normally take the form of legislation; in the common law, especially in earlier periods, reliance is largely on judicial decisions.

A second difference relates to the influence of Roman law. In the case of the civil law, the Roman influence was various and profound; on the other hand, the common law was little influenced by Roman law.

A third difference relates to the style of legal analysis and thinking. Although various forces have today reduced the differences between the two traditions, the civil law still states legal propositions more abstractly and systematically than does the common law. Moreover, the civil law also generally places greater value than does the common law on coherence, structure, and high-level generalization.

Such differences raise an historical question that deserves attention before the more particular history of the development of American law is explored: How did it come to pass that these two distinctly different legal traditions emerged even though at the crucial historical periods the West was culturally, economically, philosophically, and religiously relatively unified?

For roughly the first millennium of western European history, there was no reason to believe that legal developments on the Continent would be dramatically different from those in England. True, England was on the Roman frontier but so were parts of continental Europe. Moreover, the fall of the Roman Empire in the West at the end of the fifth century and the rise of Islam in the course of the seventh century produced similar and profound economic, legal, and social changes throughout western Europe. The commercial civilization that Rome had built slipped back to an essentially rural way of life with land the source of substance and the condition of wealth. Everywhere the law, like the political order, was fragmented.

The great compilation and systematization of Roman law – the *Corpus iuris civilis* – was accomplished between 528 and 534 in Constantinople, but had no importance for western Europe until early in the second millennium. The distinct civil and common law traditions arose in large measure because of two events that occurred between 1000 and approximately 1200. The first was the Norman Conquest of England in 1066. The second was the rediscovery at the very end of the eleventh century of Justinian's *Corpus* and the beginning, first at Bologna and then at other continental European universities, of university legal education grounded on the *Corpus iuris civilis*.

The Norman Conquest created conditions such that in England, an effective, centralized administration of justice could be put in place. In consequence, the King's court was able, in the course of the administration of justice, to declare one law *common* to the whole realm. Between the accession of Henry I and the death of Henry III (1100–1272), a common law was declared for England. Several consequences followed that were of profound importance for the theory and practice of English law.

Within less than two centuries, the English legal order had matured along lines that were until modern times to preclude the English university from playing for law a role comparable to that assumed by continental European universities. The university study of law that began at Bologna at the end of the eleventh century without difficulty crossed the Channel to Cambridge and Oxford but did not profoundly affect the emerging common law. By the end of the thirteenth century, English law was a practitioner's law, and practitioners – lawyers and judges – firmly controlled the legal order and legal education.

The law declared by the King's courts over time satisfied, by and large, the society's needs and aspirations. Centralization of justice called forth a small, closely knit profession. Because the legal rules relevant for the practice of law were largely a product of the courts' administration of justice, practitioners enjoyed a monopoly of the knowledge and skills required for the practice of law. This state of affairs had consequences of great importance: Legal education was provided by the practicing profession and concentrated on the work of the courts. In these circumstances, the education of jurists naturally focused on specific problems and their solutions. There was little concern for or interest in either the systematic or theoretical implications of particular results. By the end of the thirteenth century, practitioners' concerns and perspectives shaped English legal education and thinking about law.

In all essentials, in England the situation would remain basically unchanged until the twentieth century. Aspirant lawyers were formed as apprentices rather than scholars. Legal education and legal thinking – at least as far as the law in action is concerned – were not the province of the university or the scholar. The legal science that developed from the twelfth century onward in the continental European universities had no place on the English legal scene. English legal analysis was concerned with deriving precedents from decided cases, a process that gives great importance to nuances of fact. Legal materials were, for the most part, structured in terms of remedies; to the continental European jurist, English legal thinking appears unsystematic if not disorderly, but the small, close-knit profession ensured predictability and brought about a kind of coherence.

England's achievement by the end of the thirteenth century of a law common to the realm through a slow and organic growth meant that its law would for centuries exhibit the characteristics described previously. Had the legal systems of continental Europe achieved legal unity at roughly the same period, they would doubtless have exhibited the same characteristics. For several reasons, including the slow pace of economic and social change, in the twelfth century the West saw law as a declaration or articulation of community standards and practices rather than an instrumental resolution of actually or potentially competing claims and interests. This vision found congenial the emergence of law in the course of resolving particular controversies. With the courts at center stage, the legal profession dominated legal education and legal thinking.

On the continent of Europe, legal unity was not achieved until the nineteenth century. By then, the intellectual and institutional setting differed profoundly from that which had shaped the common law. The rate of economic and social change was by then much greater. Law was no longer seen as "declared" but rather as "made." Perhaps most important of all, scholars in the universities had developed from the twelfth century onward a legal science derived from the efforts of jurists to make the *Corpus iuris civilis* understandable and useful for their economies and societies. The lack of legal unity on the continent of Europe had resulted in the law in action being of less interest and importance than in England and in the practicing profession enjoying less prestige and influence; the universities, consequently, could dominate legal education.

From the twelfth century onward, the rediscovered *Corpus iuris civilis* provided material for the work of generations of jurists. These materials were not only extensive and complex, they were also obscure. They had been developed for a society that no longer existed and that differed in many important respects from the society with which contemporary scholars were familiar. In these circumstances, the effort to unlock for contemporary purposes the *Corpus iuris civilis* ultimately led scholars to search for the general principles that might inform particular solutions or examples.

The effort to understand in these terms was reinforced by other considerations. Because the law actually administered was fragmented and undeveloped, especially when compared with the *Corpus iuris*, there was little scholarly interest in the particularized solutions reached by the law in action. Furthermore, the university environment in which the study of law was pursued naturally favored those characteristics generally associated with the scholar rather than the judge or lawyer: the love of system, structure, and generalization. Although no simple formula can capture the complexity and variety of the court systems that emerged on the European continent, approximate generalizations can be offered respecting the relationship between judge and university. From at least 1300 onward, men trained in law at the universities were increasingly appointed judges in seigniorial as well as royal courts. Furthermore, the personal responsibility that rested in some parts of Europe on judges for erroneous decisions led to another form of reliance on the university scholar; his advice on the law was obtained by the judge as a means of self-protection.

When the moment came for legal unification on the continent of Europe, the situation thus differed greatly from that in which England had achieved legal unity. Generations of university study of law had created a legal science admirably fitted to the task of creating a uniform national law; moreover, economic, political, and social changes were now proceeding relatively rapidly. For both philosophical and sociological reasons, by the end of the eighteenth century, law could no longer be looked upon as "declared"; law was "made." Nor was it acceptable to the political thinking of this period that law should be a judicial creation; lawmaking was a legislative or executive task. Indeed, quite aside from political and philosophical considerations, the sheer pace and depth of change meant that neither France nor Germany could now embark upon the creation of a common law by gradual accretion through the work of the courts.

When France, Germany, and other nations of continental Europe finally were in a position to establish legal unity, the forces at work thus were such that codification was inevitable. The legal science developed in the universities had accustomed the societies in question to aspire to a generalized, systematic statement of legal rules and principles. This approach was both manageable and congenial to the legislator. Just as the common law of England, French and German law thus carry in their form and theoretical assumptions the mark of the period in which the societies they serve first achieved legal unity.

## B. THE RECEPTION OF THE COMMON LAW ON THE NORTH AMERICAN CONTINENT

The colonization of the American Continents began in the sixteenth century. The Spanish and Portuguese controlled the southern continent; the northern continent was taken over by Dutch, English, French, and Spanish settlers. Each group brought its own culture and institutions.

Not all of the areas that ultimately were to form part of the United States of America were initially settled by the English. There were, for example, Spanish settlements in what is today the state of Florida, Dutch settlements in New York, and a French colonization in Louisiana. As a result, the laws of some of the states of the United States still contain elements that derive from the civil rather than the common law. However, the course of political and economic development was to be such that, as far as law was concerned, the English tradition – as modified to take into account the conditions of the New World – ultimately achieved almost complete dominance.

In 1607, the first English permanent settlement was established in Jamestown, Virginia. In the course of the seventeenth and eighteenth centuries, these and other English colonists brought to the New World the common law as well as some British legislation. After the American Revolution, which began in 1775, most of the thirteen former colonies formally "received" in their constitutions or by statutory provision the common law of England together with related statutes. In a few states, the reception was accomplished by judicial decision alone. Various cutoff dates – for example, 1607 (the year of the first settlement at Jamestown) or 1776 (the year of the Declaration of Independence) – established the date of these receptions. The common law tradition was thus continued by the states that formed in 1776 a new nation.

The environment into which the common law was thus introduced differed greatly from England. From an early period, the American scene was characterized by a rich diversity in religion, in nationality, and in economic groups. These pluralistic societies included Anglicans, Baptists, Huguenots, Presbyterians, Puritans, Quakers, and Roman Catholics. Already in the early days of colonization, English, Dutch, Germans, Irish, Scots, and Swedes had come to the New World. This diversity was inevitably accompanied by diverse cultural values and ways of life.

To diversity on the cultural and social levels was added diversity at the level of political institutions. Some colonies were royal provinces; others were proprietary provinces and some were corporate colonies under royal charters. Each colony was, as far as government was concerned, essentially separate from the other colonies and remained so for more than a decade after the Revolution.

Despite these elements of diversity, the common law established itself in those colonies that revolted in 1775 from Great Britain and in due course established the United States of America. In the early seventeenth century, conditions of life in the colonies were not such as to require a well-developed legal system and legal profession. At the beginning, trained jurists were few, local legal training was poor, and law books were scarce. By the Revolution, however, English private law was generally well regarded and each colony had trained, able, and respected professionals capable of working with a sophisticated and technical system. Especially in the cities, the colonial legal profession had achieved both social standing and economic success. A measure of the profession's importance – and of its political involvement – is that twenty-five of the fifty-six signers of the Declaration of Independence (1776) were lawyers.

The English common law was never applied fully and without modification in the colonies. Indeed, English legal doctrine itself took the position that the colonists carried with them only such of the mother country's laws as were suitable to their new conditions. For example, the English rule of primogeniture was not considered appropriate for a frontier society that thought in far more egalitarian terms than did English society. The English rule that owners of cattle had to fence them in did not survive in the open space of New World. Nor did arrangements specific to the conditions of professional legal life in England – for example, the English distinction between solicitors and barristers, the tradition that judges could be drawn only from among the barristers, and the profession's monopoly on legal education – maintain themselves.

However, the more general and essential features of the English legal system and tradition persisted. The style of legal thought and the law's technical vocabulary were maintained. In the administration of both civil and criminal justice, the jury continued to play a central role. The distinction, so deeply rooted in English legal history, between courts of law and of equity and between the rules administered by each endured.

In the area of public law, continuity was far less marked. American developments early departed, in fundamental ways, from British practices and institutions. These divergences resulted in considerable measure from the disrepute into which some aspects of the British system had fallen by the time of the Revolution. Kingship and its associated institutions were thoroughly discredited in the revolutionaries' eyes. The distinctive features of American public law – federalism, the presidential system, and the role of the courts in constitutional questions – were generated by the problems that the revolting colonies faced in forming a nation from thirteen separate states. The American experiment with federalism required institutional arrangements very different from those that served Great Britain.

## C. THE POST-REVOLUTION DEVELOPMENT OF AMERICAN LAW

For public law, unlike private law, the Revolution was a watershed. In the decades that followed 1775, new traditions and institutions were developed through constitutional conventions, legislation, executive actions, and judicial decisions. Some aspects of these developments are considered in Chapters 4 and 5, which are devoted to the American federal system, American constitutional law, and the role of the U.S. Supreme Court.

The Revolution did not bring about a comparable break with English practices and traditions in the development of the American common law. The ties with England did loosen, however, and American judges, jurists, and legislators began in a more independent and self-conscious fashion than before to develop – using the received English law as a basis – legal institutions and doctrines that reflected the economic, political, and social realities of the new American polity. This formative period of American law can be seen as lasting until the Civil War (1861–1865). The judicial contribution during this period was of great importance; the courts did yeoman service in adapting existing rules and principles and establishing new propositions of law.

The need to develop a law appropriate for a new and expanding economy and society caused American courts to take a more relaxed view with respect to the precedential value of previously decided cases than that held at some periods by the English courts. The American conception of *stare decisis* permitted much greater judicial innovation than English practice in the nineteenth century tolerated. For example, unlike its English counterpart, an American court could overrule its own earlier decision; of course, this step was never to be taken lightly. Extremely restrictive views had not prevailed in earlier periods in England, nor is the contemporary English position as restrictive as that held in the nineteenth century. But the generalization remains fair that American courts are by and large less precedent bound than are their English counterparts.

The Formative Period also saw the emergence of significant American legal scholarship. Indeed, the writings of such jurists as Chancellor Kent and Justice Story were influential not only in the

United States but also in Great Britain. During this period, legal education in America – unlike England – began to be centered in universities. Joseph Story (1779–1845) was renowned not only for his service as Associate Justice of the Supreme Court of the United States (1811–1845) but also for his tenure as one of the early Professors of Law in Harvard University (1829–1845).

The question of the ultimate authority for judge-made law lies at the heart of the common law system. Civil law codes enjoy the legitimacy of enacted legislation and can be said to be the will of the people, regardless of whether the propounders of the codes also asserted some resonance with an order inherent in nature. The ultimate authority of judge-made law is far less clear. For a long time, common law jurists asserted that judges did not "make" law with their legal decision but merely "found" a law that was inherent in nature. Later, it was thought that judges sensed the inherent order in society and decided cases in a way to maintain that order.

By the end of the nineteenth century, American jurists were beginning to question whether the common law was really an inherent feature of the natural or social order. The final break came with Oliver Wendell Holmes, Jr., a Boston lawyer, law professor, judge, and ultimately a Justice of the U. S. Supreme Court. Holmes asserted that common law judges did not find any inherent law, but rather that they decided cases according to their own senses of the correct resolutions of the policy conflicts presented. In other words, judges decided cases in order to reach results that they deemed correct based on their own individual social, economic, and political views. The fabric of precedential judicial decisions and the common law principle of *stare decisis* channeled and disciplined this lawmaking and kept individual judges from getting out of control. The presence of the legislature to observe and, if necessary, correct judicial lawmaking ensured that the policy resolutions of the judges did not stray too far from community norms and values.

Since the times of Holmes, American legal realism has become the dominant school of legal thought in the United States. American jurists live with the reality that their common law is very much the product of mortal judges, and the rules derived from the common law process are not holy writ. Such systematic coherency as the common law fabric exhibits reflects a human preference for consistency and predictability rather than an inherent order from nature.

In recent years, American legal realism has given rise to sub-schools of legal thought such as Critical Legal Theory, Critical Feminist Theory, and Critical Race Theory. These versions of American legal realism focus on the darker side of a regime that acknowledges that law is the product of mortal human beings rather than some higher authority. Judges and other lawmakers often come from or are associated with traditionally privileged social and economic groups. That the rules they create tend to perpetuate and enhance the positions of these groups, often to the disadvantage of others, is the central theme of these critical versions of legal realism.

Economic, political, and sociological developments in the late nineteenth and early twentieth centuries resulted in legislatures and administrative agencies becoming much more important for American law than had previously been the case. By the turn of the century, national law schools – beginning with Harvard – began to dominate American legal education. The apprenticeship system was in decline and, as geographical mobility increased, law schools that prepared for practice only in a particular jurisdiction could not attract the best students. The national law school provided a training that, with some additional work to master the particularities of a given jurisdiction's law, prepared the student for practice in any state of the United States.

As economic and social activity within the United States flowed with increasing frequency across state boundaries, the problem of maintaining legal unity assumed great importance. The problem is inevitably troubling for federations where the constitutional arrangements leave law-making authority in private-law matters largely in the hands of the member states. One could imagine that the supreme courts of the different American states might develop a plethora of different legal doctrines, which could constitute a serious indirect burden on interstate activity and weaken Americans' ties to each other and their sense of nationhood.

As discussed in Chapter 4, the retention by the American states of comprehensive spheres of private and public law has resulted in considerable legal diversity among the various American jurisdictions. Common law doctrines, as well as statutory rules on a variety of subject matters, vary significantly among states. The variety of solutions to social and policy problems reached by the various states has sometimes been regarded as a political strength of American federalism. The states form a "laboratory of democracy" in which different legal solutions can be tried and studied so that the best can emerge and eventually be adopted by all.

Ultimately, this divergence in common law as well as statutory doctrine among the states has never been crippling. In recent years, it has greatly diminished due to a number of key factors. First, American culture is largely unitary, with a common language and largely common national values and identity. Second, the national government has taken cognizance of certain key areas, such as those directly affecting interstate and foreign commerce, where state-by-state diversity would otherwise cause real problems. Third, national law schools and a national legal culture have contributed to a harmonization of approaches to legal questions that promotes convergence. Fourth, the American Law Institute (ALI), through its Restatements of the chief areas of the common law, has provided a helpful structuring of the best common law principles that leads to harmony if not uniformity. In the areas dominated by legislation, the ALI, through its Model Laws and the National Conference of Commissioners of Uniform State Laws through the Uniform State Law process, has also contributed to harmonizing the landscape of American private as well as public law.

## D. COMMON LAW REASONING AND ANALYSIS

Although much has been made of the special fact-based style of common law analysis and reasoning in contrast to the abstract logic that prevails at civil law, in fact, any difference is more in degree than in kind. Factual distinctions are as important to the application of civil law principles as to the application or distinction of case law. The vital difference is that the common law argument starts with the facts, and the principles are derived from the facts, rather than starting with an abstract principle and deciding which factual patterns fit within it.

Common law judges address solutions to legal disputes largely unaided by the kind of consistent and logical framework of abstract legal principles that are available to their civil law counterparts. Instead, judges must resort to the reported decisions of countless prior colleagues as reviewed, explained, rationalized, and modified by courts of last resort over a long period of time. It is the maintenance of logical consistency and integrity within this body of reported decisions and the discernment and identification of the public policies on which the respective decisions are based that lie at the heart of common law analysis.

## 1. Public Policy and Legal Decision Making

A common law judge deciding a civil dispute basically attempts to reach a decision that best effectuates somewhat generalized public policy in the context of the case at bar. As these public policies become more identified as the bases for judicial decisions, they assume greater significance as precedents for later decisions.

For instance, in the contracts context, as common law judges were faced with attempts to enforce various kinds of promises, they concluded that as a matter of public policy, only certain kinds of promises should be legally enforceable. Otherwise, the courts would be clogged with controversies about all sorts of casual interactions that might be characterized as promises. The policy considerations associated with enforcing at least some promises that bore consideration, in the sense that the promisor had received something of value or a promise of something of value in return for the promise, appeared significantly more weighty than enforcing gratuitous promises. The presence of consideration became associated with policy considerations favoring enforcement and the common law doctrine of consideration became established. For a comparative discussion of the common law doctrine of consideration and civil law efforts to address similar policy issues through abstraction, see Chapter 3.

Almost any legal dispute can present a multitude of policy considerations that could serve as the basis for deciding the case. The role of the common law in the form of precedent is to identify precedents that will "count." The function of the judge in identifying and defining the policy considerations that will drive the decisions of individual cases in their respective factual contexts is the creative part of the common law decision. Historically, this activity was thought to be governed by underlying principles of a legal order that was innate in nature. Since the emergence of American Realism at the end of the nineteenth century, however, judges and legal scholars have acknowledged that judges identify relevant and decisive legal policies based in large part on their own view of how the world is or should be governed and regulated.

## 2. Precedent and Case Distinctions

The common law obtains its integrity from the implicit principle that cases that present the same relevant facts (i.e., cases with the same policy considerations) should be decided the same way by all courts within the system. This principle is fundamental to the coherence and predictability of the common law system.

The principle is implemented hierarchically. Courts are only required to follow their own prior decisions and the prior decisions of courts that are above them in the appellate hierarchy, with the decisions of the court of last resort having final authority. Thus, a court of first instance is required to follow the prior decisions of the court of final appeal in all cases. Its own decisions, however, are binding on no court other than itself and no parties other than the parties to the case.

A second principle of common law adjudication is that courts must decide cases based on policies of general application. A case cannot be decided on policies that are of relevance only to a single party. Most of these policies are grounded in values and perceptions held in common by society in general.

A companion principle of the common law is that a court's determination is limited to the facts of that case. Regardless of how generally the court states the legal and policy considerations being implemented by a decision, its precedential value extends only to cases that, to all intents, purposes, and policies, are factually identical with the case at hand. It is the decision itself, not what is said in support of the decision that has the precedential effect. Broad statements by judges about why they decided cases in particular ways are called *dicta* and are not precedent. They may be helpful in revealing how the judges are approaching policy conflicts in particular contexts, but they are not binding on that or any other court in future decisions.

Once a court of last resort has reached a determination of how a conflict of policies should be resolved in a particular case, that determination becomes binding precedent for future proceedings in that case and in any cases that are highly similar to it in all relevant aspects of the policies involved. To the extent that the facts of subsequent cases diverge in some respect that may involve some policy, the force of the precedent is diluted.

So, for example, if a court of last resort had decided in a particular case that a driver who ran through a red light and caused an auto accident should be liable to the driver and passengers in the other car for the damages sustained by them in the accident, that determination would be binding precedent for other cases involving running a red light. It would be strong but not binding precedent for cases involving, say, running stop signs. Although running a stop sign involves policy issues similar to running a red light, the policy considerations are not identical. It is possible to imagine situations in which the policy issues involved in disobeying a stop sign should have different resolution than those involved in running a red light. The red-light case would be weaker precedent for cases involving driving derelictions other than failing to stop for a signal. Although the overall policy resolution of associating driving derelictions with civil liability would still apply, the different kinds of derelictions could well involve differences in policy that would support different resolutions of different cases.

An important element of common law advocacy and judicial decision making is the technique of "distinguishing" prior decisions based on differences between the relevant facts of the prior case and those of the case at bar. Of course, no two cases can be factually identical; in this sense, all cases are distinguishable. The question is, however, whether the fact distinctions between the precedent case and the case at bar are of such significance as a matter of policy that some or all of the considerations supporting the prior decision do not support the same decision in the present case. Sometimes a case that appears highly similar to a precedent decision on the facts can be shown to be different in some significant way by identifying and highlighting some fact or circumstance not readily apparent at first blush. By the same token, a case may exhibit many factual differences that do not have policy implications sufficient to distinguish it from a seemingly dissimilar precedent that is on all fours on the key facts that count.

Consider, for example, a precedent decision that adjudicated a motorist who failed to stop for a red light liable for the injuries suffered in the ensuing auto accident. Differences in the kind of vehicle involved in the accident ordinarily would not be sufficient to distinguish the red-light case as precedent, unless perhaps the vehicle that ran the red light was an ambulance on its way to the hospital. Nor would the location, urban or rural, generally be of legal significance. One could argue that the red-light case should be precedent for a case involving failure to stop at a stop sign, and that the crucial fact that "counted" was the existence of a traffic signal requiring a motorist to stop. However, one could also argue that the nature of a stop sign and the obligations thereby imposed on a driver are sufficiently different from a traffic light that the red-light case should not automatically be accepted as establishing the rule for a stop-sign accident.

The ability to recognize potential fact distinctions that might dilute or eliminate the precedential force of a prior decision and articulate them in argument or in judicial opinions is an important skill of a common law lawyer or judge. Law students are trained in these techniques by writing briefs and arguing cases in moot court proceedings during law school.

### 3. Overruling and Departing from Precedent

Although distinction of prior cases by identification of new facts that are of legal significance to a decision is a major source of common law flexibility and growth, American courts have shown themselves ready to overrule or expressly depart from prior precedent when social conditions or the legal environment have changed so that the prior rule does not produce decisions that are in accord with contemporary policies. A lawyer faced with an adverse precedent decision is always free to argue that despite factual applicability of some precedent, the case at bar should be differently decided because the precedent case was wrongly decided or that some relevant conditions or policies have changed so that a different decision is now indicated.

Case law is always subject to modification or supersession by action of the legislature. If the legislature is dissatisfied with any doctrine developed by the court in case decisions, it is always free to abrogate this decisional law by statutory provisions of almost any level of generality. Indeed, often a court decision will spur legislative activity in a particular area.

By the same token, when a court is asked to overrule a prior decision, the court will sometimes be faced with the argument that the legislature's failure to intervene up to that time means that the legislature favors the continuance of the common law rule. If there is going to be a modification of established doctrine, the legislature should have the first crack at it, and the court should decline to initiate a change by common law decision until the legislature has at least considered remedial legislation. On the other hand, it can also be argued that law created by the court should be amended by the court and that failure of the legislature to enact reform legislation can be due to political considerations having little to do with the advisability of the change.

For instance, in the 1970s, many American courts were forced to consider whether the doctrine of charitable immunity, established in most states by judicial decision in the nineteenth century, should be modified or abrogated. There were good reasons why the policy reasons that gave rise to the doctrine no longer applied with the same force. Over the past century, charities had become, in many cases, major business enterprises able to pass their costs along to patient, governmental, and insurance communities. The availability and common use by charities of liability insurance were also of significance.

In some states, the judicial response to these efforts was cautious. Courts deferred to the legislature and cited past legislative inaction as evidence that the legislature wished the traditional rule to continue. In other states, courts acted on their own to overrule prior decisions establishing immunity by promulgating new decisions permitting liability under the circumstances presented by the cases before them. In some cases, courts expressly deferred for a limited time to permit the legislature to act. In default of legislative action within a particular time, the court would feel free to take remedial action in the next case presenting the opportunity.

## E. AMERICAN COMMON LAW AT THE BEGINNING OF THE THIRD MILLENNIUM

The great attention paid to American common law in the first year of law school and in comparative discussion of legal systems and cultures should not obscure the fact that, at the beginning of the Third Millennium, the role and scope of common law in the United States has considerably shrunk from its nineteenth century heyday. The great development of public and regulatory law during the first half of the twentieth century has been entirely a matter of statute law and administrative regulation on both state and federal levels. The same is true of criminal law. Although most American states received a common law of crimes from Great Britain, in most cases criminal law was legislatively enacted relatively early in the nineteenth century and has remained statute law ever since. Family law and the law of probate and inheritance have been made the subject of comprehensive statutory treatment in every American jurisdiction.

At present, common law is dominant only in the areas of tort and personal injury law, contract law, and certain overlapping areas such as promissory estoppel, restitution, and the like. Although these are important areas of any legal regime, it cannot be any longer said that common law is a predominant part of the legal fabric of the United States.

### F. AN EXAMPLE OF THE COMMON LAW IN ACTION

The process of common law reasoning and development can be observed by studying a series of cases addressing a single policy issue over time. The development of the common law defining the scope of the remedy for loss of consortium in Massachusetts during the 1970s and 1980s is a good example.

The concept of "consortium" relates to reciprocal services and benefits such as personal care, companionship, society, and sometimes sexual intimacy conferred on each other by family members who generally live together and are bound to one another by emotional as well as economic ties. If one member of such a family group is injured by the wrongful act of a third party, should any other members of the group be entitled to monetary compensation from the tortfeasor for the loss of these kinds of services and benefits as formerly provided by the injured family member?

Historically, the Massachusetts courts had ruled that a family member could recover for personal injuries negligently inflicted on another family member by a third party only if the claimant had sustained a direct economic loss by reason of the injury. So, for instance, in *Lombardo v. D. F. Frangioso and Co.*, 359 Mass. 529, 269 N.E. 2d 836 (1971), the Massachusetts court acknowledged that a husband required to pay medical expenses for an injured wife would generally have the right to recover those expenses from a third party who had negligently caused the injuries. On the other hand, loss of companionship, society, sexual relations, and the like, which were not readily translatable into economic terms, went unreimbursed.

The issue of whether a spouse of an injured party has a legal claim for loss of consortium had been posed to the Massachusett Supreme Judicial Court in 1909, in the case of *Feneff v. New York Central Railroad*, 203 Mass. 278, 282, 89 N.E. 436 (1909). In that case, the Massachusetts court refused to recognize a claim for loss of spousal consortium.

By 1970, the common law doctrine denying recovery for loss of spousal consortium in Massachusetts had become well established. In the intervening years since the *Feneff* decision, the other courts of Massachusetts had followed *Feneff* as precedent and had denied recovery for consortium. In 1970, a lawyer looking up the law of Massachusetts on claims by spouses for loss of consortium would have found citations to the *Feneff* decision. Text writers on Massachusetts tort law would have generalized the rule announced in the *Feneff* decision as a rule denying loss-of-consortium recovery not only to wives but also to husbands and other family members.

In the late 1960s, a lawyer representing an injured party and his spouse decided to seek a change in this legal doctrine of some sixty years' standing. The lawyer did not seek this change by proposing a bill in the Massachusetts Legislature, although that body certainly would have been competent to change this doctrine by legislation. Instead, the lawyer asked the Massachusetts Supreme Court to reconsider the *Feneff* ruling in the context of his new case raising the same issue.

What caused the lawyer to raise this issue and confront the prior adverse doctrine head on? There could have been intervening changes in social norms and values that cast doubt on the ongoing validity of the policy resolution reached by the court in 1909. Courts in other jurisdictions, or even legislatures, might have reached different results on the doctrinal issue. Scholars and text writers might have suggested that the no-recovery rule was ripe for reform. Other recent decisions by the Massachusetts Supreme Judicial Court on apparently similar issues might have hinted at a social and political orientation different from that reflected in the 1909 decision. A lawyer aware of these developments might have concluded that the Massachusetts Supreme Judicial Court could conceivably be willing to reconsider and possibly modify its earlier pronouncement.

Another consideration that would have been crucial in deciding whether to seek judicial change in precedential doctrine would be the facts of the lawyer's case. A case with facts that cry out for a particular result in terms of common social values and a sense of rightness and justice is the best vehicle to seek reform of the common law.

Having decided to seek a change in Massachusetts common law to permit a spouse of an injured party to recover for loss of consortium, the lawyer filed suit in behalf of Anna T. Lombardo against D. F. Frangioso & Co. in the Massachusetts Superior Court, a trial court of first instance, and asserted in the suit a loss of consortium for which the claimant spouse sought damages. The Superior Court judge, bound by the precedent of the *Feneff* decision, dismissed the consortium claim as without legal basis. The lawyer then appealed that dismissal to the Massachusetts Supreme

Judicial Court, which had the power to declare, affirm, and modify Massachusetts' common law.

In 1971, the Massachusetts Supreme Judicial Court issued its decision in *Lombardo v. D. F. Frangioso & Co.*, 359 Mass. 529, 269 N.E. 2d 836 (1971). Its reasoning was as follows:

> Since *Feneff v. New York Cent. & H.R.R.R.*, 203 Mass. 278, 282, 89 N.E. 436, was decided in 1909, it has been generally accepted as Massachusetts law that neither spouse has any right of recovery for lack of consortium or loss of marital and other services growing out of a defendant's negligent injury to the other spouse. . . .
>
> We are aware that there is much authority in the United States which differs from the Massachusetts rule. We regard our rule, however, as having been well established throughout the more than sixty years since the *Feneff* decision. If a rule of such long standing is to be changed, we are of opinion that any modification should be accomplished by the Legislature and not by judicial decision. A change of this type by judicial decision is not as easily applied (as in the case of legislation) prospectively or after sufficient notice of a forthcoming change to ensure adequate insurance arrangements. If applied retrospectively to pending cases or to past accidents, the consequences of a change may be unfair to defendants or to their indemnitors.
>
> We note that the *Feneff* case is discussed in the Forty-sixth Report of the Judicial Council (1970) Pub.Doc. No. 144, pp. 76–78, in the course of its consideration of 1970 House Bill No. 2364 (a proposed legislative overruling of the *Feneff* case). The Judicial Council has recommended strongly that no bill allowing either spouse to recover for lack of consortium be enacted. Plainly there is not unanimity that the rule growing out of the *Feneff* case should be altered in any respect. In the circumstances we are of the opinion that the matter is not one appropriate for revision by judicial decision.
>
> Order sustaining demurrer affirmed.

Not all of the seven Justices of the Massachusetts Supreme Court agreed that the *Feneff* rule should not be changed. Three of them dissented, stating why they believed that the Massachusetts

Supreme Court, not the Legislature, should act to enable a right to recover for loss of consortium:

> The majority opinion upholds a Superior Court order sustaining the defendants' demurrer to a declaration in tort for loss of consortium, the mutual right of the marriage partners to each other's fellowship, companionship, affection, cooperation in every conjugal relationship, including sexual relations. I am unable to agree with the majority view. . . .
>
> The right of a spouse to recover for the loss of consortium after acts constituting criminal conversation, enticement or adultery, has been consistently upheld in Massachusetts. [Cases Cited]. . .
>
> In 1950, the United States Court of Appeals for the District of Columbia held that a wife could sue for loss of consortium where the injury to her husband resulted from the negligence of a third party. . . . In the intervening two decades, a substantial number of jurisdictions have recognized the existence of this cause of action, the most recent being Florida. . . . Indeed, of the forty-three jurisdictions now recognizing a right of action for such loss of consortium, twenty-six allow it both to the husband and to the wife. The remaining seventeen restrict it to the husband, a distinction of dubious validity in the present state of the law. . . .
>
> It has been contended that loss of consortium includes within its scope loss of support and that, since this is an element of damages implicitly contained in the husband's recovery for diminished earning capacity, allowance to the wife for loss of consortium might result in double recovery. [Cases Cited] A proper charge by the trial judge could eliminate this problem. . . . The problem may be further minimized by a joint trial of both the husband's and wife's causes of action. If brought separately, motions to consolidate should be allowed. . . .
>
> When dealing with a rule of law originally established by judicial decision I believe that its change, when required, should come by means of a judicial decision. In these circumstances, I do not believe that we should look to the Legislature for change. To do so is a distortion of the concept of judicial review whereby the Legislature is invited, in effect, to reverse judicial decisions. If the courts are to assert and maintain their rightful independence and inherent

powers within their proper sphere, they should not pass on to the Legislature the task of altering by statute the holdings of prior judicial decisions in non-statutory matters. The mere passage of time does not shift the burden to the Legislature. . . .

The American Law Institute has tentatively approved a rule permitting a wife to recover, after bodily harm tortiously inflicted on her husband, 'for resulting loss of his society, including any impairment of his capacity for sexual intercourse, and for any reasonable expense incurred by her in providing medical treatment.' Restatement 2d: Torts, s 695 (Tent. draft No. 14, April 15, 1969). . .

Beyond dispute, 'there is, in a continuing marital relationship, an inseparable mutuality of ties and obligations, of pleasures, affection and companionship, which makes that relationship (consortium) a factual entity. . . .We see no valid reason why that concept should not be extended to permit recovery for wrongs negligently caused to the legal unity through physical injury of either spouse. . . That both spouses suffer when the marriage relationship is adversely affected by physical injury to either is a fact' (emphasis supplied). . . .

It is argued that the right to loss of consortium should be accorded to the husband before it is given to the wife. I see no basis for such a discrimination. The short answer is that the court can provide husband and wife this 'equal protection' at the same time.

The defendants' demurrer should be overruled.

An examination of the majority and the dissenting opinions reveals that the majority buttressed its resolution of the policy conflict, not only by the policy considerations that produced the rule in the *Feneff* case but also by additional policy considerations based on the stability of the doctrine itself. These include possible damage to interests such as insurers that may have relied on the existing rules, deference to the legislature as the body closest to the community and its values, and anticipated difficulties in administering a court-initiated change.

The dissent, on the other hand, argued that the *Feneff* doctrine had indeed become out of step not only with the country's social values and mores but also that many other states had granted common law remedies for loss of consortium, and that the American Law Institute, a leading body of common law scholars, had opined that the common law did or should allow a remedy for loss of consortium at least to wives, if not all married persons. Indeed, the dissent noted that the *Feneff* doctrine was difficult to logically reconcile with the Massachusetts court's own rulings in claims for intentional deprivation of a spouse's services, society, and companionship. Although the *Feneff* doctrine remained law, the dissent heralded the winds of change in the Massachusetts common law of consortium.

The Massachusetts Legislature did not act following the decision of the Massachusetts Supreme Court in *Lombardo v. D. F. Frangioso and Co.* Two years later, the case of *Diaz v. Eli Lilly and Company* reached the court. Again, a Massachusetts lawyer must have concluded that there was a possibility that the Massachusetts Supreme Judicial Court would reconsider its decision in the *Lombardo* case based on intervening developments and the particular facts and circumstances of the lawyer's case.

In *Diaz* as in *Lombardo*, the plaintiff's wife sought damages based on loss of consortium of her injured husband. The lower court had denied the claim based on the authority of the *Feneff* case as recently reaffirmed in *Lombardo*. However, in the intervening two years, the trend that the Massachusetts court had resisted in *Lombardo* had continued. Almost all of the other American states had recognized such claims. The ALI had revised its Restatement of the Law of Torts to recognize a right of either spouse to recovery for loss of consortium by reason of injuries inflicted on the other spouse by a third party. Also, the personnel of the Massachusetts court had changed. Justices Cutter and Spalding from the majority and Justice Spiegel from the minority in *Lombardo* had retired and been replaced by new appointees, including Justices Kaplan and Braucher, who had formerly been professors at

Harvard Law School. The Massachusetts Supreme Judicial Court was urged to reconsider its decision in *Lombardo* and join the overwhelming majority of American jurisdictions in judicially recognizing a claim of a wife for the loss of consortium of her husband. A new majority of the court responded in *Milagros Diaz v. Eli Lilly and Company*, 364 Mass. 153, 302 N.E. 2d 555 (1973):

> A spouse suffers bodily injuries through the negligence of a third party. Does the other spouse have a claim against the tortfeasor for a loss of consortium that results from the injuries? The present appeal provides us with an opportunity to reconsider this question upon which the common law has spoken in recent years with exceptional vigor. . . .
>
> In *Lombardo v. D. F. Frangioso & Co. Inc.*, . . ., the majority of the court considered it to be the law of the Commonwealth that a spouse had no enforceable right for loss of consortium resulting from personal injury negligently inflicted on the other spouse. The majority declined to reconsider the question in any detail, believing that a change must come about by legislative action if at all; the minority would have reconsidered the question and upheld the right equally for husband and wife. . . .
>
> We conclude that the reasoning of the *Feneff* case is vulnerable, and its result unsound, and we are strengthened in this view by the movement of opinion in this country since 1950 toward recognizing a right of action in either spouse for loss of consortium due to negligent injury of the other. We should be mindful of the trend although our decision is not reached by a process of following the crowd. Without attempting a count of the decisions, we may summarize the position roughly as follows. The right of the husband has long been acknowledged in a very substantial majority of the jurisdictions. The right of the wife . . . has now been established in perhaps half the American jurisdictions; the result has been achieved in some States by overruling relatively recent precedent in point. In certain jurisdictions the wife's right has been denied although the husband's right is still affirmed—a regrettable solecism. A few jurisdictions have followed our *Feneff* case or another route to a conclusion denying the right both to husband and wife.

Having in the first Restatement of Torts published in 1938 affirmed the husband's right and denied the wife's in accordance with the then weight of authority, the American Law Institute in Restatement Second will state that husband and wife have the right on equal terms, adding the requirement—in recognition of the significant procedural point—that where possible the consortium claim must be joined with the claim for bodily injury. This resolution of the problem conforms to the prevailing ideas of the commentators. . . .

The reform is not a drastic or radical incursion upon existing law. In no serious way will an existing interest be impaired or an expectation be disappointed or a reliance be defeated. . . . Accordingly there is no occasion to take full precautions to confine our decision to prospective operation. As a matter of sound administration and fairness, however, we declare that where the claim for the physical injuries has been concluded by judgment or settlement or the running of limitations prior to the coming down of this opinion, no action for loss of consortium thereafter instituted arising from the same incident will be allowed, even if that action would not be otherwise barred by limitations. In this we follow the declarations made in similar circumstances by the courts of New York, New Jersey and Maryland.

Overruling the Lombardo decision, and holding that either spouse has a claim for loss of consortium shown to arise from personal injury of the other spouse caused by negligence of a third person, we reverse the order sustaining the demurrer to the present declaration.

The opinion in Diaz resolved the policy conflict originally resolved in *Feneff* and revisited in *Lombardo* in a new and different way. Times had changed and community values and expectations have changed with them. These changes were interpreted and applied not by a legislature, acting prospectively and abstractly, but rather by a court, deciding a particular dispute laid before it by private parties. The resolution reached applied only to parties and the case before the court. It was precedent only for future cases that had the same facts, or facts so similar that there would be no policy reason to make a distinction between them. On the other hand, unlike a legislative enactment, which generally applies to conduct taking place after the legislation becomes effective, the doctrine announced in *Diaz* applied to all cases that would subsequently come before the courts, including cases based on conduct that predated the *Diaz* decision.

Once the winds of change had started to blow, it was not long before the ingenuity of lawyers was applied to test the extent to which these winds would carry Massachusetts legal doctrine. It was only a matter of time, and not much time at that, before the court would be faced with a case in which a family member other than a spouse would raise a claim for loss of consortium. In *Ferriter v. Daniel O'Connell's Sons, Inc.*, 381 Mass. 507, 413 N.E. 2d 690 (1980), the children of an injured employee had brought suit against the employer on the grounds that the employer's negligence had caused them the loss of their father's companionship and society. The Massachusetts Supreme Court had to decide whether to apply its newly adopted law for loss of consortium to children as well as spouses. In this case, the lower court concluded that the reasoning announced by the Massachusetts Supreme Court in *Diaz* was applicable to the plaintiffs' claim and allowed the claim. The defendant then appealed to the court of last resort. That court analyzed the claim as follows:

> . . . According to the statement of agreed facts, the plaintiffs are the wife and two children, aged five and three, of Michael Ferriter. While working as a carpenter for the defendant, Michael was seriously injured on May 18, 1979. A one- to-two-hundred pound load of wood beams, which was hoisted in a nylon sling from the boom of a crane, fell fifty feet, and at least one beam struck Michael on the neck. The persons hoisting the lumber, operating the crane, monitoring site safety, and supervising the work were O'Connell

employees. The defendant also supplied the materials and equipment used.

Since the accident, Michael Ferriter has been hospitalized and paralyzed from the neck down. The plaintiffs first saw him in this condition in the hospital. . . .

The question whether a child can recover for loss of a parent's companionship and society caused by a defendant's negligence is a matter of first impression in Massachusetts. However, in *Feneff v. New York Cent. & Hudson River R.R.*, . . ., rejecting a wife's claim for loss of consortium for injuries to her husband, the court in essence equated a wife's interest in spousal consortium with a minor child's interest in parental society. In *Diaz v. Eli Lilly & Co.*, . . ., we characterized as "vulnerable" the *Feneff* court's reasoning supporting rejection of the wife's claim. We recognized a wife's right to recover for loss of consortium resulting from personal injuries to the husband. The wife's interest encompassed not only sexual relations with her husband, but also his society and companionship. . . . The combination of *Diaz* and the dicta in *Feneff* force recognition that a minor child has a strong interest in his parent's society, an interest closely analogous to that of the wife in *Diaz*. The court in *Diaz* expressly reserved the question whether a child has a right to recover for loss of a parent's society caused by a defendant's negligence. . . . We are skeptical of any suggestion that the child's interest in this setting is less intense than the wife's.

These cases supply analogous precedent for a child's right to recover for loss of a parent's society resulting from the defendant's negligence. The common law has traditionally recognized a parent's interest in freedom from tortious conduct harming his relationship with his child. As in husband-wife relations, albeit to a more limited extent, our law has compensated parents for sentimental as well as economic injuries. If the common law sometimes protects a parent's sentiments in the parent-child relationship, we might expect similar protection for the fledgling needs of the child. But the common law has been nearly silent concerning a child's right to recover damages for loss of parental society. . . . Furthermore, the question was not clearly presented until *Nelson v. Richwagen*, 326 Mass. 485, 95 N.E.2d 545 (1950). . . .

In *Nelson*, a minor child sought relief against the defendant for enticing her mother to desert her and her father. The child prayed for damages for loss of support, maintenance and maternal care. This court affirmed an order sustaining a demurrer to the child's claim. The court acknowledged that one spouse has a right to the personal presence and care of the other. However, a minor child has no comparable right to the presence and care of a parent. "So far as the parent is bound to support the child the parent may be compelled to do so by other proceedings.". . . The court also raised four practical objections to the child's action: "(1) Possibility of a multiplicity of suits, . . .; (2) Possibility of extortionary litigation . . .; (3) Inability to define the point at which the child's right would cease, (i.e., the point at which the child becomes an adult); (4) Inability of a jury adequately to cope with the question of damages" both because the damages are too speculative and because overlapping recovery is probable. The court then likened the policies involved to those underlying parent-child tort immunity. . . .

*Nelson* is the only Massachusetts case to discuss in any detail a child's right to recover damages for loss of parental society. Because it involves the disfavored action for alienation of affections, it is distinguishable from the present case. The court implied a distaste for tort litigation among family members. . . . Also, the court was concerned with the likelihood of extortionate litigation. However, when a third party's negligence causes injury to a parent and the child suffers loss of society, the litigation does not typically pit family members against each other. . . . And the potential for extortionate litigation is absent . . .

Despite the conceded natural justice of a child's claim and extensive commentary favoring such actions, only one jurisdiction presently permits recovery. *Berger v. Weber*, 82 Mich. App. 199, 267 N.W.2d 124 (1978). . . . We believe that Michigan's approach is the correct one. Scrutiny of the reasons for denying recovery finds them unsound. Moreover, many of the objections to the child's claim raise anew the questions that we laid to rest in *Diaz*. . . .

The other objections in *Nelson* were the subject of discussion in *Diaz*, supra. We dealt at length with such problems as possible multiplicity of suits, . . . purported remoteness of the damages, . . . and dangers of redundant recovery, . . . As for the argument that we should withhold our hand until the Legislature acts, we need only repeat: "In a field long left to the common law, change may well come about by the same medium of development. Sensible reform can here be achieved without the articulation of detail or the creation of administrative mechanisms that customarily comes about by legislative enactment . . . . In the end the Legislature may say that we have mistaken the present public understanding of the nature of the (parent-child) relation, but that we cannot now divine or anticipate.". . .

We hold that the Ferriter children have a viable claim for loss of parental society if they can show that they are minors dependent on the parent, Michael Ferriter. This dependence must be rooted not only in economic requirements, but also in filial needs for closeness, guidance, and nurture. In so holding, we do not abandon our determination to "proceed from case to case with discerning caution" in this field. . . . As claims for injuries to other relationships come before us, we shall judge them according to their nature and their force.[1]

The court's opinion in *Ferriter* extending the newly recognized doctrine making loss of consortium compensable is noteworthy in two respects. First, the facts of the case, recited in some detail, seem to have been particularly compelling. The severe nature of the parent's injuries would have made the children plaintiffs' losses of parental companionship and nurture particularly palpable and plausible. Second, the court was faced with the need to deal with its contrary resolution of the same policy issue in cases of alienation of affections. The court had to identify the factual characteristics that would make a different resolution of the policy conflicts in these cases acceptable in terms of ordinary values and morals.

---

[1] For reasons similar to those expressed in *Diaz*, we declare that, where a spouse's claim for loss of consortium has been concluded by judgment or settlement or the running of limitations before this opinion comes down, no child's action for loss of parental society thereafter instituted and arising from the same incident will be allowed, even if that action would not otherwise be barred by limitations. See *Diaz v. Eli Lilly & Co.*, 364 Mass. 153, 167, 302 N.E.2d 555 (1973).

Once the Massachusetts Supreme Judicial Court had accepted the idea that a child should be able to recover for the loss of a parent's companionship, the next question would be: Can a parent recover for the loss of the companionship and society of a child? This was the question posed by Paul and Meg Norman, who sued the Massachusetts Bay Transportation Authority for negligently injuring their son, Mathew. Mr. and Mrs. Norman included in their complaint a claim for their loss of Mathew's society and companionship. The Superior Court again assumed that the reasoning of the Court in *Diaz* and *Ferriter* would support such a claim. The defendants appealed to the Massachusetts Supreme Court, which decided *Norman v. Massachusetts Bay Transportation Authority*, 403 Mass. 303, 529 N.E. 2d 139 (1988) as follows:

> The principal question in this case is whether a parent may recover for the loss of a child's consortium due to injuries negligently inflicted on the child by a third party. The complaint alleges that Matthew Norman sustained severe injuries when he was struck by a Massachusetts Bay Transportation Authority (MBTA) vehicle, negligently operated by its employee, the defendant, Steven DeDominici. Mathew's asserted damages include his medical expenses. Meg Manderson Norman, Mathew's mother, and Paul M. Norman, his father, seek damages for the loss of Mathew's consortium and they, too, seek damages for his medical expenses. The defendants moved to dismiss the parents' claims, and that motion was denied. . . .
>
> In *Diaz* and *Ferriter* we recognized that the relationship between a negligently injured person and a person seeking recovery for loss of consortium may be such that recourse for the consortium loss must be available despite the strong public interest in not expanding tort liability beyond tolerable limits. Accepting that proposition, but also accepting the proposition that the possibility of recovery cannot wisely be extended to every relationship in which a loss of consortium has been sustained, we must draw a principled, defensible line between those relationships to which a right of recovery should attach and those relationships with respect to which no

such right should be recognized. "Every effort must be made to avoid arbitrary lines which 'unnecessarily produce incongruous and indefensible results.' ". . .

By the very nature of marriage, spouses depend on one another's society, companionship, love and support (consortium) to a degree of intensity not normally present in other relationships. An injury to a spouse that impairs his or her ability to fulfil the other spouse's needs in that regard ordinarily is uniquely serious, identifiable and predictable. Our recognition of a right of recovery for the loss of spousal consortium in *Diaz* reflects that fact. Subsequently, in *Ferriter*, . . . in concluding that a dependent minor child should be entitled to recovery for the loss of a parent's consortium, we characterized a minor child's interest in his parent's society as "closely analogous" to the interest of a wife in her husband's society recognized in *Diaz*. We expressed our skepticism "of any suggestion that the child's interest . . . is less intense than the wife's." In the ordinary course of things, the dependence of spouses on one another for love and support is found to the same degree in no other relationship except, perhaps, in the relationship of a minor child to his or her parents. The key to our holding in *Ferriter* was our recognition that ordinarily minor children are critically dependent on their parents for the spiritual and physical necessities of life. Thus, we concluded that the Ferriter children had "a viable claim for loss of parental society if they [could] show that they are minors dependent on [their injured father].". . . We added: "This dependence must be rooted not only in economic requirements, but also in filial needs for closeness, guidance, and nurture.". . .

Although parents customarily enjoy the consortium of their children, in the ordinary course of events a parent does not depend on a child's companionship, love, support, guidance, and nurture in the same way and to the same degree that a husband depends on his wife, a wife depends on her husband, or a minor or disabled adult child depends on his or her parent. Of course, it is true that such dependency may exist in a particular situation, but it is not intrinsic to the parent-child relationship as is a minor child's dependency on his or her parents and as is each spouse's dependency on the other spouse. Thus, a principled distinction can be made between the situations governed by the *Diaz, Ferriter,* and Morgan cases and the instant case. On the other hand, if a plaintiff parent is permitted to recover in the circumstances of this case, there will be no defensible reason in the future to deny recovery to other relatives or even to friends who can establish that a defendant's conduct has adversely interfered with their relationship with the physically injured person. . . .

If, as a result of the defendants' negligence, Mathew Norman had died, his parents, as next of kin, would have been entitled to recover under the wrongful death statute, G.L. c. 229, § 2, for the loss of his consortium. Does consistency require that the parents be entitled to recover for the loss of Mathew's consortium due, not to Mathew's death, but to his injuries? Does consistency require that recovery for loss of consortium be available to anyone who would have been the injured person's next of kin had the injured person died? We think not. In a wrongful death action, damages are not recoverable both for the injured person's losses and the derivative losses of others. In a wrongful death action, although the next of kin may recover for loss of consortium, no one recovers for the losses sustained by the injured deceased party. Here, the plaintiffs seek to recover for both. We conclude that the plaintiff parents cannot recover for the loss of their injured child's consortium.

Not all of the judges believed that the Court should refrain from a further extension of the *Diaz-Ferriter* rule to include claims by parents for the loss of the companionship and society of their children. Three justices joined in a dissent stating:

> . . . At the outset, based on the facts alleged in this case, I would rephrase the court's statement of the issue before us as follows: The principal question in this case is whether a parent has a cause of action for the loss of an adult child's society and companionship when that child has been severely and permanently injured due to the defendant's negligence. In my view it is legally significant that the complaint not only alleges that Mathew Norman was struck by a Massachusetts Bay Transportation Authority (MBTA) vehicle, negligently operated by its employee, the defendant, Steven DeDominici, but also that, as a result, Mathew suffered "serious injury to his brain," which has rendered him "largely incapacitated,"

"permanently disabled," and "totally dependent on his parents for financial, physical and emotional sustenance.". . .

The notion of allowing loss of consortium for an injured child is neither new nor in disrepute. It has been accepted in Florida since 1926, and a number of jurisdictions permit parents to recover either by statute or by common law. . . .

As we indicated in *Ferriter v. Daniel O'Connell's Sons*, . . ., economic dependence is just one factor to be considered in awarding damages for loss of consortium. Moreover, it has become an increasingly less significant factor in determining consortium rights. In recent years several courts have recognized that "the pecuniary-loss test is outmoded and does not, by itself, provide a proper vehicle for assessing the damages incurred by a parent when his child has been injured.". . . A child today is valued not because he is a source of income, but because he is a source of emotional sustenance and joy . . .

I acknowledge that there are differences between the way in which parents depend on their children and the way in which spouses depend on each other and children depend on their parents. However, I am not persuaded that such differences should preclude the recovery of a parent for loss of consortium of his or her child who has been seriously injured by defendant's negligent acts, especially when the severity of the injuries has resulted in the child's continued dependence on his parents and the parents' continued subordination to the needs of the child. . . . Such a position is more "consistent with the humane policies underlying the *Ferriter* decision," than the position the court takes today.

In my view, the court should hold that Mathew's parents have viable claims for loss of filial society if they can show that Mathew's injuries are of such severity and permanence as to render him physically, emotionally, and financially dependent on them and that, as a result, their lives have been significantly restructured and their expectations of enjoying those experiences normally shared by parents and children have been seriously impaired. If the plaintiffs can prove such a parent-child relationship and that Mathew's negligently inflicted injuries severely affected their relationship with him, recognition of a filial consortium right would be justified. I dissent.

The majority opinion found a difference between the facts of the *Norman* case and those of the *Ferriter* case that had policy implications that required a different result. The nature of the dependent relationship between spouses and of a child on its parents was seen to be different than the dependence of a parent on a child. Thus, the majority distinguished the *Ferriter* result and declined to apply the doctrine allowing compensation for loss of consortium to parents whose children were injured. The dissent acknowledged that the degree of dependence of parents on their children for care, companionship, and society is less than that of either spouses or minor children. The dissenters, however, stressed the severity of the child's injuries and introduced a new slant to the concept of dependence, suggesting that the increased dependence of an injured child upon her or his parents for services, care, and companionship should support a compensable claim for loss of consortium by the parents.

This was not the end of the matter. Within several months after the Massachusetts Supreme Court had decided *Norman*, a bill was introduced in the Massachusetts Legislature to overrule the decision and legislatively establish the right of a parent to sue for the care, comfort, society, and companionship of a child of any age, dependent on his or her parents for support. Ultimately, the Legislature enacted Section 85X of Chapter 231 of the General Laws of Massachusetts:

**§ 85X. Loss of consortium of a dependent child; cause of action**

The parents of a minor child or an adult child who is dependent on his parents for support shall have a cause of action for loss of consortium of the child who has been seriously injured against any person who is legally responsible for causing such injury.

Section 2 of Chapter 289 of the Statutes of 1989, the session law making the change, also provided:

This act shall be effective to all causes of action which accrued on or after September first, nineteen hundred and eighty-six and to all similar causes of action now pending in any court in the commonwealth.

As can be seen from the text of the law, the Legislature attempted to create an abstract norm based on the concept of dependence identified in the *Norman* dissent. Only parents of minor children or adult children who are dependent on them for support would have this new right of action for loss of the child's consortium.

Passage of this new law, of course, did not mean that there was no more work for the courts. The new law had to be interpreted and applied. Like any generalization, the new provisions had ambiguities. What kind of support is required? How serious is "seriously injured"? What kinds of services and companionship are contemplated by "loss of consortium" of a dependent child?

In 1990, the Massachusetts Supreme Judicial Court considered the claim of Robert and Eileen Monahan for loss of the society and companionship of their son, Robert Monahan, who was injured in a fall from a hose-drying tower allegedly caused by the negligence of his fellow firemen. The new statute applied to the case because the case had been pending at the time the law was passed by the Legislature. In *Monahan v. Town of Methuen*, 408 Mass. 381, 558 N.E.2d 951 (1990), the Supreme Judicial Court tried to give some guidance on how to apply the abstract norm of the statute to concrete situations.

> In order to determine whether the parents in this case have a viable consortium claim, we must decipher the meaning of the dependency clause of the statute in question. We think that, in creating the consortium cause of action for parents of minor and adult children, the Legislature looked to the definition of dependence in our previous consortium cases. . . . In *Ferriter v. Daniel O'Connell's*

*Sons*, . . ., we stated that the plaintiff "children have a viable claim for loss of parental society if they can show that they are minors dependent on [their] parent. . . . This dependence must be *rooted not only in economic requirements*, but also in filial needs for closeness, guidance, and nurture" (emphasis supplied). We also think that the Legislature, in devising a statute to overturn the *Norman* decision, considered the dissent in that case. By virtue of § 85X, in order for an adult child to be considered "dependent on his parents for support," that child must be, at the very least, financially dependent on his parents, either prior to or after the accident, or both.

With the above considerations in mind, we conclude that Monahan's parents may not recover for loss of consortium because their son was not dependent on them financially either before or after the accident. Prior to the accident, Monahan was employed as a fire fighter and was financially independent, paying his parents $40 a week for room and board. After the accident, Monahan remained financially independent, for he continued to receive his pay pursuant to G.L. c. 41, § 111F, and continued to pay his parents $40 a week for room and board. The parents do not make any argument or point to any facts which would suggest that their son was financially dependent on his parents either before or after the accident. Therefore, judgment may now be entered for the town as to the consortium claims.

The Supreme Judicial Court chose to construe the legislature's expansion of the law of consortium conservatively, finding that the legislature had intended that only parents of children dependent on them for financial support should be entitled to recover. The court mentioned the concept of increased dependence as spelled out in the dissent in *Norman* and recited facts of the case that would suggest that such an increase in dependence applied in the *Monahan* case. However, the court declined to adopt the theory wholesale and restricted application of the statute to cases of more or less traditional financial dependence.

Whenever there is a change in the law, whether by court or legislature, there is a potential question of retroactivity. Section 2 of the statute by which the Massachusetts Legislature recognized a claim for loss of consortium of a dependent child attempted to address the issue of retroactivity. Only cases pending at the time the new statute was passed would be entitled to retroactive application of the new law.

Retroactive application of a statute can involve the due process clause of the Federal Constitution as well as similar guarantees in state constitutions. In 1987, before there was any statute permitting a claim for loss of a child's consortium, Mark D. Antonellis was sued by the Liebovich family for loss of the comfort, care, and companionship of Philip Leibovich, the plaintiffs' son, because of injuries sustained by Philip in an auto accident that had taken place in 1985. Does the application of the 1989 law to a 1985 accident violate the defendant's right to due process of law? The Massachusetts Supreme Court answered this question in the case of *Leibovich v. Antonellis*, 410 Mass. 568, 574 N.E.2d 978 (1991):

Retroactive application of G.L. c. 231, § 85X. The defendant claims that retroactive application of G.L. c. 231, § 85X, to this case, violates his constitutional right to due process under the Massachusetts and Federal Constitutions. See Declaration of Rights to the Mass. Const. arts. I, X, and XII; U.S. Const. Amend. XIV, § 1. There is no question of statutory construction in this case, as the Legislature's intentions with regard to retroactivity are expressly stated. . . . The statute is clearly intended to apply retroactively, and covers the plaintiffs' action, as their case was pending when the statute was passed.

The defendant's argument, thus, amounts to a facial challenge to the constitutional validity of G.L. c. 231, § 85X, itself, or at least to that portion of the statute which applies retroactively. . . .

In the case of retroactive statutes, we have stated the following rule: "Only those statutes which, on a balancing of opposing considerations, are deemed to be unreasonable, are held to be unconstitutional.". . . In evaluating the reasonableness of a retroactive statute, we have weighed three principle [sic] considerations: the nature of the public interest which motivated the Legislature to enact the retroactive statute; the nature of the rights affected retroactively; and the extent or scope of the statutory effect or impact. . . .

The Legislature's passage of G.L. c. 231, § 85X, was clearly a response to this court's decision in *Norman v. Massachusetts Bay Transp. Auth* . . ., which had held that a parent has no common law cause of action for loss of his or her child's consortium resulting from injuries to the child. . . . The new statute explicitly provides for such a cause of action. The Legislature may have been motivated by at least three considerations of public interest to enact G.L. c. 231, § 85X. First, the statute furthers "the long established policy of this Commonwealth of protecting the integrity and sanctity of the family unit.". . .The Legislature may have determined that because of the long-standing existence of this policy, the statute should apply not only to future lawsuits, but also to lawsuits which were pending.

In addition, by applying the statute retroactively, the Legislature may have intended to correct what had been an inconsistency in the law. As then Justice Liacos stated in his dissent in *Norman*: "Parents, as next of kin, may recover for loss of consortium after the death of a child in a wrongful death action. . . . There should be a consistency between our statutory law and our case law. It would be anomalous to take the position that, if a child is severely injured, but does not die, the parents may not recover. . . . The reasons for allowing the former militate in favor of the latter.". . . Finally, the Legislature may have decided that, in order to effectively spread the costs of accidents such as this throughout society, the statute should be applied retroactively. . .

We next address the nature of the right affected retroactively by G.L. c. 231, § 85X. The defendant essentially asserts a right not to be subject to loss of consortium claims by parents when he negligently injured their child, as provided for by the law as it existed when the accident occurred and when the plaintiffs' lawsuit was filed. . . .

Generally, persons challenging a retroactive statute must show that they acted in reasonable reliance upon the previous state of the law. . . . The defendant does not make, and could not credibly make, any argument that he would have acted differently had he known that G.L. c. 231, § 85X, would be enacted. . . . The new statute in no way alters the standards for determining what kind of behavior constitutes negligence. The defendant always had the obligation to drive in a non-negligent manner, and this obligation was not affected by G.L. c. 231, § 85X. . . . The statute merely expands the class of potential plaintiffs who may recover for their injuries caused by the negligence of tortfeasors such as the defendant.

It is not important that the statute increases the consequences of the defendant's prior negligence. The defendant cannot reasonably claim a right to act negligently without an effect on his liability in damages beyond what had been provided for in the case law. . . . This is especially true given the fact that, prior to our decision in *Norman*, the case law had arguably been moving toward allowing parents to bring loss of consortium actions for injuries negligently inflicted on their children. . . .

Finally, the scope of G.L. c. 231, § 85X, is not excessive. Because the statute will affect a relatively small number of pending cases, it is highly unlikely that "society's exposure to the threat of financial ruin will be intolerable.". . . In addition, the statute is narrowly drawn to treat the problem perceived by the Legislature. . . . Given the strength of the public interest that motivated the Legislature to enact the statute, the comparative weakness of the rights asserted by the defendant, and the narrow range of cases that will be affected by the statute, we conclude that retroactive application of G.L. c. 231, § 85X, is reasonable and therefore does not violate the defendant's constitutional guarantees of due process. . . .

Thus, over a period of twenty years, through a series of decisions, the Massachusetts Supreme Judicial Court recrafted, redefined, and redeclared the law of family consortium of the Commonwealth of Massachusetts. This process ultimately involved the Massachusetts Legislature, which extended the new doctrine to an area in which the court had not dared to go. The final word, however, was for the court, which applied the new statute and declared what it meant and whether its terms were in accord with the Constitution.

This series of decisions is an example of the common law in action and the process by which litigants ask courts to make resolutions of conflicting policies in litigated cases. The courts balance these policies and reach resolutions that reflect contemporary moral, social, economic, and political values. The courts attempt to identify and describe the policies driving their decisions in a way that is consistent with their prior decisions in cases that could be considered similar from a fact-policy standpoint. The courts consider systematic policies of predictability, reliability, consistency, and ease of application and administration.

To the extent that the court's application of contemporary social values is at variance with political perceptions of these values, the Legislature can step in and bring the common law into line through legislative pronouncements. Unlike case decisions, which operate primarily on the facts of the case at bar, these legislative pronouncements are abstract and generalized. So, the courts are called on to decide what the legislature meant and how the legislative provision is to be applied to specific cases. This process in turn generates a common law of statutory construction and application.

Finally, all declarations of law, whether by a court or by a legislature, are subject to the ground rules of constitutions. It is the responsibility of all courts to assess the conformity of both case law and statutes to the requirements of the applicable constitutions.

## 3

# Comparative Perspectives on American Contract Law

## A. LOOKING AT LAW COMPARATIVELY

There are many ways in which a body of law can be studied and learned. At this point, we can probably ignore obsolete approaches such as rote memorization. Among the current methods, the historical approach focuses on the evolution of law and legal institutions over time, the systematic method looks at the way with which the various elements of the law work together as a system, and law and economics analyzes the way legal precepts form and reflect economic interrelationships.

The comparative method of law pedagogy attempts to analyze the way legal doctrine and institutions of the body of law under study compare with doctrine and institutions of other legal systems. The techniques of comparative law enable the student to take a social, economic, or governmental problem common to the respective political economies of both of the legal systems under study and study how the respective systems address and solve this particular problem. The solutions can be compared in terms of economic efficiency as well as systemic consistency and harmony with common social, political, and moral values.

For students already familiar with the doctrine and systemic elements of one legal system, the comparative method presents particular advantages in learning and coming to terms with a new body of law. Comparative analysis enables one not only to acquire familiarity with another legal system but also to obtain new and critical insights into one's own legal system. By learning how other systems solve problems that also exist within one's own society and by comparing those solutions with the solutions with which one is already familiar, the student learns in two directions at once.

Of course, for any jurist already familiar with one legal system, learning the doctrine and institutions of another legal system involves unconscious comparisons with the preexisting legal knowledge. By subjecting these unconscious comparisons to the discipline of comparative law methodology, the depth and value of the bi-directional insights may be increased.

This chapter takes some basic problems of contract law – or, more accurately stated, of the economic dealings that contract law proposes to regulate – and compares how those problems are addressed by American common law and by German civil law, respectively. Comparative law references in later chapters of this text are intended to continue its comparative flavor and to encourage students from other legal cultures to learn American law and legal institutions as they compare with the elements of the legal system with which they are already most familiar.

## B. COMPARATIVE LAW METHODOLOGY

As indicated previously, the core of comparative law methodology is the identification of particular social, political, or economic problems common to two political economies and then juxtaposing the legal and institutional measures adopted by those respective economies to deal with the identified problem. The respective measures can then be evaluated in terms of various social, economic, or political values.

It is not the purpose of this text to delve into comparative technique in great detail. Von Mehren and Gordley, *An Introduction to the Comparative Study of Private Law: The Civil Law System* (Cambridge 2006, Aspen 1999) and Zweigert and Koetz, *Comparative Law, 3ᵈEd.*) (Oxford 1998) are appropriate introductory texts. For the purpose of the present discussion, only a few basic observations are in order.

First, it is important that one be fairly rigorous in identifying the problem or problems that will serve as the frame of reference for the comparison. The best comparisons are made in terms of basic economic, social, and political problems that are experienced in most (or at least two) social, economic, and legal systems. Problems caused by social or political elements of one system that are not shared by another system cannot serve as the basis for a comparison. For instance, the American problem of enforceability of contracts made on Sundays could form a basis for comparison with other legal systems that have social policies of restricting business activity according to day of the week or time of the year. However, there is no point in trying to compare the American "solution" to this problem with legal systems in which this kind of social choice does not exist.

By the same token, social or legal problems caused by the solution of another underlying problem are good bases for comparison only with systems that have chosen to solve the underlying problem more or less in the same way. The comparison then becomes a second-level comparison of how problems caused by a commonly chosen solution to an underlying problem are in turn solved in the respective systems. For instance, both English and American procedural law attempt to deal with the problem of evaluating secondhand evidence by restricting the admission of hearsay. This solution engenders its own problems of accessibility to evidence, particularly in nonjury matters. The differing English and American solutions to these common second-level problems can be compared but only in the context of two systems that create the common issue by creating a hearsay rule of nonadmissibility to address the underlying primary problem of information accreditation.

Once a common problem has been identified, one must also be rigorous in focusing on all ways in which the respective political economies address this problem. It is not sufficient to compare just those elements of doctrine or institutions that bear similar names or seem to fulfill similar functions in the systems to be compared. One must look at all ways in which the basic problem under consideration is addressed. Some of these ways may not be in the same doctrinal terms or institutional form in both systems. Sometimes social, economic, customary, or even religious structures will address a problem that is largely a matter of doctrinal law or public institutional structure in another.

In seeking those elements of another legal system that solve the underlying problem under consideration, it is important to focus on function rather than facial similarity to the elements of doctrine or institutions that address the problem in the system with which one is already familiar. The issue is whether some element in the foreign system functions to solve the problem, not whether it looks like the element that solves the problem in the comparatist's own system or whether it solves the problem in the same way.

> [E]ach system functions as a whole. Its general tendencies depend on the interaction in concrete situations of all of the elements discussed . . .Only after analyzing for each system the full range of historical, institutional and social facts here considered, can comparative generalizations be offered.[1]

---

[1] von Mehren, "The Judicial Process: A Comparative Analysis," 5 *Am. J. Comp. L. 197* (1956). See also Zweigert (Kötz, *An Introduction to Comparative Law*, 3$^{rd}$ ed.(1998), pp. 33 ff. For a good survey on the most recent development of comparative law as a body of knowledge, see Reimann, "The Progress and Failure of Comparative Law in the Second Half of the Twentieth Century," 50 *Am. J. Comp. L. 671* (2002).

An example of this is the problem of mass torts, cases in which unintentional wrongs such as defective products, drugs, or environmental pollution cause harms that may affect large numbers of victims. The American system addresses this problem in large part by a robust civil litigation system, including the possibility of class actions. European civil litigation systems may suffer by comparison in the context of this problem until one takes into account the role of criminal law and administrative proceedings, which in Europe are much more actively employed to address these issues than in the United States. It also cannot be ignored that Europe's more pervasive system of social insurance may serve to mitigate the impact of these mass torts and reduce the need for a massive and expensive private civil justice system to secure indemnification from the responsible parties.

Once the respective solutions to the basic social or economic problem have been identified and understood, then one must be sure that the evaluation of those solutions is in terms of values that are basic and common to both systems. Frequently, cultural, historical, and traditional factors will mean that particular values will have greater or less significance to individuals of different cultures. For instance, to some cultures, economic efficiency is the single most important touchstone for any legal or social institution. In other cultures, harmony with underlying moral and religious values is of greater importance than mere economic efficiency. In some legal cultures, a kind of logical coherence is a value in itself. Comparatists must be sure that they are talking in terms of the same values when they evaluate legal institutions from different cultures.

For these reasons, comparative law dialogue rarely exhibits that degree of declarative certainty that jurists sometimes employ with respect to the internal structure or doctrine of their own domestic systems. The comparatist speaks and writes of other legal systems with some tentativeness and restraint. Comparative value assessments of legal systems are couched in terms that respect diversity of values as well as the limitations of cross-cultural knowledge and understanding. In studying, analyzing, comparing, and evaluating the legal fabric of each other's society, we must be respectful of each other's history, values, institutions, and traditions, especially as our understanding of those cultural elements is by necessity more limited than our understanding of our own. Bold blanket assertions of comparative value or efficacy tend to stifle productive discussion and have little place in comparative law dialogue. Questions rather than declarations, qualified rather than indisputable conclusions, and a little humility about one's own legal system go a long way to foster productive comparative discussion.

### C. CONTRACT LAW – OFFER AND ACCEPTANCE

In both the common law and the civil law, agreement is an idea central to the law of contract. How then is assent or agreement manifested, channelized, and made legally effective? Important aspects of these problems are illuminated by considering the rules respecting offer and acceptance described herein. A comparison between contract law rules of the American common law and those found in one civil law system – that of the Federal Republic of Germany – is then undertaken to illustrate some of the problems and possibilities of comparative analysis.

### 1. The Common Law of Offer and Acceptance

Various questions arise in connection with offers. A pervasive problem is whether the stage of *offer* – as distinguished from that of preliminary negotiation – has been reached. In all contemporary legal systems, this issue raises essentially a problem of interpretation. Questions also arise as to how long an offer remains open and whether an offeror can legally bind himself or herself to keep an offer open for a stated period or for a reasonable time.

In the common law, an offer is open for the period stated or, if the offer is silent on the point, for a time period that is reasonable in the circumstances. However, under traditional common law, an offeror cannot bind himself or herself to keep an offer open for a stated period or for a reasonable length of time. The doctrine of consideration permits a promisor to revoke a promise freely until he or she has received for it a counter-promise or counter-performance. Accordingly, the traditional common law position was that an offeror could lose the right freely to revoke the offer only if a separate contract were concluded in which, for a price, the offeror agreed to hold the offer open for a period of time or until certain conditions were met.

In the United States, this view has been modified to some degree in the course of the last half century. Doctrines such as promissory estoppel can be invoked to protect an offeree who reasonably relies to his or her detriment on an offeror's promise to hold the offer open. In addition, Section 2–205 of the Uniform Commercial Code treats as binding a firm offer to buy or sell goods made in writing by a merchant; however, for the common law, it remains true that even firm offers are, in principle, revocable.

A classic problem arising at the stage of acceptance is when an acceptance manifested by the offeree is effective to form a contract where the parties are not in instantaneous and continuous communication. In the famous case of *Adams v. Lindsell*, 1 B. & Ald. 681, 106 Eng. Rep. 250 (K.B. 1818), the common law took the position that the acceptance was effective to form the contract at the time the acceptance was dispatched. This view is often referred to as the "mailbox" rule. From the time of dispatch onward, therefore, an offeror can no longer withdraw his or her offer. Indeed, delay or loss of the acceptance in transmission usually does not prevent the contract from arising if the transmission of the acceptance was by a means appropriate in view of the method used by the offeror to transmit the offer.

As already explained, the justification for the offeror's right to withdraw his or her firm offer is the absence of consideration to support the promise to keep the offer open. The doctrinal explanation originally advanced for the rule that the acceptance was effective upon dispatch is of a different order. The mailbox rule follows from the idea that when consent is effectively manifested on both sides, the contract is in existence. The rule can thus be seen as an implication from the metaphor that contracts rest on "meeting of the parties" minds.

One difference of importance that flows from the different doctrinal bases for the two rules is that the rule of no firm offer without consideration is *ius cogens* whereas the mailbox rule is *ius dispositivum*. The requirement of consideration cannot be set aside by party agreement; accordingly, the rule that an offer not supported by consideration is revocable is mandatory. On the other hand, because the mailbox rule rests on the idea of agreement, by stipulating in the offer that agreement depends on receipt of the acceptance, the offeror can postpone the meeting of the minds until the stipulated event has occurred. The mailbox rule yields, therefore, to a contrary expression of intention.

## 2. Comparative Analysis

The common law rules respecting the free revocability of offers and the effectiveness of acceptances on dispatch provide the basis for a simple exercise in comparative analysis; the exercise illustrates methodology and suggests some of the kinds of insights that can be derived from comparative work.

For purposes of this comparative exercise, it is convenient to look to German law for rules to be compared with the common law rules discussed previously. Section 145 of the German civil code (*Burgerlichesgesetzbuch*, or BGB) provides that an offer is, in principle, binding either for the time stated or, if no period is stated, for a reasonable time. The rule of Section 145 yields, however, to an offeror's expression of a contrary intention.

The problem of when an acceptance is effective to form the contract is dealt with in German law as an aspect of the general problem of when a declaration of intention (*Willenserklärung*) is effective. German legal scholarship prior to the drafting of the BGB analyzed this problem in terms of four theories: the *Äusserungstheorie*, the *Übermittelungstheorie*, the *Empfangstheorie*, and the *Vernehmungstheorie*. As of the time the BGB was being drafted, none of these had achieved supremacy. The drafters of the BGB ultimately preferred the *Empfangstheorie* on practical as well as theoretical grounds. However, the rule of Section 130 (1) can, as far as the effective date of the acceptance is concerned, be displaced by the offeror stipulating otherwise in the offer.

An interesting pattern of rules thus emerges. In the common law, the offer is revocable and the rule is mandatory; in German law, the offer is, in principle, irrevocable but the rule yields to a contrary stipulation by the offeror. The two legal systems also deal differently with the acceptance. In the common law, the acceptance is effective upon dispatch. In the German law, the acceptance is effective upon receipt. In both systems, these rules yield to contrary stipulation by the offeror in the offer.

What is one to make of all this? Does the contrariness of the rules in question indicate that the two systems view these problems quite differently? Or are the two systems really in fairly substantial agreement as to the policies at stake so that the differences in rules reflect technical or doctrinal difficulties or differences rather than different conceptions of policy?

We thus encounter a problem of comparative law methodology: What significance is to be assigned to facial similarities or differences? And how can we penetrate to the reality that lies beneath the surface of described rules and doctrines?

To accomplish this task successfully, one must analyze the rules in question in functional terms. In undertaking such an analysis of rules in American and German law dealing with offer and acceptance, a convenient starting point is Section 145 of the BGB. Why did the drafters of the BGB provide that the offer was, in principle, irrevocable for a stated period or a reasonable time? The drafters' thinking is explained in their 1888 commentary or *Motive* to the proposed new BGB (Vol. I, pp. 165–166), in which it is said that the binding effect of the offer is a requirement of commerce. The recipient of an offer needs a sure point of departure for the decision he is to make. He must often change his position even to consider the offer. Commerce would be rendered more difficult and would decrease if offers were not binding.

In effect, therefore, the German rule respecting the irrevocability of offers rests on a policy of offeree protection. The same considerations can be advanced to support the identical policy in common law. However, the common law doctrinal imperative of consideration stands in the way of advancing this policy through a rule comparable to that contained in Section 145 of the BGB. Accordingly, the question arises whether another route is available through which the common law can provide offeree protection.

The contemporary policy justification of the mailbox rule is in terms of offeree protection. By making the acceptance effective upon dispatch, the offeree's period of uncertainty is made as short as possible. Moreover, the offeror's freedom to revoke the offer is constrained because he cannot be sure that the offeree has not already accepted the offer and thereby created a binding contract. In this connection, it can be noted that the common law considers a revocation of an offer effective upon its receipt by the offeree rather than upon its dispatch by the offeror.

If this analysis is correct, the American and German systems are pursuing the same policies but with different techniques because of the different doctrinal possibilities available to each of them. It can also be noted that the irrevocable-offer rule pairs naturally with the rule that the acceptance is effective only upon receipt, just as the revocable-offer rule finds its natural counterpart in the mailbox rule.

It is interesting to consider which of these patterns of rules more effectively carries out the shared policy of offeree protection. Theoretically, the German irrevocability rule would seem to provide the offeree with the higher degree of protection. It is not clear, however, that matters have in practice worked out that way. The rule of Section 145 is, as has already been remarked, not a mandatory rule. It follows that offerors, once their attention has been drawn to the possible consequences of the rule, may routinely exclude the operation of Section 145. The economic dislocations in Germany after World War I and World War II had the effect of encouraging such exclusions. So-called *freibleibend* offers became very common and the policy of offeree protection suffered seriously.

Of course, an analogous possibility exists in the common law. The offeror can exclude the mailbox rule. This does happen but arguably less frequently than in German law. There are two reasons why this may be the case. First, the relationship between offeree protection and the mailbox rule is more subtle than is the connection of offeree protection to Section 145 of the BGB. Presumably, therefore, an offeror would be less likely to expressly stipulate that the other party's acceptance would occur only upon receipt than to exclude the binding effect of one's own offer. Second, economic dislocations that might have caused offerors to exclude the mailbox rule on a widespread basis have never occurred in the United States on the scale experienced in Germany. However, an assured and definitive answer to how these rules work out in practice would require extensive field investigation.

A further question can be asked based on this comparative exercise. If one were charged today with drafting the provisions of a civil code dealing with this area of the law, what rules should one propose? Probably one would begin with the German rules. But would it not be wise to provide that in cases where the offeror has stipulated that the offer is not binding, the acceptance would take effect upon dispatch rather than receipt? In this way, offeree protection would be advanced in some situations where use of the German rules alone would not accord the desired protection.

Could one go further? For example, would it be possible to make the German rule respecting the binding effect of offers or the common law's mailbox rule mandatory? The answer is probably no. A mandatory rule in the offer-and-acceptance area could presumably be avoided if the offeror were to cast the proposition in the form of an invitation to the other party to make an offer along the lines of a proposal set out in an invitation to deal. The regime of private autonomy, of which contract law is the institutional expression, thus sets a limit to the degree of offeree protection that is possible. Conceivably, ideas of reliance and doctrines such as *culpa in contrahendo* could be used to provide some measure of offeree protection for situations where the offeror seeks to avoid or make inapplicable rules designed to protect the offeree. However, the complications and administrative difficulties involved are probably too great to be overcome effectively.

## D. THE DOCTRINE OF CONSIDERATION

A civil law jurist undertaking a study of the common law of contracts will find some areas or topics more accessible than others. Offer and acceptance and the learning relative to such problems as the effects of mistake or of changed or unforeseen circumstances deal with doctrines and rules that, at least in general outline, are familiar to jurists trained in the civil law tradition. Greater difficulty is experienced when a civil law jurist confronts the complex and subtle doctrine of consideration.

## 1. The Common Law Doctrine of Consideration

Consideration stands, doctrinally speaking, at the center of the common law's approach to contract. The doctrine performs a variety of functions that are quite unrelated except as they can be joined by a verbal formula.

The literature on consideration is enormous. Yet, the great bulk of the writing is only indirectly helpful to one who seeks to understand consideration from a perspective whose points of reference are external to the common law. Direct comparison of the doctrine of consideration with doctrines of other legal systems is out of the question; the doctrines differ too greatly in formulation and technique. A basis for comparison can be found only in the functions that consideration performs, in whole or in part, in a common law system.

The discussion that follows considers three problem areas that the American common law approaches – to a greater or lesser degree, depending on the area in question – through the doctrine of consideration: the position accorded abstract obligations; the problem of unenforceability, relative and absolute; and the screening of individual transactions for unfairness. Before undertaking this investigation, a few words are in order respecting the doctrinal statement or formulation of the consideration requirement.

A standard, contemporary American statement of the doctrine is given in Section 71 of Restatement Second, Contracts 2d (1979):

Requirement of Exchange; Types of Exchange.

(1) To constitute consideration, a performance or a return promise must be bargained for.
(2) A performance or return promise is bargained for if it is sought by the promisor in exchange for his promise and is given by the promisee in exchange for that promise.
(3) The promise may consist of
    (a) an act other than a promise, or
    (b) a forbearance, or
    (c) the creation, modification, or destruction of a legal relation.
(4) The performance or return promise may be given to the promisor or to some other person. It may be given by the promisee or by some other person.

At traditional common law, an agreement or a promise, except a promise under seal, was not enforceable unless supported by consideration. Today in American law, some agreements or promises not supported by a consideration are enforceable as contracts. Indeed, in Restatement Second of Contracts, Topic 2 of Chapter 4 on contract formation is entitled "Contracts Without Consideration." The most general of the relaxations, set out in Section 90(1), covers:

> A promise which the promisor should reasonably expect to induce action or forbearance on the part of the promisee or a third person and which does induce such action or forbearance is binding if injustice can be avoided only by enforcement of the promise. The remedy granted for breach may be limited as justice requires.

Although in the last century the requirement that promises or agreements present an element of bargain or reciprocity has eroded, the consideration doctrine remains central to the American common law's approach to the problem of unenforceability, relative and absolute. The doctrine has also a role to play, although one of lesser importance, with respect to abstract obligations and the screening of individual transactions for unfairness.

## 2. The Problem of Unenforceability, Relative and Absolute

Consideration's most central and pervasive role is in handling the problem of unenforceability. In the first instance, the doctrine operates to mark off various classes of transactions either as always unenforceable or as unenforceable unless there is present an element not necessarily or naturally associated with the transaction – for example, reliance on a formality. No legal system is prepared to enforce all types of promises or agreements. Some are not enforced because they are inherently too dangerous for one party or for the society; others are too unimportant or marginal to justify the effort; still others are denied enforcement because they do not make sense in terms of the level of social and economic development achieved by the particular society.

For the American common law, as for other contemporary Western legal systems, there are four general, interrelated concerns that lead the system to treat a given transaction type – as distinguished from a discrete transaction – as unenforceable: (1) concern for evidentiary security, a desire to protect both the individual citizen and the courts against manufactured evidence and difficulties resulting from insufficiencies in the available proof; (2) the individual is also to be protected against his or her own rashness and the importuning of others; further, (3) the potentially *enforceable* obligation is to be marked off or signalized so as to ensure an awareness on the individual's part that his or her action may have legal consequences and to simplify the administration of justice; and, finally, (4) there is a reluctance to commit the legal order's resources to enforce transaction types considered suspect or of marginal value. These four concerns can be referred to as evidentiary, cautionary, channeling, and deterrent policies.

Transaction types are considered unenforceable that present, in their natural or ordinary configuration (taking into account community habits and conceptions), one or more of these difficulties in a sufficiently acute degree. Speaking very generally, the unenforceability is absolute or incurable if the introduction of an element – say, reliance or a formality – extrinsic to the transaction in its natural state cannot remove or sufficiently meet the concern. If the introduction of extrinsic elements can satisfy the objection, the unenforceability is curable and the transaction will be enforced if appropriate extrinsic elements are present.

The problem of unenforceability has three aspects. Consideration is involved in all of these, although the degree of involvement varies: (1) delineating *transaction types* unenforceable in their natural or normal state; (2) classifying a *discrete or specific transaction* to determine whether it falls within an unenforceable transaction type; and (3) determining and devising extrinsic elements – for example, affixing a seal or contriving an exchange (nominal consideration) – capable of rendering enforceable otherwise unenforceable transactions.

*a. Delineating Transaction Types Unenforceable in Their Natural or Normal State.* The American common law uses two quite different techniques in classifying transaction *types* with respect to their enforceability. The first, seen in the Statute of Frauds and similar legislation, proceeds by delineating the transaction type in functional or economic terms. Statute of Frauds legislation speaks of contracts to sell goods, the value of which exceeds a certain amount; contracts to sell any interest in land; agreements not to be performed within a year of their making; agreements upon consideration of marriage; suretyship agreements; and undertakings by an executor or administrator to be surety on a debt of the deceased for which the estate is liable.

The other technique, seen in the doctrine of consideration, is less direct. A generalized, abstracted characteristic – the absence of a bargained-for exchange – defines the transaction type that is unenforceable. Therefore, for example, gift contracts are not enforceable.

Two traits of the traditional common law approach to the handling of the problem of unenforceability through the doctrine of consideration – traits that are still present in the American common law – should be noted. The first is that the common law considers suspect and denies enforcement to certain transaction types that, when evaluated not in terms of the abstract characteristic of bargained-for exchange but in terms of their economic and social characteristics, should not be enforceable in their natural state. A clear example is the option given in a business context but without any price being paid. In other situations, the court may be either (1) striking down the transaction as a *class* (and without regard to the fairness of the particular arrangement) because the element of bargained-for exchange is too tenuous, or (2) refusing, in view of the unfairness of the *discrete* transaction, enforcement although a fair arrangement in which the element of bargained-for exchange was equally tenuous would be given effect. Examples of commercial transactions that present this ambiguity because the element of bargained-for exchange is tenuous are (1) business arrangements (e.g., requirements and output contracts) in which only one side undertakes in advance a substantial commitment, and (2) compromise agreements – or contract adjustments – in which the duties incumbent on one party remain substantially unaltered while those falling on the other are reduced in amount but unaltered in kind.

*b. Classifying Individual Transactions to Determine Whether They Fall Within an Unenforceable Transaction Type.* Once a legal system treats certain transaction *types* as relatively or absolutely unenforceable, the problem of classifying arises: Does an *individual* situation fall within an unenforceable type so that, unless the unenforceability is curable and appropriate extrinsic elements are present, no legally enforceable obligation arises?

For purposes of the Statute of Frauds, the classification process proceeds in terms of legislatively enumerated contractual provisions or characteristics. For example, is the contract to be performed within a year of its making; does the price of goods covered by a contract of sale exceed a certain amount; does the contract transfer an interest in land? Where the doctrine of consideration marks off the general area of unenforceability, that doctrine furnishes – in the form of its judicially developed criterion of an element of bargained-for exchange of economic values – as well as the technique for classifying the individual transaction.

The results reached in classifying *individual* transactions in terms of whether they present an element of bargained-for exchange can be examined under three headings: (1) transactions in which an element of liberality is combined with an onerous element (promises of mixed gifts); (2) promises made in recognition of a preexisting situation of fact that does not, at the time of promising, give rise to a legally enforceable obligation against the promisor; and (3) promises of liberalities made in the public interest (the charitable subscription).

When one party promises because he wishes to confer a benefit on the other party and to obtain as well from that party a desired advantage, the transaction presents elements of both an onerous transaction and a liberality. A promise of a mixed gift is present, for example, when an uncle agrees to sell his house, worth $100,000 on the current market, to his favorite nephew for $50,000. Should this transaction be considered wholly or partially suspect because it can be notionally divided into two transactions, only one of which presents an element of bargained-for exchange? The common law strongly tends to classify all mixed gifts as enforceable; doctrinally, the result is both required and justified by the proposition that a court is not to investigate the adequacy of the consideration.

Viewed from a less doctrinal perspective, the issue in our hypothetical case is whether the court believes the element of onerousness in the situation affects the uncle's behavior in such measure that the cautionary and channeling concerns – which are decisive for a purely donative situation – are obviated. The legal system here ultimately relies on psychological assumptions that are untested and perhaps untestable. In all events, approaching such problems through the doctrine of consideration and an irrebuttable presumption that consideration – if present at all – is adequate may well result in enforcing mixed gifts where the onerous element present would not, were the question put directly, be considered sufficiently important to affect the parties' behavior in a manner that removes cautionary and channeling concerns. Here as elsewhere, a tension sometimes arises between the result that flows from the logic of the consideration doctrine and an evaluation of the situation in more realistic or factual terms. For example, where an uncle promises to sell his valuable house to the nephew for $10, the rule that courts do not investigate the adequacy of consideration could make the uncle's promise enforceable even if, as a psychological matter, one were prepared to conclude that serious cautionary and channeling concerns remained.

The problem a legal system faces in handling situations in which a party, in recognition of a preexisting situation of fact, purports to assume an obligation is similar to that raised by mixed gifts: Should a situation that combines onerous and gratuitous elements be handled as though it were entirely gratuitous or entirely onerous? The answer should ultimately turn on whether the policies thought to justify treating wholly gratuitous situations as unenforceable carry over to these special cases. But, the common law usually approaches these situations through an analysis based on the doctrine of consideration.

Consider (1) a promise to fulfill an obligation contracted while a minor; (2) a bankrupt debtor's promise to pay a released or discharged debt; and (3) a promise to pay an obligation on which the period of limitation has run. American common law classifies promises made in these three situations as enforceable. Though the result is clear, considerable dispute exists on how it is to be explained in view of the doctrine of consideration. Just as did the first Restatement of Contracts, Sections 82, 83, and 85 of the Restatement Second resolve the problem by treating these situations as contracts enforceable without consideration. Another explanation sometimes encountered is that from the beginning a moral obligation exists that supports and serves as consideration for the later promise. By his promise, the debtor recognizes the moral obligation and becomes liable. A third theory posits that the creditor has, prior to the debtor's new promise, not merely a moral claim but also a legal claim. This legal claim is unenforceable because the defense of infancy, of the statute of limitations, or of discharge in bankruptcy is available to the debtor. Therefore, when a new promise is made, the effect is not to create a legal right in the creditor where none existed before (for this, it is asserted, would require consideration) but rather to remove a defense of the debtor against the assertion of an already existing legal right.

These special situations can be contrasted with the general problem of promises made in subsequent recognition of past situations out of which no legal obligation had arisen (or now exists) on the promisor's part. Classifying these situations with respect to enforceability has produced considerable difficulty and uncertainty in the common law. The courts tend to be mechanical, refusing enforcement because of logical compulsions deriving from consideration even though cautionary, evidentiary, channeling, and deterrent policies do not require this result.

Lord Mansfield attempted to introduce a more flexible approach in a series of decisions between 1774 and 1782. He proposed to consider each case individually, finding consideration – and thus classifying the transaction as enforceable – whenever a "moral obligation" could be said to exist. In *Hawkes v. Saunders*, 1 Cowp. 289, 290, 98 Eng. Rep. 1091 (K.B. 1782), an executrix, who had promised to pay a legally unenforceable legacy, was held liable in assumpsit on her promise. Mansfield reasoned that "[w]here a man is under a moral obligation, which no Court of law or equity can inforce, and promises, the honesty and rectitude of the thing is a consideration. . . . [T]he ties of conscience upon an upright mind are a sufficient consideration." This view at first achieved some general acceptance but was repudiated in *Eastwood v. Kenyon*, 11 Adol. & El. 438, 113 Eng. Rep. 482 (Q.B. 1840). Since that decision of 1840, the English courts have usually classified promises made in recognition of moral obligations as unenforceable.

The contemporary position in the United States is less clear. In the case of *Mills v. Wyman*, 20 Mass. (3 Pick.) 207, 209, a promise made by a father to reimburse a stranger for food and shelter given to the promisor's adult son (whom the father was under no legal duty to support) was held unenforceable because consideration was lacking. The court reasoned that:

> It is said a moral obligation is a sufficient consideration to support an express promise; and some authorities lay down the rule thus broadly; but upon examination of the cases we are satisfied that the universality of the rule cannot be supported, and that there must have been some pre-existing obligation, which has become inoperative by positive law, to form a basis for an effective promise. . . .

On the other hand, *Webb v. McGowin*, 27 Ala. App. 82, 86, 168 So. 196, 198 (1935), *cert. denied*, 232 Ala. 374, 168 So. 199 (1936), held enforceable a promise made by an employer (defendants' intestate) to pay an employee (the plaintiff) $15 every two weeks for the remainder of the employee's life. The promise was made after the employee had saved his employer from severe bodily injury or death by diverting, at the cost of serious injury to himself, a falling block that would otherwise have struck the employer. The employer had faithfully performed during his lifetime. The court, in giving judgment for the plaintiff, explained the result as follows:

Some authorities hold that, for a moral obligation to support a subsequent promise to pay, there must have existed a prior legal or equitable obligation, which for some reason had become unenforceable, but for which the promisor was still morally bound. This rule, however, is subject to qualification in those cases where the promisor, having received a material benefit from the promisee, is morally bound to compensate him for the services rendered and in consideration of this obligation promises to pay. In such cases the subsequent promise to pay is an affirmance or ratification of the services rendered carrying with it the presumption that a previous request for the services was made. . . .

The position taken by Restatement Second of Contracts 2d accommodates the results reached alike in *Webb v. McGowin* and *Mills v. Wyman*. Section 86 treats "Promise for Benefit Received" and provides that

    (1) A promise made in recognition of a benefit previously received by the promisor from the promisee is binding to the extent necessary to prevent injustice.

    (2) A promise is not binding under Subsection (1)

        (a) if the promisee conferred the benefit as a gift or for other reasons the promisor has not been unjustly enriched; or

        (b) to the extent that its value is disproportionate to the benefit.

The approach builds on the law of restitution; hence, the section does not operate unless the promisor was enriched. The result reached in *Mills v. Wyman* is thus accepted. On the other hand, where enrichment has occurred but restitution would be "denied by virtue of rules designed to guard against false claims, stale claims, claims already litigated, and the like [,] . . . [the] subsequent promise to make restitution removes the reason for the denial of relief, and the policy against unjust enrichment then prevails." Accordingly, the result – although not the reasoning – of *Webb v. McGowin* is approved.

The charitable subscription raises a basic policy issue: Do the reasons that lead to the classification of ordinary promises to give as unenforceable also apply to promises of gifts to charity? The common law does not give a direct answer to this question; its position must be derived from the manner in which the doctrine of consideration is applied to charitable subscriptions.

In England, the charitable subscription has been treated like an ordinary promise to give and is not, in the absence of special circumstances, legally enforceable. In the United States, many courts have treated subscriptions as an enforceable transaction type by finding consideration through a variety of analyses, none of them doctrinally very satisfying. Each subscriber's promise is taken to support, by serving as consideration, the promise of every other subscriber. Or, it is said that the acceptance of the subscription by the beneficiary or its representative imports a promise to apply the funds properly, and this promise supports the subscriber's promise. Section 90(2) of Restatement Second treats a charitable subscription as enforceable when the subscription could reasonably induce action or forbearance regardless whether action or forbearance was induced.

*c. Determining and Devising Extrinsic Elements Capable of Rendering Enforceable Otherwise Unenforceable Transactions.* When a legal order treats a given transaction type as unenforceable, two further questions must be faced: Is the unenforceability absolute; and, if not, what elements extrinsic to the transaction in its normal configuration will render the transaction enforceable? Aside from immoral or illegal transactions and transactions against public policy, no clear examples of a radically unenforceable transaction type is found in the common law. However, as is developed herein, the gift-promise arguably presents a case of absolute unenforceability.

Transactions that fall within the ambit of the Statute of Frauds or similar legislation are clearly only relatively unenforceable; they are rendered enforceable by the use of various extrinsic elements – embodying the obligation in a signed writing or preparing an adequate memorandum is always effective, part performance or the giving of earnest money often suffices. These elements are legislatively determined, set out in the same statutory source that ascribes relative unenforceability to the transaction types in question.

The situation is far more complex when in question are extrinsic elements capable of rendering enforceable transaction types marked off as unenforceable by a consideration-based analysis. First, the general doctrine of consideration as developed by judicial doctrine does not state whether the unenforceability is relative or absolute. Nor are extrinsic elements prescribed that will cure the unenforceability in the event that it is not absolute. Second, unless a limiting principle is implicit in the consideration doctrine, arguably any element capable of removing the policy concerns taken to justify treating as unenforceable the transaction type in question should satisfy the court. Moreover, because the doctrine of consideration is a judicial creation that has in good measure developed in terms of logical rather than functional premises, the relative strengths of the various policy concerns that underlie these applications of consideration are unclear. Indeed, as pointed out previously, business options and other business arrangements that lack – when abstracted from their commercial context – any element of reciprocity may be treated as unenforceable because they technically fall within consideration's scope rather than because strong policy concerns so require.

A final element of complexity in the common law situation is uncertainty respecting the effectiveness of the extrinsic elements that parties might utilize in an effort to render enforceable gift-promises, option arrangements, and other transactions lacking an element of bargain or reciprocity and thus suspect under the general doctrine of consideration. Indeed, because no suitable extrinsic element has been developed, some American jurisdictions may today treat gift-promises as absolutely unenforceable.

The two extrinsic elements that at once come to mind as possibilities are the seal and nominal consideration. Various states of the United States no longer recognize the seal as an effective extrinsic element. The seal's decline is rooted in its changed significance in the modern, literate, democratic world. The seal was originally an impression, usually in wax, of a device or design representing an individual or a family. In modern times, the courts, with legislative assistance in a fair number of states, have recognized easygoing substitutes for the wax seal. Accordingly, today according to Section 96 of the Restatement (Second) Contracts, "[a] seal may take the form of a piece of wax, a wafer or other substance affixed to the document or of an impression made on the document." Indeed, "[b]y statute or decision in most States in which the seal retains significance a seal may take the form of a written or printed seal, word, scrawl or other sign." Despite this erosion of the seal, Section 95 of the Second Restatement sets out the general proposition that

(1) In the absence of statute a promise is binding without consideration if
  (a) it is in writing and sealed; and
  (b) the document containing the promise is delivered; and
  (c) the promisor and promisee are named in the document or so described as to be capable of identification when it is delivered.

The status of nominal consideration in contemporary American common law is precarious. In a Comment (i.e., *d – Pretended exchange*) to Section 79, Adequacy of Consideration; Mutuality of Obligation, the Second Contracts Restatement rejects nominal consideration as a formality:

> . . . Disparity in value, with or without other circumstances, sometimes indicates that the purported consideration was not in fact bargained for but was a mere formality or pretense. Such a sham or 'nominal' consideration does not satisfy the [consideration] requirement of § 71. Promises are enforced in such cases, if at all, . . . as promises binding without consideration under §§ 82–94. . . .

In taking this position, the Second Restatement departs from the position taken by the First Restatement. Although the latter does not use the term, its Section 76 is to the effect that: "Any consideration . . . is sufficient . . . (c) The transfer of money or fungible goods is consideration for a promise to transfer at the same time and place a larger amount of money or goods of the same kind and quality."

At least in jurisdictions that do not recognize the seal, an argument can be made against the Second Restatement's rejection of nominal consideration on the ground that the effect is to treat gift-promises as absolutely unenforceable. The opposing argument is, of course, that nominal consideration is too poor a formality to be accepted; the interjection by the parties of the element of contrived exchange into their transaction simply cannot meet the cautionary, channeling, deterrent, and evidentiary concerns that stand in the way of enforcement.

Restatement Second does recognize in Section 90(1) an extrinsic element – a party's reliance – of a very different kind as effective to render enforceable transactions, such as gift-promises, lacking an element of bargain. The fact of reliance argues in favor of enforcement both because it indicates that an underlying understanding existed between the parties and because a question of fairness is raised.

### 3. The Problem of Abstractness

In various situations, a contractual obligation will be more readily enforced if it can be effectively divorced from the environment and motives that gave rise to the obligation. Civil law theorists, especially German writers, have discussed such divorcement in terms of whether the legal system allows the creation of "abstract obligations." A fully abstract obligation would be enforceable regardless of the underlying transaction or the existence of collateral agreements. For example, an abstract obligation could be enforced even if obtained by fraud; similarly, a party's failure to perform his or her part of the bargain would not affect the enforceability of an abstract obligation. Nor could collateral agreements be argued by way of defense. In sum, the abstract obligation would lead a legal existence completely independent from the transaction out of which it arose.

At various stages in the development of some legal systems, it has been possible to render an obligation at least partially abstract by casting it in special forms. The "stipulation" of Roman law had some of the effects of an abstract obligation. In the old common law, a promise under seal was presumably enforceable even though the promisee failed to render the agreed exchange that was the economic basis for the promise.

For an analysis of consideration, a full discussion of the abstract obligation takes one too far afield. However, a relationship exists between the problem of abstractness and the consideration doctrine. The requirement that consideration be shown before a contract is enforced makes it necessary to reveal, in some degree at least, the transaction's motivational and economic background. Consideration thus requires a degree of contextualization for all contractual obligations. In some jurisdictions, a promise under seal still has certain characteristics of an abstract obligation – in particular, a *prima facie* case for relief can be made out by proving that the instrument is genuine. In other jurisdictions, similar results flow from statutory provisions, making a written instrument presumptive evidence of consideration. Furthermore, in all jurisdictions, a transaction can be rendered partially abstract by embodying it in an integrating agreement. Such an agreement operates under the parol-evidence rule to exclude contemporaneous oral – and prior oral or written – agreements relating to the same subject matter. However, parties can never by an integration foreclose the consideration issue. As is set forth in Section 218(2) of the *Restatement of Contracts, 2d*, "Evidence is admissible to prove whether or not there is consideration for a promise, even though the parties have reduced their agreement to a writing which appears to be a completely integrated agreement."

American common law thus basically rejects – as do contemporary legal systems generally – the abstract obligation.


### 4. The Screening of Individual Transactions for Unfairness

The consideration doctrine is also of importance – although less so today than at times in the past – in the policing of individual transactions with a view to refusing enforcement if the arrangement is too unfair. An American court has available several techniques through which the actual or potential unfairness of a particular transaction can on occasion be mitigated. The learning on mistake, impracticability, impossibility, frustration, and conditions provides in some situations grounds for relief. On occasion, the court can use its power to interpret contractual provisions to achieve a fair result in the particular case.

Another approach to this range of problems rests on the doctrine of consideration. To the extent that this last approach is used, consideration performs a screening function that is different from its previously discussed roles. Where the existence of an element of exchange is open to question – as, for example, in agreements

of compromise, adjustments in an ongoing contractual relationship, and certain requirement and output contracts – a court that
perceives the contract, on its particular facts, as unfair – or likely
to become so – may be able to rationalize a refusal to enforce in
terms of consideration. Thus, in cases involving dealers, jobbers,
and parties without established businesses, courts have refused to
enforce fixed-price requirement contracts that give one party the
right to demand unlimited deliveries in a rising market and to
cease all purchases in a falling one. On the other hand, requirement and output contracts can usually pass muster for purposes of
the doctrine of consideration if the amounts that can be demanded
or supplied are not unlimited and the price varies with the
market.

The doctrine of consideration is obviously a blunt and limited
tool with which to deal with the problem of unfairness. In contemporary American law, the fairness issue is increasingly approached
through the more direct and comprehensive techniques mentioned
previously.

## 5. Conclusion

Not a few writers, responding to the complexity and ambiguity
of the consideration doctrine, have raised the question whether it
should not be radically modified. Lord Wright concluded that

> the common law doctrine of consideration is one which other sys-
> tems successfully dispense with, . . . the doctrine is no natural or
> essential part of the theory of contractual liability. Modern legal
> thought has either adopted or is tending to adopt the simple idea
> that (subject to the obvious qualifications that the subject matter is
> lawful) "*conventio* without more = *contractus*". . .[2]

---

[2] Wright, "Ought the Doctrine of Consideration to be Abolished from the Common
Law?," 49 *Harvard L. Rev.* 1225, 1238 (1936).

The English Law Revision Committee, after briefly discussing French and German law, concluded in its 1937 report "that highly developed systems of modern law can function quite satisfactorily without the aid of the artificial common law doctrine of consideration with its subtle distinctions and refinements."

These writers are obviously overstating their case if they mean to suggest that other systems either enforce all promises seriously intended by the promisor to have legal effects or have managed to render easy solutions of all the problems approached in the common law through consideration. For example, French and German law in many ways deals strictly with gift-promises. Various problems handled by consideration arise in French and German law and at least some are not found notably easier to resolve. However, it is probably fair to criticize consideration as a complicating and obscuring doctrine, one that at times gets in the way of an intelligent handling of basic functional issues.

Several examples may serve to illustrate this proposition. In the common law, as has already been pointed out, difficulties arise respecting the enforcement of various perfectly normal business arrangements, in particular the option contract. Would the common law courts have reached these results if they could have ignored the doctrine of consideration and approached the option situation directly, considering its enforceability in terms of cautionary, evidentiary, channeling, and deterrent policies? It is hard to escape the conclusion that, at least in cases involving two businesspeople, the treatment in the past of firm offers and options can only be explained as a logical deduction from the general doctrine of consideration without proper regard to the policies at stake.

A more pervasive difficulty is the confusion that the doctrine of consideration engenders between the problem of unenforceability and the policing of individual transactions for unfairness. It is not entirely clear whether compromise agreements, modifications in existing contractual relations, and long-term, fixed-price output and requirement contracts require for their enforcement the addition of an extrinsic element, such as a seal or nominal consideration, or whether the courts simply check on the fairness of the individual transaction. A court could require both an extrinsic element and police the particular arrangement for unfairness. Or, a court might not feel free to strike down an unfair or improvident agreement if it is under seal or, where the doctrine of nominal consideration is accepted, was made for such a consideration.

The confusion of the two different problems does more than render difficult the proper handling of individual cases. It may also hamper the development of a satisfactory approach to the general problem of policing individual transactions for unfairness. The consideration doctrine cannot provide a comprehensive solution for the problem; however, use of the doctrine diverts attention and effort from a full analysis of the question and the development of comprehensive solutions. In 1941, Professor Sharp observed that

> [m]uch of the work that is being done by doctrines of consideration could be handled more discriminatingly and systematically by notions of duress, fraud, mistake, supervening difficulty, forfeiture, or more general and less easily defined notions of public policy. . . .[3]

It is the emergence in recent decades of such more comprehensive solutions that explain the contemporary decline, discussed previously, of consideration as far as the policing of individual transaction for unfairness is concerned.

Consideration also tends to blur, with unfortunate results, two distinct aspects of the problem of unenforceability: (1) Is a particular transaction type considered absolutely unenforceable?; and (2) What extrinsic elements are accepted as adequate to render enforceable a transaction unenforceable in its normal state? In many American jurisdictions, it is today unclear whether the

---

[3]  M. Sharp, "Pacta Sunt Servanda," 41 *Columbia L. Rev.* 783, 796 (1941).

unenforceability attaching to gift-promises is relative or absolute. Nor is the acceptability of nominal consideration as a formality always clear. When the two issues are blended, the real difficulty is obscured. Is the problem a lack of a well-conceived extrinsic element, for both the seal and nominal consideration have obvious shortcomings in the contemporary world? If so, a more appropriate formality should be developed. Or is the difficulty more basic; is the real question whether to enforce some gift-promises while denying enforcement to gift-promises in general?

Why has the American common law experienced such difficulties? Several explanations can be ventured. A partial explanation lies in consideration's conceptual nature. A doctrine based on a notion of bargained-for exchange is, in its very nature, too all-inclusive, too expansive to handle appropriately the problems under discussion. Almost inevitably, a doctrine embodying the idea of exchange will be called upon, as consideration has been, to handle too may different and separate problems. Moreover, the exchange idea does not lend itself well to the handling of all aspects of the several problems that can fall within its ambit. Exchange is, for example, too restrictive a standard to handle some aspects of the problem of unenforceability. Witness the difficulties given by the option agreement. In screening individual transactions for unfairness, reliance on an element of exchange can carry one both too far and not far enough. Finally, a doctrine whose central element is a notion of exchange may tend to obscurantism, toward a substitution of logical refinements for analysis based on a weighing of policy concerns. In handling problems of unfairness, an approach through the doctrine of consideration may thus cause one to lose sight of the ultimate goal.

# 4

# American Federalism

AN UNDERSTANDING OF THE CONTOURS AND FUNCTION OF American federalism is vital to comprehension of the workings of the law in the United States. The division and sharing of power between the fifty American states and their federal government in both public law and private law spheres is more fundamental and intricate than is the case with any other modern federal nation-state.

When considering American federalism, it must be constantly kept in mind that the American nation-state is the result of the voluntary association of thirteen independent former colonies, each with a degree of individual sovereignty and its own complete system of public and private law. The American states are not provinces or regions of a larger comprehensive whole; rather, the national government that binds them together is the product of a voluntary fusion of the sovereign states that had been there before.

This historical development stands in contrast with that of other modern democracies, even those with some federal characteristics. In most of these jurisdictions, political consolidation had preceded or accompanied the development of a national legal order. Even in European federal democracies such as Germany, private law as well as much of public law is and remains national despite the increased federalization of the German state following World War II.

## A. THE AMERICAN GOVERNMENTAL SCENE PRIOR TO THE CONSTITUTION OF 1789

Prior to the Declaration of Independence in 1776, the thirteen American colonies did not form part of a federal system. Each was a separate governmental unit that had its own direct relationship with the mother country. The relationship of the colonies to Great Britain can be thought of as a hub (England) and spokes (the various American and other colonies). There was no particular governmental system linking the colonies to each other outside of their common relationship to the mother country. For example, appeal lay in appropriate cases from the highest court of a colony to the Privy Council in England, not to any common court for the American colonies.

Relations between and among the former colonies were not fundamentally changed by the Declaration of Independence or the Articles of Confederation (1781). The colonies had separated from Great Britain and attained independent statehood, but they had not united. There was no national executive or judiciary nor did the Congress established by the Articles of Confederation have significant law-making authority. It lacked, for example, power to tax, to regulate interstate or foreign commerce, and to ensure state compliance with treaties. The only confederation courts envisioned by the Articles were courts to try felonies on the high seas and prize courts for cases of capture on the high seas; Congress was itself "the last resort on appeal in all disputes and differences . . . between two or more states concerning boundary, jurisdiction or any other cause whatever. . . . " Articles of Confederation, Article IX (effective March 1, 1781).

The Convention called in 1787 to revise the Articles of Confederation produced a radically different document: the Constitution of the United States. The confederation of independent states that existed under the Articles was replaced by a federation with a central federal governmental structure upon the Constitution's entrance into force in 1789. This was clearly a stronger federation than had existed before. However, the extent to which the centralized powers of the new federal government supplanted the preexisting powers of the respective states and the division of power between the federal government and the states were carefully circumscribed in the new Constitution. These issues were very much in contention from the earliest days of the new republic and remain somewhat in play to the present day despite two centuries of constitutional construction and experience.

## B. THE FEDERAL SYSTEM ESTABLISHED BY THE U.S. CONSTITUTION

The Constitution as originally written and understood clearly contemplated a federal government that possessed only assigned powers. Unassigned residual power, as the Tenth Amendment made explicit in 1791, was "reserved to the States respectively, or to the people." The corollary of this conception was that each state enjoyed essentially unlimited authority except as limited as a result of the powers delegated to the federal government. Accordingly, each state required the full panoply of government – executive, legislative, and judiciary – even though the Constitution established a federal executive, legislature, and (at least potentially) judiciary.

Article I of the Constitution grants certain "legislative Powers" to the federal government and vests those powers in a Congress of the United States, to consist of a Senate and a House of

Representatives. Section 8 of Article I enumerates the powers granted; these include the power to tax and to "provide for the common Defence and general Welfare of the United States"; "to borrow money on the credit of the United States"; to "regulate Commerce with foreign Nations, and among the several States, and with the Indian Tribes"; to "coin Money [and] regulate the Value thereof"; and to "make all Laws which shall be necessary and proper for carrying into Execution the foregoing Powers, and all other Powers vested by this Constitution in the Government of the United States, or in any Department or Officer thereof."

Although a significant federal authority was thus granted, Article I left to the several states broad powers, including authority over the general subject matters of criminal law and private law. The extent of the law-making authority that remained with the states is emphasized by the Tenth Amendment (1791) to the Constitution:

> The powers not delegated to the United States by the Constitution, nor prohibited by it to the States, are reserved to the States respectively, or to the people.

The powers of the federal system thus established were unclear. The delegations contained in the commerce clause, in the necessary and proper clause, and in other provisions could sustain far-reaching claims of federal authority. However, the history and records of the Constitutional Convention throw little light on how well the delegates understood the possible implications of these provisions. The U.S. Supreme Court's most significant task for much of the nineteenth and early twentieth centuries was to spell out the constitutional allocations of federal and state legislative authority. Today, reflecting economic and political changes deriving from the emergence of a nation-wide economy and the decline of *laissez-faire* thinking, in many fields potentially almost plenary powers rest in Congress, so that Congress now exercises in practice broad powers to resolve allocation issues by legislating or refraining from legislating.

Article II, Section I, of the Constitution provides that "The executive Power shall be vested in a President of the United States of America." Section 2 provides for the appointment of various federal officers. The most important positions are filled by the president with the "Advice and Consent" of the Senate. The same section gives the president power to conclude treaties with the advice and consent of the Senate and the concurrence of two thirds of the senators present.

Just as in the case of the legislative power, the federal executive has its counterpart in the executive branch of the government of each of the several states. The federal executive establishment is concerned, in principle, with the administration of federal laws and regulations. The executive establishment of each state handles, by and large, the administration of that state's law and regulations. Today, areas of overlap exist because of federal-state cooperation in some fields and federal grant-in-aid programs; however, the state and federal executive establishments remain essentially separate in their responsibilities and work.

The Constitution deals somewhat differently with the federal judiciary than with the legislature or the executive. Article III establishes only the Supreme Court; inferior federal courts are permitted but not constitutionally required. This approach resulted from a great constitutional debate on whether the existence of such courts would pose too great a danger to state authority. In all events, the Judiciary Act of 1789 promptly exercised Congress's Article III power and established a full-blown federal judiciary. Accordingly, there are complete and parallel systems of federal and state courts. However, the relationship between the federal and state judicial establishments is quite different from that between the Congress and the federal executive on the one hand and their state counterparts on the other. Unlike the legislative and executive branches, the functions of state and federal judicial systems overlap to a significant extent. The federal judicial establishment is not concerned with federal law alone, nor are state courts responsible only for state law.

## C. THE SPHERES OF FEDERAL AND STATE AUTHORITY – INTERSTATE COMMERCE

At the time the American Constitution was adopted and ratified by the original thirteen states, there were two competing schools of political thought on the nature of the federal entity created by the constitution and the source of its powers. One group, headed by Thomas Jefferson, maintained that the independent American states, acting as political bodies, had delegated certain of their sovereign powers to the new federation, but that they otherwise retained full power and sovereignty. Powers delegated to the federal government should be narrowly construed in order to avoid infringing on the sovereignty of its creators.

The other position was advanced by John Adams and later Chief Justice John Marshall. These jurists regarded America's federal government as a direct creation of the people. It should be afforded the power and authority necessary for it to perform the function that the people expected of it.

Adherents of these competing schools of thought regarded each other's positions with suspicion. The Jeffersonian Democrats feared a central government so strong that it would dominate the legitimate spheres of activity of the respective states. The Adams Federalists were concerned that a weak federal government would lead to disunity of the new nation and regional squabbling that could eventually lead to the dissolution of the union.

Ultimately, the ideological division was resolved largely in favor of a stronger central government. Key to this resolution was a series of early nineteenth-century U.S. Supreme Court decisions that addressed the division, overlapping, and sharing of powers between the states and the United States in various crucial contexts.

One of the most important early questions of American Federalism was the nature and extent of the authority of the federal government to regulate commerce between the states as granted by Section 8 of Article III of the new Constitution. Conflicting regulations of commerce, even to the point of state tariffs or duties, had plagued the Confederation during its short life. The commerce clause had been inserted in the new compact to prevent at least the worst of such abuses. The questions remained: How much farther did the power of Congress go to forge a national economy, and how much power did states retain in matters that may have some interstate character? The tension over the meaning of "interstate commerce" and its effect on the division of powers between state and federal governments has continued to the present day.

This question first came before the U.S. Supreme Court in the case of *Gibbons v. Ogden*, 22 U.S. 1 (1824). In recognition of his contribution to the development of maritime propulsion by steam, the New York Legislature had granted to Robert Fulton and his associate John Livingston the exclusive right to operate "boats moved by fire or steam" on the waters of the State of New York. These included the New York half of the Hudson River, which served as a part of the boundary between New York and New Jersey. This legislative franchise had been assigned to Aaron Ogden.

Thomas Gibbons was the owner of the steamboats *Bellona* and *Stoudinger*. These vessels had been duly licensed pursuant to an early Act of the U.S. Congress, which limited the "coasting trade" between U.S. ports to American vessels licensed pursuant to the Act. Gibbons began to offer steamboat service crossing the Hudson between New York and New Jersey.

Ogden brought suit in the New York State courts seeking an injunction prohibiting Gibbons from operating in New York waters in violation of his statutory monopoly. The New York Chancellor (i.e., equity court judge) granted the injunction and the decision was affirmed on appeal by New York's highest court, the Court for the Trial of Impeachments and the Correction of Errors. Gibbons then appealed to the U.S. Supreme Court on the grounds that the Ogden statutory monopoly violated the laws and Constitution of the United States.

Gibbons's basic position was that the power to regulate interstate commerce was reserved to the federal government, and that any state regulation that had the effect of restricting interstate commerce was *ipso facto* void. Ogden asserted that even if Congress had the right to regulate purely interstate intercourse, the states retained the right to regulate activities occurring within their own boundaries, and that the Ogden monopoly was limited to operations occurring within New York. The case thus presented a direct conflict between the two main constitutional schools of thought.

Chief Justice Marshall's opinion in *Gibbons v. Ogden* is considered one of the foundation stones of American constitutional law. Speaking for a unanimous court, Marshall posed the issue as outlined previously. He then reasoned that "interstate commerce" does include navigation of the kind carried on by Gibbons and extends to acts that take place within a single state as a part of commerce between the states. Acknowledging the existence of various forms of valid state regulation and taxation that also affect interstate commerce, the Court declined to find in those laws a coordinate state power to regulate interstate commerce. The opposing argument that the power to regulate interstate commerce was exclusively delegated to the federal government and that even in the absence of exercise of this power, the states were powerless to act, had, in the words of the Chief Justice, "great force" such that the Court was "not satisfied that it has been refuted."

In a delicate twist that is found in several Marshall opinions, the Court expressly refrained from establishing an exclusive congressional power over interstate commerce of the kind carried on by Gibbons. Instead, the Court found that in this case, Congress had acted in the premises. The U.S. statute licensing vessels for the coasting trade, although originally aimed at preventing foreign vessels from carrying on this trade, also had the effect of preventing the states from enacting inconsistent or more stringent requirements. Gibbons's vessels were licensed under the federal act. The New York regulation had to yield to federal enactments within the scope of the authority granted to Congress.

The *Gibbons v. Ogden* decision, like most of the other great Marshall opinions, established a kind of diplomacy in judicial dialogue that has been a core element of the successful development of constitutional law in the United States ever since. Although the U.S. Supreme Court claims and insists upon the last word in construing and applying the strictures of the U.S. Constitution, it plays this role with a kind of judicial and political sensitivity and respect for the political roles of the coordinate branches of federal government and for the American states. In *Gibbons*, the Court cut the cloth of interstate commerce generously in favor of federal power, at the same time acting with seeming restraint vis-a-vis the role of the states.

The effect of the federalization of regulation of interstate commerce can be seen in the dramatic increase in steamship traffic on the Hudson River following *Gibbons v. Ogden*. The number of steamboats plying back and forth between New York and New Jersey exploded from a mere handful of steamboats before the U.S. Supreme Court decision to more than two hundred vessels only a few years later.

Congress was slow to exercise the commerce power; it was little used until an industrial society emerged after the Civil War. However, from the beginning, the Court held that, even in the absence of congressional action under the Commerce Clause, a state's regulation of activity that affects interstate commerce might be in violation of the commerce power. In defining the scope of the power, content had to be given to the Commerce Clause's two key phrases: "to regulate" and "Commerce with foreign Nations, and among the several States." The endlessly varied forms of trade and the manifold methods and objectives of regulation make this task one that the Court must still on occasion discharge today.

Certain types of state legislation are obviously unconstitutional interferences with interstate commerce. Clear discrimination in favor of local commerce – for example, restrictions on the importation of goods or preferences given to the sale of local goods – plainly run afoul of the Commerce Clause. However, the problem is often much more complex. What if a state imposes regulations that favor local trade but purportedly are required to protect the health of its citizens? Is such a law a legitimate measure for the protection of health or an illegitimate interference with commerce? And what about other areas of state concern? Can a state where natural gas is produced prohibit its export until the needs of its own inhabitants are met? Can a similar embargo be imposed on water?

Of course, there are many borderline issues. Can a state refuse to permit disposal within the state of refuse originating from outside the state? Can a state prescribe minimum prices for particular key products (e.g., milk) sold within the state even though some of the product comes from outside the state? Can the State of Maine prohibit the sale in Maine of lobsters that were legally caught in New Hampshire but do not meet Maine's size restrictions for lobsters caught in Maine? Can a state government give a preference in its own purchases for items manufactured within the state? The answers to these questions are not always clear. As anyone familiar with the experience of the European Union will recognize, such problems are inherent in any meaningful federal structure. At first, the U.S. Supreme Court sought to resolve these issues by classifying a particular state law either as a regulation of commerce and, therefore, unconstitutional, or as an exercise of police powers and, therefore, valid. This approach was soon seen to be too simplistic. A law may well be a regulation both of commerce and of health; ultimately, the burden on the national market must be weighed against the degree of local need. In this calculus, it is appropriate to consider, *inter alia*, whether other alternative measures, less burdensome to commerce, are available to safeguard the local interest.

Similar approaches are seen in the handling of controversies over state taxation of interstate commerce. Recourse has been to simplistic propositions, such as interstate commerce must not be taxed directly and interstate commerce must pay its own way. Taxation problems may not yield to such general formulas; often, the choice of one or the other solution rests on specific judgments and wise results may be best achieved by using a particularistic approach.

For example, in considering whether a state may impose a sales tax on an interstate sale, the Court has considered whether such a tax is forbidden in principle and, if not, whether the tax may be imposed both by the state of the market and by the state of the origin of the goods. The Court has, in effect, concluded that the state of the market can tax but not the state of the origin. In the market state, because the goods will be competing with local products that must pay a similar tax, the burden of the tax will fall equally on local and imported goods. Accordingly, no special burden is being placed on interstate commerce.

Of course, Congress has power by legislation under the Commerce Clause to expand or contract such state authority over commerce as the Court recognizes in the absence of federal legislation. However, the problems in this area are so varied in their incidence and call for such continuing scrutiny that Congress has in the main left their resolution to the Court. When Congress does act, it generally takes over the field and subjects it to national regulation.

There is also a range of activity that may admit of overlapping federal and state regulation, at least in the absence of action by the federal government. Some activity may involve both local and interstate interests. *Gibbons v. Ogden* was decided as if it were in this category. In areas in which both the federal government and states have power to legislate or regulate, the constitutional question becomes whether the federal regulation grounded on the Interstate Commerce Clause is inconsistent with the state regulation and whether it is intended to preempt the field occupied by the state regulation. For instance, at one time, cigarette companies that were sued under state law for misrepresentation of the hazards of smoking asserted that the federal regulatory requirement that cigarette packages bear a particular warning label occupied the field of consumer warning in this area and prevented the states from imposing common law liability on cigarette manufacturers for other kinds of misrepresentation relating to smoking dangers.

The Interstate Commerce Clause has been the foundation for a great deal of federal economic regulation, much of which was enacted during the 1930s in response to the Great Depression. Broad federal regulation of the issuance and sale of securities, collective bargaining, stock exchanges, agricultural marketing, and competition in general was all founded on the powers granted the federal government under the Commerce Clause. Over the years, the Court has sustained federal legislation regulating even apparently intrastate activities that "have such a close and substantial relation to interstate commerce that their control is essential or appropriate to protect that commerce from burdens and obstructions."[1]

Once Congress began to act in the areas of industrial and business regulation, the Court faced an issue that was not necessarily central to its control over state interferences with interstate commerce: Is the federal legislation within Congress's power under

---

[1]  *NLRB v. Jones & Laughlin Steel Corp.*, 301 U.S. 1, 37 (1937).

the Commerce Clause? Although the clear tendency has been to sustain federal power if supported by any direct or indirect connection with interstate commerce, there have been exceptions. From time to time, the U.S. Supreme Court has taken a restrictive view of the federal commerce power. Indeed, it was not until the late 1930s – in the course of reviewing challenges to President Franklin Roosevelt's New Deal legislation – that the Court gave the Commerce Clause the broad reading it has today. The commerce power is now taken to reach activity that, although not in itself interstate or commercial in nature, affects interstate commerce. For example, the placing of quotas on basic agricultural crops has been upheld as a regulation of interstate commerce. Under its authority to regulate business and labor when engaged in production for interstate commerce, Congress can control trade and labor relations.

In view of the sweeping interpretation given the commerce power, some have maintained that federal-state balance in the realm of economic legislation is today maintained not by the Court but by the Congress. Elected by the localities and with each state represented by two members in the Senate, Congress is sensitive to state views. It is this sensitivity that in part explains why the Uniform Commercial Code was not enacted under the commerce power as federal legislation. Such enactment would have provided a federal law for commercial transactions in interstate commerce but only at the price, considered too high to pay, of removing from state control areas for which the states had traditionally been responsible.

Recently, the U.S. Supreme Court has revived the notion that federal authority under the Commerce Clause has limits that can be enforced by the courts. *United States v. Lopez*, 514 U.S. 549 (1995), is a recent example of a somewhat more restrained Commerce Clause jurisprudence. In that case, the defendant had been convicted of a violation of the federal Gun-Free School Zones Act of 1990, which made it a federal crime to have a gun on school property. He appealed the conviction to the U.S. Supreme Court on the ground that there was no constitutional basis for the federal legislation. He asserted that, in particular, there was no relationship between gun possession at a local school and interstate commerce.

The U.S. Supreme Court agreed and vacated the conviction by a 5–4 decision. Although Congress had purported to enact the federal Gun-Free School Zones Act of 1990 pursuant to the inter-state commerce power, the enacting law did not contain legislative findings explaining how the activities of public schools related to interstate commerce. In the absence of a legislative declaration, the Court should not be expected to speculate on potential remote connections between the regulation at issue and some form of interstate commerce that could justify action by Congress. The dissenters asserted that it is indeed the responsibility of the Court to discern any possible connection between the legislation and the constitutional basis for it, regardless of whether Congress chooses to make this connection explicit, and noted that legislation with apparently even less connection to interstate commerce had been routinely upheld as grounded on that constitutional power.

## D. THE FEDERAL AND STATE JUDICIAL SYSTEMS

Because none of the powers delegated by the Constitution to the federal authority limits directly or by implication the general scope of a state's judicial power, the scope of that power depends on the constitution and legislation of the state in question. In principle, these constitutions entrust to the state judicial establishment the plenary administration of justice regardless of whether the claims or issues arise under the forum law, federal law, the law of sister states, or the law of a foreign state. It follows that unless the federal Constitution, treaties, or federal laws prescribe otherwise, the state system handles litigation without regard to whether the claims or issues are state, federal, or foreign in nature.

The structure of the state-court system is controlled by the constitution and laws of the state in question. Courts of first instance normally sit as a single judge. In many cases, both criminal and civil, use of a jury is mandatory unless waived by the parties. When a jury is used, it decides disputed issues of fact; the judge instructs the jury on issues of law. With variations from state to state, special court divisions exist; for example, there are criminal courts, family or domestic-relations courts, juvenile or children's courts, and probate or surrogates courts for decedents' estates. However, special administrative or commercial courts are generally not found.

Each state also has a complete system of appellate justice. In most states today, there are intermediate appellate courts. These courts handle most routine appeals from state courts of first instance. Each state's justice system is capped by a state supreme court, which is the court of last resort on questions of the construction of the law and constitution of that state. In many states, appeal to the highest court is discretionary based on the importance of the issues raised by the appeal.

In both state and federal appellate courts, the scope of review is limited to legal questions, including whether the evidence adduced in first instance reasonably supports the findings made. The scope of review also includes the constitutionality of the law applied and of the decision applying it.

The grant of power on which the federal judicial establishment rests is contained in Article III of the Constitution. That Article creates the "judicial Power of the United States" and provides for the establishment of a Supreme Court with original jurisdiction over cases to which a state is a party, as well as cases involving ambassadors, other public ministers, and consuls. Congress is authorized – but not required – to create lower federal courts and to vest, insofar as it desires, the federal "judicial" power, as defined in Article III, in a federal judiciary.

The Judiciary Act of 1789 set up the first federal judicial establishment. For trial-court purposes, the eleven states then in the union were divided into thirteen districts, each of whose boundaries corresponded to state lines, except that the parts of Massachusetts and Virginia that later became Maine and Kentucky, respectively, were made into separate districts. Although not constitutionally required, a precedent – still in principle respected today – was thus established that the boundaries of federal judicial districts for courts of first instance should not overlap state lines. In most other respects, the arrangements provided by the Act have since been greatly modified.

Today, the federal system has courts of three instances. The first-instance courts are the U.S. District Courts. Each state consists of one or more federal districts for purpose of division of the business of the district courts. Each district court is normally composed by a single judge, who sits in many cases with a jury. (For a few extraordinary matters, a three-judge district court can be constituted.)

The work of a single-judge district court is reviewable in a Court of Appeals. There are Courts of Appeals for each of eleven "circuits" and for the District of Columbia. There is also a special Federal Circuit Court of Appeals that hears appeals in patent cases, appeals in claims against the federal government, appeals involving customs duties, and a handful of other specialized federal matters. A Court of Appeals usually sits with a bench of three judges; occasionally, the entire court sits *en banc*.

At the apex of the federal judicial system is the Supreme Court of the United States, composed of nine justices who sit as a single bench. Only exceptionally is review in the Supreme Court a matter of right. Usually, the final instance in the federal judiciary is the appropriate court of appeal.

One who approaches the question independently of its historical context might well assume that Article III would define the "judicial Power of the United States" either in the broad terms permitted to state judicial power or in narrower terms limiting the federal power to cases implicating the Constitution, laws, or treaties of the United States. Indeed, the uninitiated would probably expect to find constitutional arrangements designed to limit state-court jurisdiction, on the one hand, to nonfederal matters and federal-court jurisdiction, and to federal matters on the other hand.

How such an allocation of judicial authority would have worked in practice will never be known. In the circumstances of 1789, it would have been unthinkable for the federal constitution to limit state-court jurisdiction. At the time, many were suspicious of the untried federal judicial establishment and were unwilling to grant it the plenitude of jurisdiction enjoyed by state courts.

Article III, Section 2, thus imposes limits on the federal judicial power that do not attach to the judicial power of the several states. Speaking generally and omitting detail, the federal power extends only to controversies "between Citizens of different States," "between a State, or the Citizens thereof, and foreign States, Citizens, or Subjects," and to "Cases, in Law and Equity, arising under this Constitution, the Laws of the United States, and Treaties made, or which shall be made, under their Authority. . . ." It follows that where both parties are citizens of a single state and the claim does not raise a federal question, Congress cannot provide for federal-court jurisdiction.

Stated in general terms, the federal judicial power comprises a diversity jurisdiction – the parties belong to different legal orders – and a federal-question jurisdiction. However, Congress has never given the federal courts the full jurisdiction that Article III would permit. One who is not a student of American history is surprised that the Judiciary Act of 1789, which first implemented Article III, did *not* provide for a general federal-question jurisdiction in the lower federal courts. Instead, Section 25 of that Act foresaw

Supreme Court review of state court decisions on federal questions. It was not until 1875, nearly a century later, that the lower federal courts acquired a general federal-question jurisdiction.

On the other hand, the Act of 1789 did provide for "diversity jurisdiction" over cases and controversies between citizens of different states. This fact suggests that in the beginning, the only agreement on the proper role of the federal judiciary was that it should provide an impartial tribunal for those situations in which there was a reasonable fear that the state-court system might be prejudiced in favor of one party. However, from the beginning, this jurisdiction has been subjected to a significant amount-in-controversy threshold.

The role originally assigned the federal judiciary rested, therefore, in substantial measure on the fact that independence did not really create a new nation. At the end of the eighteenth century, one still thought of oneself as a Virginian or a New Yorker rather than as an American. It is a measure of the change in sentiment that has taken place since 1789 that today there is a substantial body of opinion that favors ending the general diversity jurisdiction. However, for a variety of reasons, this change will probably not occur in the foreseeable future.

### E. INTERACTION BETWEEN THE STATE AND FEDERAL SYSTEMS OF JUSTICE

The state and federal systems intersect to ensure the integrity of federal law when, in exercising plenary state-court jurisdiction, a state court decides a federal issue. Intersection also occurs to ensure the integrity of state law when, in carrying out the nonprejudice philosophy of federal diversity jurisdiction, federal courts decide issues within state legislative competence. Complications arise in handling each of these situations. The solutions provided are described herein in general and necessarily incomplete terms.

Basically, two problems are presented. Preserving the unity of federal law requires that state instances do not determine finally the interpretation and application of federal law. On the other hand, the preserving integrity of each state's law requires that federal instances do not determine finally the interpretation and application of state law.

In the context of the American federal system, a variety of mechanisms could be devised to handle these problems. Exclusive jurisdiction could be given federal courts over some or all issues of federal law and to state courts over some or all issues of state law. Ultimate review of issues of federal law litigated in state courts could lie to federal courts; state courts could review federal-court determinations of state law. Removal to a federal court of a cause initiated in a state court – or to a state court of a cause initiated in a federal court – could be permitted where important issues of federal – or of state – law were raised. The judicial system that entertained a given matter could seek – either as a matter of law or in its discretion – the view of an appropriate state or federal court on important issues arising under the requested court's law. Finally, courts – whether federal or state – could be required by their own law to apply rules and principles derived from another legal order.

All of these techniques are encountered. Some – ultimate review of certain discrete issues of law and removal of causes – are utilized essentially to ensure the integrity of federal law and, in the case of removal, to carry out as well the nondiscrimination policy that underlies the federal diversity jurisdiction. There is no state counterpart to removal of causes from state to federal courts nor to the Supreme Court's power to review issues of federal law that arise in matters litigated in state courts. Jurisdiction over certain areas of state law (e.g., general criminal law, except as to federal constitutional issues, and domestic relations) is exercised only in state courts. Federal courts have exclusive jurisdiction over certain federal matters: admiralty, crimes created by federal statutes, and civil actions for patent infringements and Sherman Act (anti-trust) violations.

Occasionally, federal courts request the views of the supreme court of a state on issues of state law, but such reference is not required. Reference by a state court of an issue either to another state court or to a federal court, as may be appropriate, seems very rare.

Both federal and state courts are, of course, required by their own law in many cases to apply rules and principles derived from other legal orders. Chapter 9 explores some aspects of this area of law. The federal courts differ here from state courts in one highly significant respect: Where federal courts exercise diversity jurisdiction, their choice of law is regulated, as explained later, by the conflict of laws, rules, and principles applicable in the courts of the state in which sits the federal court that handles the matter in first instance.

With these general observations as background, the interactions of the federal and state courts are explored from the federal perspective.

In 1789, the Judiciary Act provided for exclusive jurisdiction in the federal courts over "cases of admiralty and maritime jurisdiction." As already discussed previously, this technique to ensure unity of federal law has been extended to other areas – for example, most crimes created by federal statute and civil actions for patent infringement and for anti-trust violations.

Until 1875, however, most federal-question litigation had to be brought in the state courts. Since 1875, in these matters the plaintiff often has a choice whether to proceed in a federal or in a state court. Accordingly, two further mechanisms are utilized to ensure the unity of federal law. First, the U.S. Supreme Court can review final decisions of state courts on federal questions. This review is limited to federal issues. The state court's determination of other matters is not disturbed. The technique was introduced by Section 25 of the Judiciary Act of 1789; however, it did not provide for review in all situations. For example, it was not until 1914 that Supreme Court review was made available for cases in which the state court had upheld a claim that the federal Constitution or a federal statute rendered a state statute invalid.

A second technique to ensure the unity of federal law permits the defendant to remove to a federal court for trial a case brought in a state court if the plaintiff's claim rests on federal law. Removal is today available in various situations. The technique is hardly feasible as a practical matter, however, where the federal issue arises not as a part of the plaintiff's case but in the defendant's pleading or at a later stage in the proceedings. Accordingly, removal in these situations is only exceptionally permitted.

The removal technique is also used to ensure that the federal courts' diversity jurisdiction will provide a neutral, national forum in which it could reasonably be feared that the state court might prefer one party because of that party's connection with the forum state. Exclusive jurisdiction could have been given to the federal courts in this class of cases, but this solution was unacceptable for political reasons and because of the great additional burden that would thereby have been placed on the federal judicial establishment.

An intermediate solution was found in the removal technique. The Judiciary Act of 1789 opened the federal courts for litigation in which the parties are citizens of different states. (The requirement imposed by the Act of 1789 that one party be a citizen of the state in which the federal court is sitting was later dropped.) The plaintiff makes an initial choice between the federal and state forum. If he chooses the federal forum, that ends the matter. On the other hand, if he selects the state forum, the defendant can remove the case to the federal forum *unless* the defendant is a citizen of the state whose court is seized of the matter. Removal is inappropriate in this latter case because the defendant's own legal order is presumably not prejudiced against him. The resulting system is not entirely symmetrical. The plaintiff in a diversity case can choose whether to litigate in the courts of the defendant's state or in the federal court sitting in that state, but the defendant cannot make a comparable choice by removing to the local federal court an action brought by the plaintiff in a court of the defendant's state.

There are, of course, many complications and intricacies that arise where removal is sought in diversity cases. For example, if the diversity is not complete – that is to say, if even one plaintiff and one defendant among many are citizens of the same state – the federal courts do not have diversity jurisdiction and removal is not possible. The judicially created requirement of complete diversity constitutes a restriction on diversity jurisdiction of greater significance than the legislatively imposed amount-in-controversy requirement.

Another problem that arises from the interaction of the state and federal judicial systems in the United States is how to ensure to the states ultimate control over matters within their legislative competence. This problem can be seen as the counterpart to the problem, already discussed, of ensuring the unity of federal law. However, state control over rules and principles governing issues within state legislative competence raises two difficulties that are not encountered where the unity of federal law is in question. It would be awkward, perhaps impossible as a practical matter, to construct a system in which the relevant state's courts could review determinations of last resort made by another state's court or by a federal court. Theoretically, the party who was unsuccessful could be allowed to seek review on issues of state law in the supreme court of the state whose law was applied, just as issues of federal law decided in a state court can be taken to the Supreme Court of the United States. However, this approach would be exceedingly complex and cumbersome; consider, for example, the complications that would arise in a proceeding in which the law of more than one state was involved or in which both state and federal law were at issue.

One reason why the possible approach outlined previously was not provided for in the Constitution of the United States may lie in a concern felt by its drafters for legal unity – especially in private law. The problem of legal unity is endemic to federal systems, where legislative authority over private law matters is in the states rather than in the central government. Lacking both a unitary source of private law and a uniform judicial administration of that law, how can a law common to the whole society and economy be created and maintained? In 1789, much of private law was judicially created. Perhaps the drafters subconsciously took comfort in the thought that the common law was, after all, a common heritage whose unity the courts would maintain. In 1789, common law rules and principles could be seen as elements in a shared tradition rather than as expression of a particular sovereign's authority. In all events, in 1789 no one came upon the idea of providing for an ultimate review by the state which, in Austinian terms, had the ultimate authority to lay down for a given matter common law rules and principles. The way jurists thought about the common law in 1789 and the connection that mode of thought had with the desire for legal unity militated against the provision of institutional arrangements along the lines canvassed previously.

The influence of the non-Austinian view of the common law widely held in 1789 and the desire for legal unity, therefore, help to explain the position the federal courts sitting in diversity jurisdiction enjoyed when they had to decide questions of common law. The Judiciary Act of 1789 required application of state *legislation* but did not clearly provide for the application of state *decisional* law. The relevant provision of the Judiciary Act – Section 34 – provides that:

the laws of the several states, except where the Constitution, treaties, or statutes of the United States shall otherwise require or provide, shall be regarded as rules of decision in trials at common law in the courts of the United States in cases where they apply.

For more than a century, the term "laws" in Section 34 was interpreted as referring to statutes and as not including decisional law. Justice Story, in his opinion for the Supreme Court, wrote as follows in *Swift v. Tyson*, 41 U.S. 1, 19 (1842):

> It never has been supposed by us, that the section did apply, or was designed to apply, to questions of a more general nature, not at all dependent upon local statutes or local usages of a fixed and permanent operation, as, for example, to the construction of ordinary contracts or other written instruments, and especially to questions of general commercial law, where the state tribunals are called upon to perform the like functions as ourselves, that is, to ascertain upon general reasoning and legal analogies, what is the true exposition of the contract or instrument, or what is the just rule furnished by the principles of commercial law to govern the case. . . .

The view that the federal courts exercising diversity jurisdiction were entitled to generate and apply their own rules and principles of decisional law to issues within state – rather than federal – governmental authority persisted until 1938. In that year, *Swift v. Tyson* was overruled in *Erie R. R. Co. v. Tompkins*, 304 U.S. 64 (1938). In *Erie*, the Supreme Court held that in a diversity case, a federal court had to apply not only the statutory law but also the decisional law of the state in which it was sitting. In contrast, procedural questions are governed by federal law. In a subsequent decision, *Klaxon Co. v. Stentor Electric Manufacturing Co.*, 313 U.S. 487 (1941), the Court made it clear that the *Erie* principle extended to the state's rules respecting choice of law. Since then, in diversity cases the Court has struggled to evolve principles to distinguish between "procedural" or "substantive" matters. The basic test offered asks whether the relevant issue is "outcome-determinative." As far as legal rules determine the outcome of a litigation, state law has to be applied.

Since *Erie* and *Klaxon*, there has been difficulty in applying the seemingly simple doctrine there enunciated. Many rules that seem to be procedural, such as rules specifying forms of service of process or the standard of review for evidentiary rulings of a first-instance court, can be outcome-determinative under the circumstances of individual cases. At the borderline, decisions applying the Erie doctrine can be difficult to harmonize and, therefore, are favorite subjects of discourse in American first-year law school classes and examinations.

The demise of *Swift v. Tyson* had basically two causes. First, an Austinian view of law had come to dominate legal thinking. Second, the federal common law had not, as it turned out, advanced significantly the cause of legal unity.

Justice Holmes addressed the jurisprudential issue posed by *Swift v. Tyson* in his dissent in *Black and White Taxicab and Transfer Co. v. Brown and Yellow Taxicab and Transfer Co.*, 276 US 518, 532, at 533–534 (1928):

> If there were . . . a transcendental body of law outside of any par-
> ticular State but obligatory within it unless and until changed by
> statute, the Courts of the United States might be right in using
> their independent judgment as to what it was. But there is no such
> body of law. The fallacy and illusion that I think exist consist in
> supposing that there is this outside thing to be found. Law is a
> word used with different meanings, but law in the sense in which
> courts speak of it today does not exist without some definite author-
> ity behind it. The common law so far as it is enforced in a State,
> whether called common law or not, is not the common law gener-
> ally but the law of that State existing by the authority of that State
> without regard to what it may have been in England or anywhere
> else. . . .

Had *Swift v. Tyson* enabled the federal courts to create a uniform, national body of commercial law, Holmes's jurisprudential objection might not have prevailed. However, many state courts refused to accept the federal version of the common law. As a result, instead of ensuring legal unity, the rule in *Swift v. Tyson* facilitated forum shopping; each party jockeyed to litigate in a state or a federal court depending on which court's view of the common law favored the party's cause.

It is worth remarking that 1938, the year of the *Erie* decision, saw as well a revolution in the procedural law applicable in the federal courts. Section 5 of the Conformity Act of 1 June 1872 had provided:

> That the practice, pleadings, and forms and modes of proceedings in other than equity and admiralty causes in the circuit and district courts of the United States shall conform, as near as may be, to the practice, pleadings, and forms and modes of proceeding existing at the time in like causes in the courts of record of the State within which such circuit or district courts are held, any rule of court to the contrary notwithstanding: *Provided, however*, that nothing herein contained shall alter the rules of evidence under the laws of the United States, and as practiced in the courts thereof.

Variations of this conformity approach had been in effect since 1789.

The result of the conformity requirement was that procedure within the federal court system was as varied as the procedure of the courts of the states in which the federal courts sat. Reform of federal civil procedure obviously could not occur so long as conformity was the rule. As early as 1886, David Dudley Field pressed for a federal code of procedure. In 1912, the American Bar Association began an extended campaign for uniform federal procedure. In the Act of June 19, 1934, Congress authorized the Supreme Court to prescribe rules of procedure "in civil actions at law" and "at any time [to] unite the general rules prescribed by it for cases in equity with those in actions at law so as to achieve one form of civil action and procedure for both. . . ."

Under Chief Justice Hughes's leadership, the Supreme Court in 1935 vigorously exercised the new power. An advisory committee was appointed to draw up proposed rules. On 20 December 1937, Hughes transmitted the Federal Rules of Civil Procedure, whose adoption all the members of the Court (except Justice Brandeis) had approved, to the attorney general of the United States with the request that the rules be reported to Congress. The rules came into effect on September 16, 1938. They have since been reviewed and amended on various occasions.

The year 1938 thus saw state law lose ascendancy over procedural matters in actions at law in federal courts but gain ascendancy over substantive matters in diversity cases. One of the arguments for the development of a system of federal civil procedure had been the hope that procedural uniformity would be advanced because many states would follow a federal model. In the decades since 1938, the federal rules haves certainly engendered more uniformity in the procedural field than *Swift v. Tyson* in its day produced for substantive law.

Long before *Erie Railroad* was decided in 1938, it had been clear that a common law developed by the federal courts in diversity cases would not produce a uniform commercial law. Accordingly, already by the early decades of the twentieth century, other approaches were being explored. The ALI's contribution, as well as that of American legal education and scholarship, to the goal of legal unity have been considered in Chapters 1 and 2; another force for legal unity deserves mention here.

The American Bar Association, which was organized in 1878, appointed a Committee on Uniform State Laws in 1889. Under the leadership of this committee and of the State of New York, the National Conference of Commissioners on Uniform State Laws was organized with the specific purpose of advancing legal unity. The conference's first meeting was held in 1892. By 1912, all the states were participating.

The conference has been quite successful, especially in commercial areas. Its most ambitious and successful project – undertaken after World War II – is the Uniform Commercial Code. The code is now law in every state. Despite the civil law antecedents of its private law, even Louisiana has adopted six of the code's nine articles.

The code is adopted as state law. Accordingly, its text is not entirely uniform and, more important, may be interpreted differently in different states. The conference seeks to avoid divergent interpretations in various ways. For example, it monitors state-court litigation and appears as *amicus curiae* to support what the code's sponsors consider to be its correct interpretation. During the last thirty years, the activity of the conference has increased and uniform state laws have been proposed and widely adopted in many fields of formerly divergent state doctrine, such as family law, interstate recognition and enforcement of judgments, and probate law.

In these ways, among others, a substantial measure of uniformity is maintained in American private law despite the potential for fragmentation that inheres in the American federal system. However, techniques are available to the system through which in various fields a significantly greater degree of unity than now exists could be achieved. These techniques are unused in part because the federal tradition still has great strength. For example, as was suggested in the 1960s, under the commerce power of Article I of the Constitution, the Congress of the United States could make the Uniform Commercial Code applicable to all transactions in interstate commerce. This step would turn the code, for most practical purposes, into federal law.

The proposal failed, largely because the private law is still seen as an area in which the states are, by and large, supreme. In addition, it was recognized that such a substantial federalization of the private law would have important – and perhaps unforeseeable – consequences for the work of the federal judiciary and, although probably to a lesser degree, of the federal Congress and executive. In particular, could the Supreme Court of the United States – at least if it were to continue to function as a single bench of nine justices – carry the additional work load that ultimate responsibility for the unity and development of American commercial law entails? If the Court could not, how might its role (considered in the next chapter) change? Concern for these questions constitutes an additional barrier to the creation of legal unity in the private law by federalizing that law.

## F. AMERICAN FEDERALISM COMPARED

Among the political economies of the modern world, federalism is found in many shapes and sizes. Many countries consider themselves more or less federal in that certain governmental powers are divided between central and more localized governmental institutions. In some nation-states, the power to enact substantive law is divided between local and federal entities. Swiss cantons, for instance, retain some degree of law-making authority in local matters, which up to now has included the power to prescribe codes of civil procedure for cantonal courts. (A proposed Swiss Federal Code of Civil Procedure was recently authorized and is currently under consideration to go into effect around 2010.) German Länder have law-making competence in certain areas of regional environmental and regulatory public law. Canadian provinces have considerable provincial law-giving authority, including some private law matters.

However, substantive American federalism is more extreme than the forms of substantive federalism in any other existing nation-state. The American states have full private and public law-making competence, except as this competence is preempted or limited by the defined authority of the federal government. Although it can fairly be said that there has been increasing feder-alization of various areas of American law over the years, the role of substantive state law remains large and pervasive at all levels. All states continue to maintain their own law and legal institutions in more or less the same form and relative competence as they were created by the Constitution of 1789.

American federalism is also at one end of the spectrum in terms of organs and institutions of justice. Each American state has its own justice apparatus, including first-instance and appellate courts, including a court of last resort as to state law. States cre-dential and license lawyers separately and choose their judiciaries in their own individual fashions. The federal judiciary starts with first-instance courts with limited and defined jurisdiction, some of which overlaps the jurisdiction of state first-instance courts. There is also a federal appellate system culminating in the U.S. Supreme Court, which has the last word on questions of federal statutory and constitutional law.

This can be contrasted with justice systems of European nation-states and Canada. In Germany, for instance, first-instance and intermediate appellate courts are organs of the respective German states, whereas the courts of last resort, the German Federal Supreme Court, its specialized counterparts, and the Federal Con-stitutional Court are all institutions of the German federal gov-ernment. However, there is no horizontal division of jurisdiction of the state courts. All are governed by the same national orga-nizational law, all apply the same statutory law, and the Federal Supreme Court has the last word not only on national law but also on the relatively few questions of state law that arise in litigation in those German states with more than one state appeals court. Thus, the state sponsorship of the lower courts becomes more a matter of local financing and administration than any form of separate judicial autonomy. Lawyers are admitted regionally but are entitled to practice nationwide and are governed by a national code.

The same is true, with some variation, in Canada and Australia. For instance, in Canada, lawyers are still admitted by individual provinces but enjoy greater reciprocity among provinces than their counterparts in the United States.

The extreme extent to which the United States preserves federalism in its substantive law as well as its legal institutions results in a degree of complexity in substantive law, choice of laws, conflicting jurisdiction, and similar issues. American lawyers have to be prepared to deal with these issues in all but the most local transactions or disputes. By the same token, the division of substantive and institutional authority in the American legal system increases Americans' sense of ownership of their law and enables state-by-state experimentation with new legal solutions to old and new problems, a so-called laboratory of democracy. For these reasons, Americans are jealous of their federalism and any perceived movement to shift power or responsibility from the individual states to the federal government is regarded with suspicion.

Harmonization of state law by Restatements and similar devices, creation of uniform state laws, and federalization of areas of law formerly governed by state law have reduced this diversity and complexity to some extent. The degree of such complexity that remains can raise the question of whether the positive virtues of the American degree of federalism throughout its legal order continue to outweigh its evident costs as the world becomes smaller and the various political economies are thrown into ever more direct competition.

# 5

# American Constitutional Law and the Role of the United States Supreme Court

## A. INTRODUCTION

About a century and three quarters ago, Alexis de Tocqueville remarked that the major issues of American life sooner or later appear as questions for decision by the courts. The truth of his remark was already apparent by the early nineteenth century; of course, different types of problems have, from epoch to epoch, held center stage.

The early decades of the nineteenth century saw the U.S. Supreme Court beginning to map out its own role in the tripartite system of government provided for in the new Constitution. In a series of important decisions, the early Supreme Court under the leadership of Chief Justice John Marshall not only established the principle of judicial review of federal legislative action but also gave meaning to important structural Constitutional provisions, such as the Commerce Clause, that defined the respective spheres of competence of the states and the new federal government.

From roughly 1885 to 1937, the judiciary was increasingly involved with economic and regulatory issues. In the 1930s, a constitutional crisis developed. The Supreme Court struck down on constitutional grounds the basic elements of President Franklin Roosevelt's "New Deal," which contemplated large-scale governmental intervention in national economic life. With a view to overcoming this judicial veto, Roosevelt proposed that the Court's membership be increased. The highly controversial proposal, which was known at the time as the "court-packing plan," was never implemented. More or less coincidentally with the plan's surfacing, significant changes in the Court's membership occurred. As a result, a majority was soon found for the position that the Court should not – except in the most egregious circumstances – invoke constitutional principles to negate legislative regulation of the economic arena. Thus, in the late 1930s, constitutional control over governmental regulation of economic life largely ceased.

This judicial withdrawal from one arena of contemporary life did not, however, presage a general retreat. Indeed, since World War II, the American tendency to address society's fundamental issues in legal terms has, if anything, become more marked. For example, issues respecting desegregation of education; discrimination on the basis of age, color, or sex; and civil rights generally are, in large measure, fought out in courtrooms. Indeed, on occasion, judges have taken over the administration of school districts, prisons, and mental health institutions.

A dramatic example of the way in which major issues are cast in legal terms is furnished by the controversy over slavery, which led in early 1861 to the outbreak of the American Civil War. In the middle of the 1850s, a man named Dred Scott, held as a slave, brought a suit claiming that he had become a free man when his owner removed him into the northerly frontier territory, once part of French Louisiana. An act of the U.S. Congress had forever prohibited slavery in the territory. Scott's case ultimately reached the Supreme Court of the United States. The Court held not only that because of his slave ancestry, he was not a "citizen" and consequently was under certain procedural disabilities, but also that the Act of Congress purporting to abolish slavery in the northerly territory was beyond the constitutional powers of the central government. *Dred Scott v. Sanford*, 60 U.S. 393 (1857) was the second case in which the Supreme Court struck down federal legislation as incompatible with the Constitution.

The slavery issue proved to be too complex and difficult for judicial decisions to resolve. Dred Scott's case became a rallying cry for antislavery sentiment in the North. The case played a role in the 1860 election of an antislavery President, Abraham Lincoln. Civil war between the northern and southern states broke out early in 1861.

The Civil War resulted in three amendments to the Constitution of the United States. The Thirteenth Amendment (1865) provides that slavery shall not exist within the United States or in any place subject to its jurisdiction. The Fourteenth Amendment (1868) is to the effect that all persons born or naturalized in the United States shall be citizens of the United States and of the state in which they reside, and that no state shall abridge the privileges or immunities of any citizen of the United States nor deprive any person of life, liberty, or property without due process of law, nor deny to any person equal protection of the laws. The Fifteenth Amendment (1870) provides that the right of citizens of the United States to vote shall not be denied or abridged by any state of the United States by reason of race, color, or previous condition of servitude.

These three amendments furnish the basis on which the issue of the civil rights of racial minorities was later fought out in the courts. In 1954, a long struggle was won; in *Brown v. Board of Education*, 387 U.S. 483 (1954), the Supreme Court held that "separate but equal" education did not satisfy the Fourteenth Amendment's injunction that no person shall be denied the equal protection of the laws. The *Brown* decision established the bases on which integration of state school systems was to proceed.

To a significant degree, the opportunity of – as well as the responsibility for – setting out the terms on which courts will deal with such major issues rest with the Supreme Court of the United States in its role as interpreter and guardian of the Constitution of the United States. The Court also ultimately resolves ambiguities in federal legislation and supervises the legislation's application.

## B. THE SUPREME COURT'S THREEFOLD ROLE

In the American view, the quintessential role of the judiciary – and, *a fortiori*, of the Supreme Court – is to ensure government under law; the exercise of power by government and by its officials is to be in accordance with law.

In the context of this overarching responsibility, the Court's role can be seen as threefold: to maintain the supremacy of the Constitution; to assure the uniform interpretation of federal law; and to resolve controversies between states or between a state and the United States. The last role is relatively infrequent. Legal controversies between states – for example, boundary disputes – or between a state and the United States are rare. The second role has assumed greater importance as the scope and volume of federal legislation have increased. However, the most complex, controversial, and important of the Supreme Court's tasks is maintenance of the constitutional order.

This task has three aspects. First, the constitutionally established allocation of powers between the central government and the states must be explicated and enforced. Second, constitutional standards that restrain the exercise of a power by the government to which that power is allocated must be interpreted and applied. (Such limiting standards are, for the most part, contained in the first eight amendments and in the Fourteenth and Fifteenth Amendments adopted after the Civil War.) Finally, where powers rest in the federal government, their allocation among the branches of that government must be determined and enforced.

## C. THE SUPREME COURT'S INSTITUTIONAL CHARACTER

The role of the Supreme Court, especially in maintaining the constitutional order, is in many respects a highly political one; nonetheless, the Court remains – although less so than in the past – a court of law. The Court exists to decide lawsuits, not to give answers to abstract questions of law, still less to render advice on political questions. The Court takes positions and states views only in the context of litigation. It does not advise the president or the Congress on the validity or interpretation of a proposed or existing law. However, over the decades, the degree to which the Supreme Court's judicial task of deciding lawsuits has submerged its concern for government under law has not remained constant.

Various requirements of a "procedural" nature are available to cabin the Court's activity within conventional lawsuits. The Constitution provides that the authority of the federal courts shall extend to "Cases" and "Controversies." In the period before World War II, the view had become orthodox that from the "case or controversy" requirement several entailments flowed that applied as well to ordinary litigation as to litigation with constitutional dimensions: There had to be a plaintiff who had suffered or was about to suffer a definable injury. Similarly, challenge to a statute had to be in terms of concrete instances of its operation in practical situations. Citizens cannot bring proceedings to attack a legislative measure that does not affect them in a direct and immediate way; in particular, the fact that one pays taxes is generally not sufficient to establish one's right to challenge the government's exercise of the spending power.

Under the orthodox view, an analogue to approaching difficult and complex issues in the limiting and factual context of an actual controversy was the Court's practice of usually resting decision on the most moderate grounds available. For example, if a law could reasonably be interpreted so as to avoid a serious question as to its constitutional validity, this interpretation was ordinarily given. In principle, constitutional issues were not addressed if there were any other way of deciding the lawsuit.

It may seem paradoxical that, although the Supreme Court passes judgment on some of the most profound national issues, it was thought that it should do so only when absolutely neces- sary to the solution of a conventional lawsuit. The orthodox view rests, in the last analysis, on concern for the Court's continuing legitimacy and the view that judicial wisdom depends in no small measure upon contextual decisions. The power of a small group of judges, appointed for life, to set aside the acts of the democratically elected representatives of the people might well be unacceptable if the power's exercise were less constrained.

Moreover, these constraints can be seen as essential to the Court's wise exercise of its powers. By declining to give advisory opinions, the Court refrains from intrusion into the law-making process. By requiring a concrete case with litigants adversely affected, the Court reduces the likelihood of premature, abstract, and ill-informed judgments. By placing a decision on a nonconsti- tutional ground wherever possible, the Court gives the legislature an opportunity to amend controverted statutes to reduce or remove potential constitutional difficulties.

Since the 1950s, the procedural restraints described previously have been somewhat relaxed. In the process,

> the view that constitutional adjudication is collateral to the essential judicial task of deciding lawsuits has yielded ground to the concep- tion that the primary function of the Supreme Court of the United States, in support of its special responsibility for liberty and equality, is to insure that other organs of government observe constitutional limitations.[1]

---

[1] A. Cox, "The New Dimensions of Constitutional Adjudication," 51 *Washington L. Rev.* 791, 805 (1976).

Recourse to the declaratory judgment procedure now permits challenge to a statute or administrative practice before the moving party is subject to an explicit threat of immediate action. Standing to sue has been extended to the point that almost any form of actual loss suffices for suit against the government. The rule has been relaxed that constitutionality of legislation is subject to inquiry only so far as its application to a litigant is in question. The use of class actions has extended the significance of relaxed standing requirements and of declaratory judgment.

## D. THE FOUNDING FATHERS' UNDERSTANDINGS RESPECTING THE SUPREME COURT'S ROLE

Among the drafters of the Constitution of 1789, various views were held respecting the role and function of the Supreme Court provided for by Article III, Section 1, of the Constitution. Presumably few, if any, foresaw the full range and importance of the role that the Court would ultimately play.

The federal nature of the new nation rather clearly required the creation of a Supreme Court. Working out the full implications of the federal structure could hardly have been left to the political process. To have done so would have risked either the decline of the federation into a loose confederation or the emergence of a central authority that would establish a unitary system. The new federal system needed a balance wheel. The only governmental process that could discharge this responsibility in a reasonably neutral and objective way was the judicial process. With the respect for law and the strong legal tradition that existed by 1789 in the new nation, giving this responsibility to the judiciary was natural if not inevitable.

This role gave the Supreme Court broad powers; the Court was charged with the ultimately political task of shaping the new federal structure. One sees today in the development of the European

Union how much can turn on whether individual states or the central authority has power to regulate important economic and social issues.

What implications, if any, did entrusting the Court with broad responsibility for federalism have for the problem of judicial review of legislation? The issue of judicial review is not directly implicated by federalism issues arising from state encroachment on federal authority. In such situations, an undisputed principle of intergovernmental hierarchy justifies the Court's exercise of authority. As Article VI of the Constitution proclaims:

> This Constitution, and the Laws of the United States which shall be made in pursuance thereof . . . shall be the supreme Law of the Land . . . .

However, if the Founders contemplated the possibility that the Court might set aside *federal* legislation that conflicted with state legislation in fields within the sole competence of states, the proposition would inescapably follow that the Court's views respecting constitutionality took precedence over the views of the Congress or the Executive. Apparently, the Founders saw only vaguely, if at all, the possibility of a conflict in this context – or any other, for that matter – between the Court and the other branches of the federal government. Certainly, the issue whether the Court was expected to have the decisive voice with respect to interpretation of the Constitution was never directly addressed.

How can the failure of this issue to surface in connection with relations between the central government and the states be explained? Clearly, in 1789 the states would not have accepted a system in which the central authority could have radically altered in its favor the allocation of powers provided for in the Constitution. The explanation presumably is that the states' control of the Senate was seen as protecting states' rights against federal encroachments. In the federalism field, the Supreme Court thus played the role with respect to state governments that the Senate performed for the states with respect to the federal government.

The Court's power of judicial review was settled less than fifteen years after the Constitution came into force in a case in which no federalism issue arose. In the famous decision of *Marbury v. Madison*, 5 U.S. 1 (1803), Chief Justice Marshall, writing for a unanimous Court, held that the Court had the power to strike down federal legislation that violated the Constitution.

*Marbury* arose out of the transfer of political power from the Adams administration to the Jefferson administration in the election of 1800. Following his election defeat, outgoing Federalist President John Adams made a number of appointments of federal officials. These were duly ratified by the lame-duck Federalist Congress. William Marbury was appointed a Justice of the Peace for the District of Columbia. Through oversight, not all of the commissions evidencing the appointments were delivered to the appointees before Adams left office. The incoming Republican[2] Secretary of State, James Madison, found Marbury's signed commission undelivered on his desk. In hopes of thwarting the appointment, Madison declined to deliver the commission. Marbury brought suit in the U.S. Supreme Court, then under the leadership of newly appointed John Marshall, Adams' former Secretary of State.

The suit was brought pursuant to the Supreme Court's original or first-instance jurisdiction. The Judiciary Act of 1790, which established the structure of the federal judiciary, defined the original jurisdiction of the Supreme Court and authorized it to grant writs of *mandamus*. *Mandamus* was a development of the English

---

[2] The Republican Party of the early days of the American republic was the historical ancestor of the modern Democratic Party. The modern Republican Party was formed in the 1850s.

common law under which citizens aggrieved by failures of officials to perform essentially ministerial tasks could seek a court order requiring the officials to perform their legal duties. Marbury sought a writ of *mandamus* directing Madison to deliver to him his commission.

That this apparently insignificant case involved a potential confrontation between the executive and the judicial branches of the American government was evident at the time. If the Court held for Marbury and directed the delivery of the commission, would the Executive obey? On the other hand, if the Court ruled that it had no power to command officials of the Executive Branch, would its power and prestige be forever compromised?

On February 24, 1803, Marshall orally delivered the opinion of a unanimous Supreme Court to a packed audience. The genius of the opinion is the ordering of the reasoning and the remarkable twist at the end.

Marshall first reasoned that Marbury had under the law a right to the commission. Withholding that commission was a violation of his legal right.

The next question was whether the law provided a remedy for that violation of right. The answer was that the ancient writ of *mandamus* provides a remedy for violations of the kind experienced by Marbury.

The stage was set for the constitutional confrontation. Once the Court had determined that Marbury was entitled to the commission and that *mandamus* was the correct remedy to secure it, it seemed inevitable that the Court would have to face the question of whether it had the power to order its coordinate branch of government. Marshall avoided this constitutional confrontation and simultaneously established a principle of even greater importance to the power of the Court by posing the third major issue: Could the writ of *mandamus* be issued from the Supreme Court? This issue had not been seriously contested by the parties. After all, the Congressional statute clearly gave the Supreme Court first-instance jurisdiction to issue writs of *mandamus*.

Marshall noted that the Act of Congress clearly authorized the Court to issue the writ of *mandamus* running against the Secretary of State. However, this was not the end of the inquiry. The Court had to determine whether that Act of Congress was in conformity with the Constitution. Here was the twist. For although Article III, Section 2, of the Constitution described the judicial power of the United States in general terms, it spelled out the "original" or first-instance jurisdiction of the Supreme Court rather specifically as extending to "all cases affecting ambassadors, other public ministers and consult, and those in which a state shall be a party." In all other cases, the jurisdiction of the Supreme Court was to be appellate. It was thus easy for the Court to determine that the Constitution did not authorize the jurisdiction conferred by the Act of Congress, and thus that the Act of Congress must be ignored as unconstitutional. Whereupon Marbury's case was dismissed as brought in the wrong court and the constitutional confrontation was averted.

The genius of the Marshall opinion is that the principle of judicial review – namely, that the courts have the last word in determining the constitutionality of legislation – was established in a case in which the result was a constriction of the Court's powers, not the powers of another agency or party. Thus, by reading that Constitution to limit its own legislatively granted powers, the Court established the principle that the Court is the branch of government to determine whether all legislation is in conformity with the Constitution.

Politically, the *Marbury* opinion went down easily. The incoming Republicans were not commanded by the Court to do anything. The Federalists felt vindicated by the ruling that Marbury was entitled to his commission, whether or not he actually got it.

Those who favored a strong federal government could appreciate the significance of the Court's assertion of its role as the constitutional arbiter. Marshall's words,

> It is emphatically the province and duty of the judicial department to say what the law is. Those who apply the rule to particular cases must of necessity expound and interpret that rule. If two laws conflict with each others, the courts must decide on the operation of each.
>
> So if a law be in opposition to the constitution; if both the law and the constitution apply to a particular case, so that the court must either decide that case conformably to the law, disregarding the constitution; or conformably to the constitution, disregarding the law; the court must determine which of these conflicting rules governs the case. This is of the very essence of judicial duty.
>
> If then the courts are to regard the constitution; and the constitution is superior to any ordinary act of the legislature; the constitution, and not such ordinary act, must govern the case to which they both apply.

continue to state the core reasoning of the doctrine of judicial review to the present day. The principle established in *Marbury v. Madison* became – and has remained – fundamental to the American theory and practice of constitutionalism.

## E. THE COURT AS BALANCE WHEEL OF THE FEDERAL SYSTEM: THE COMMERCE CLAUSE

The most creative and important task of the Supreme Court in the early decades was to work out, in general terms, the allocation of powers between the state and the federal governments. Although a number of constitutional provisions come into question, the most important and basic is the grant to Congress in Article I, Section 8, of the power "To regulate Commerce with foreign Nations, and among the several States, and with the Indian Tribes." This grant of power left many issues open. The Constitution does not set out the boundaries of the commerce power vested in Congress, particularly when Congress has not spoken. It is not textually demonstrable whether the commerce power, where it exists, is exclusive or concurrent so that, in the absence of an articulated congressional preemption, state regulation can coexist. The Court has had to decide, therefore, whether this affirmative grant of power implies, at least in some circumstances, negative, self-executing limitations on the scope of state regulation of interstate and foreign commerce.

The development of the Supreme Court's Commerce Clause jurisprudence is discussed in Chapter 4. Although the issue that preoccupied Marshall in *Gibbons v. Ogden* in the early nineteenth century is by now well settled in favor of federal power and authority, over the centuries, the Commerce Clause jurisprudence of the Court has constituted the primary means by which the Court balances the respective interests and legislative roles of the federal government and the individual American states.

### F. THE COURT AS GUARDIAN OF INDIVIDUAL RIGHTS

In discharging its function as the balance wheel of the federal system, the Court is essentially concerned with the proper allocation of governmental authority. Is the center – or the individual state – entitled to act? In its role as guardian of individual rights, the Court does not allocate authority between governments; instead, it determines whether any government has authority to act in certain ways. Since World War II, it can fairly be said that the growing point of constitutional law has been in the area of individual rights. Relying as well on the first ten amendments to the Constitution – the so-called Bill of Rights – as on the Civil War amendments – especially the Fourteenth – the Court has imposed restraints on *all* governments.

In the form that the Constitution was submitted to the states for ratification, relatively little protection was accorded to individual rights. Sections 9 and 10 of Article I provide some guarantees. Those contained in Section 9 – for example, the assured availability of the writ of habeas corpus and the prohibition of bills of attainder and ex post facto laws – run against the federal government. Section 10 applies to the states; no state shall "pass any Bill of Attainder, ex post facto Law, or Law impairing the Obligation of Contracts . . . ." Article III sets out certain protections that relate to the operation of the federal courts. Section 2 is to the effect that "[t]he Trial of all Crimes, except in Cases of Impeachment, shall be by Jury; and such Trial shall be held in the State where the said Crimes shall have been committed . . . ." Section 3 defines "Treason against the United States" and requires for conviction "of Treason . . . the Testimony of two Witnesses to the same overt Act, or . . . Confession in open Court." The section further provides that "no Attainder of Treason shall work Corruption of Blood, or Forfeiture except during the Life of the Person attained."

During the ratification process, it quickly became evident that these protections were not sufficient. Many state constitutions contained more comprehensive statements of individual rights. State legislatures made it clear that the new federal Constitution would not achieve ratification without corresponding restraints on the power of the new federal government. A series of ten initial Amendments were drafted to embody the most important of these restraints and became known as "The Bill of Rights."

The Bill of Rights was ratified by the states pursuant to Article V of the Constitution and came into force less than three years after the Constitution did. The amendments apply only to the federal government. The First and the Fifth Amendments are the most significant for protection of individual rights. The former provides that

> Congress shall make no law respecting an establishment of religion, or prohibiting the full exercise thereof; or abridging the freedom of speech, or of the press; or of the right of the people peaceably to assemble, and to petition the government for a redress of grievances.

The Fifth Amendment, after requiring the "presentment or indictment of a Grand Jury" for "capital, or otherwise infamous crime[s]", continues as follows:

> nor shall any person be subject for the same offence to be twice put in jeopardy of life or limb; nor shall be compelled in any criminal case to be a witness against himself, nor be deprived of life, liberty, or property, without due process of law; nor shall private property be taken for public use, without just compensation.

The Constitution as originally conceived thus gave little protection against infringements of civil rights by state governments. This state of affairs remained unchanged until the ratification of the Civil War Amendments: Amendment XIII (1865), Amendment XIV (1868), and Amendment XV (1870). The Thirteenth Amendment abolished slavery; the Fifteenth provided that "[t]he rights of citizens of the United States to vote shall not be denied or abridged by the United States or by any State on account of race, color, or previous condition of servitude . . . ." These provisions, as well as certain of the provisions contained in the Fourteenth Amendment, apply to the state and federal governments alike.

The most important provision of the Fourteenth Amendment applies, however, only to the states. The second sentence of the Amendment's first section echoes language applicable to the federal government in the Fifth Amendment: "nor shall any State deprive any person of life, liberty, or property, without due process of law . . . ." The section continues with language not found elsewhere in the Constitution, "nor deny to any person within its jurisdiction the equal protection of the laws."

The first important applications of the due process clauses of the Fifth and Fourteenth Amendments were in the economic sphere. For a time in the early part of the twentieth century, the Court interpreted the due process clause as if it embodied the principle of *laissez-faire*. Liberty of contract became a bar to many government controls. The bar was never, however, complete. The Court always accepted that the social interests in physical safety and health, in fair dealing, and in public morals were sufficient bases for laws regulating, for example, dangerous machinery, unsanitary working conditions, and deceptive business practices. And, where a business was "affected with a public interest" – carriers, public utilities, and banking – rates and services could be regulated.

Later, the Court allowed broader scope for legislative experiments. Legislation no longer had to be brought under the conventional heads of health, safety, and morals. A community's interest in aesthetics has, for example, been recognized as a proper basis for prohibiting advertising posters on the roadside.

But the most dramatic and important manifestations of the Court's concern for individual rights have been, as already remarked, in the area of personal rights: the right to a fair hearing, rights of free speech and press and assembly, and the right to equal protection of the laws. The great school-desegregation decision, *Brown v. Board of Education*, decided in 1954, is only one landmark in a body of decisional law that has, in the name of individual rights and civil liberties, profoundly influenced – and, in many ways, reshaped – American society.

## G. THE COURT AS ARBITER OF THE ALLOCATION OF POWERS AMONG THE BRANCHES OF THE FEDERAL GOVERNMENT

To say that under the Constitution power rests in the federal government does not put an end to discussion; questions may arise as to which branch controls exercise of the given power. The issue is of constitutional dimensions; the final word rests with the U.S. Supreme Court.

Consider, for example, the clash presented by federal seizure in 1952 of the American steel industry. When collective bargaining broke down and a nationwide strike was threatened in the steel industry, President Truman ordered the Secretary of Commerce to take possession of most of the steel mills to ensure their continued operation. The steel companies challenged the order in the federal district court on the grounds that the seizure was not authorized by an act of Congress or by any constitutional provision. The court issued a preliminary injunction, which was stayed by the Court of Appeals; the matter was then brought, under expedited procedures, to the Supreme Court on a writ of certiorari.

*Youngstown Sheet & Tube Co. v. Sawyer*, 343 U.S. 579, 589 (1952), presented the issue of whether the President's action was within his constitutional powers in the absence of authorizing legislation. The Supreme Court faced conflicting claims to authority by the executive and legislative branches. No express constitutional language granted seizure power to the President; can then authority be implied from the aggregate of the executive's powers under the Constitution? Six of the nine justices held – in six separate opinions (there was also one dissenting opinion) – that, as Justice Black wrote in the Opinion for the Court, "The Founders of this Nation entrusted the lawmaking power to the Congress alone in both good and bad times." The Supreme Court thus vindicated the exclusivity of the legislature's authority against a conflicting claim by the executive branch of the federal government.

Where claims of executive authority conflict with claims of judicial authority, the final word likewise rests with the Supreme Court. *United States v. Nixon, President of the United States*, 418 U.S. 683, 704–705, 713 (1974), involved a clash between the President's claim of executive privilege for tape recordings and documents relating to his conversations with aides and advisors, on the one hand, and the need to use the aforesaid material as evidence in a criminal prosecution, on the other.

Two arguments were made in support of the claims of presidential privilege. The first was that the principle of separation of powers precluded judicial review of the president's claim of privilege. It was further contended that, in the circumstances, the need for confidential communication between the president and his advisors outweighed the claim of the criminal prosecution. In an opinion written by Chief Justice Burger for a unanimous Court, both arguments were rejected.

Rejection of the first argument demonstrated that the judicial branch has the last word where its powers conflict with those of the executive branch:

> Notwithstanding the deference each branch must accord the others, the 'judicial power of the United States' vested in the federal courts by Art. III, §1, of the Constitution can no more be shared with the Executive Branch than the Chief Executive, for example, can share with the Judiciary the veto power, or the Congress share with the Judiciary the power to override a Presidential veto. Any other conclusion would be contrary to the basic concept of separation of powers and the checks and balances that flow from the scheme of a tripartite government. . . . We therefore reaffirm that it is the province and duty of this Court 'to say what the law is' with respect to the claim of privilege presented in this case. *Marbury v. Madison,* [1 Cranch 137] . . ., at 177.

In the exercise of its constitutional responsibility, the Supreme Court went on to hold that:

> when the ground for asserting privilege as to subpoenaed materials sought for use in a criminal trial is based only on the generalized interest in confidentiality, it cannot prevail over the fundamental demands of due process of law in the fair administration of criminal

justice. The generalized assertion of privilege must yield to the demonstrated, specific need for evidence in a pending criminal trial.

On occasion, the Court has thus set aside what it considered improper legislative or executive claims respecting the constitutional division of functions among the legislative, executive, and judicial branches. Two further illustrations from the 1980s are interesting.

Over the last half century, and especially in the last two decades, Congress has sought to maintain control of executive and administrative actions through the use of the so-called legislative veto. This "invention" allows Congress to reject regulations or decisions made by the executive branch if, within a given period of time, either House — or both — expresses disapproval. Congressional action operates, depending on the particular statutory provision involved, to either block or give effect to the regulation or decision in question.

In *Immigration & Naturalization Service v. Chadha*, 462 U.S. 919 (1983), the Supreme Court for the first time considered the constitutionality of such an arrangement; the legislative veto was held unconstitutional in principle. Exercising a discretionary authority contained in the Immigration and Nationality Act (INA), an Immigration and Naturalization Service official — pursuant to a delegation of authority from the Attorney General — suspended deportation of an alien. The INA provided that either House of Congress could set aside such discretionary suspensions of deportation. Acting pursuant to this authority, the House of Representatives disapproved the suspension. The alien obtained judicial review of the deportation order and the matter ultimately reached the Supreme Court.

The Court considered the House's veto a legislative act; as such, Article I, Section 7, of the Constitution deprived the action of effect because the measure had not been passed by a majority of both Houses and presented to the president for his signature or veto. A concurring opinion took the position that the House's veto was unconstitutional on a different ground because, in essence, an exercise of judicial power, it violated the principle of separation of powers.

The *Chadha* case raises many interesting questions: What will its legal and political ramifications be? Will the Court eventually retreat from what many consider a doctrinaire, extreme, inflexible, and nonfunctional position? Regardless of how such issues are ultimately resolved, *Chadha* illustrates in yet another context the Court's role as arbiter of the allocation of federal governmental power.

Somewhat related issues respecting the allocation of federal powers were faced in *Bowsher v. Synar*, 478 U.S. 714 (1986). There, the Supreme Court struck down a central provision of the Balanced Budget and Emergency Deficit Control Act of 1985. The Act, popularly know as the Gramm–Rudman Act after its principal Congressional sponsors, had been passed to bring the spiraling federal budget deficit under control. It placed a ceiling on the federal deficit for each fiscal year from 1986 to 1991.

The Court held that the provision in question assigned executive powers to a legislative agent – the Comptroller General – and thus violated the principle of separation of powers by allowing Congress to retain control over the execution of the Act. The Court's majority took the position that the Act's "reporting provision," which delegated to the Comptroller General the task of calculating and ordering budget reductions, required him to exercise independent judgment and to interpret the Act. By entrusting these functions – which constitute "the very essence of 'execution' of the law" – to an official subservient to Congress, the legislature impermissibly intruded into the executive function. Accordingly, the challenged provision was unconstitutional; the severability principle permitted the remainder of the Act to survive, however, and a fallback

provision provided by Congress for the eventuality that material-
ized came into operation.

The *Bowsher* case's significance may well lie less in rejection
of what could be characterized as "reverse" delegation of legislative authority than in the Court's failure to revive the delegation
doctrine as a means of limiting the kinds of administrative arrangements Congress can make. The delegation doctrine had not been
invoked to curtail legislation since the confrontation in the mid-
1930s between the Court and President Roosevelt's New Deal.
The last Supreme Court decision to rely centrally on a prohibition
against delegation of "legislative" authority was perhaps *Schechter
Poultry Corp. v. United States*, 295 U.S. 495 (1935). Of course, the
Court could revive the old doctrine were it convinced that circumstances so required.

## H. THE COURT'S STANDING IN AMERICAN SOCIETY

The immense power over American life exercised by the Supreme
Court is clear. The question naturally arises, therefore, of the
Court's standing. Is it respected and accepted by American society?

A tribunal with the Court's powers and role can hardly avoid
all conflict with popular and political forces. Jefferson and Jackson
were critics of Chief Justice Marshall. Lincoln refused to accept the
*Dred Scott* decision as definitive for the law of slavery. Theodore
Roosevelt favored the popular recall of both judges and judicial
decisions. And Franklin Roosevelt, witnessing judicial vetoes of a
number of his New Deal measures, sought by his court-packing
plan to increase the size of the Court by one for each justice who
did not retire at the age of seventy.

To some extent, these conflicts are inherent in the Court's role
as preserver of the federal balance and of individual liberties. In
part, however, the conflicts have been brought on by decisions

that were narrow and insensitive, reflecting personal or parochial preconceptions. These decisions constitute what Chief Justice Hughes once called the Court's self-inflicted wounds.

And yet the Court has, over time, managed to retain popular support. In the 1930s, realizing that its prestige and popularity had been undermined by the majority's unyielding opposition to Roosevelt's New Deal, the Court wisely relinquished enormous power. Within two decades, the Court again tackled controversial problems but this time in the civil rights field. Overall, this "activism" seems to improve the Court's standing. By the middle 1980s, the Court's prestige and popularity were at a high point in recent history.

Here, as elsewhere in human affairs, are ebbs and flows. No doubt, the Court will again generate constitutional crises. Yet, the extent to which since 1789 the Court has retained the confidence and respect of the American public is remarkable. The court-packing plan encountered strong opposition even among those who thought the Court's decisions wrong. And, of the twenty-six amendments to the Constitution, only four are directed, in whole or in part, to the overruling of Supreme Court decisions. (These amendments are XI [1798, limiting jurisdiction of federal courts to hear suits brought against states]; XIV [1868, deeming Americans of African descent citizens of the United States]; XVI [1913, expanding power of Congress to tax]; and XXVI [1971, setting voting age at eighteen]).

The Court's ability to discharge its responsibilities without forfeiting its prestige rests largely on the quality of the Court and on its methods of work. The total number of justices since the Court's establishment is only slightly more than a hundred. They have brought to the Court a wide range of experience and outlook. They have been drawn not only from the bench and practicing bar but also from academia and from positions in public affairs. The

size of the Court – six justices at the beginning and nine since
1869 – has enabled all the members of the Court to participate in
all its actions. Its opinions are reasoned expositions rather than
fiats. And there is full opportunity for individual expression of
concurring and dissenting views. Moreover, the Court has always
held itself open for reconsideration of doctrine, yielding – as Justice Brandeis put it – to the lessons of experience and the force of
better reasoning.

The Court's use of the common law method and processes of
decision also helps to maintain respect for and acceptance of the
Court's work. Absolutes are avoided by testing general maxims
against concrete particulars. The Court both achieves wisdom and
leaves open the possibility of change by deciding in the context of
specific controversies, by finding accommodations between polar
principles, and by a willingness on occasion to reconsider established doctrine.

Although many of the questions faced and decided by Supreme
Court judgments are "political" in that they define and limit the
power of organs of government, historically, the Court has tried to
avoid becoming directly involved in the process of political decision making. The Court has generally declined to intervene in
issues such as the executive-appointment function, the manner in
which Congress conducts its legislative business, and, above all,
the manner in which the electorate selects legislative representatives and political leaders. This restraint has generally been on the
grounds that the issues raised are not cases and controversies of
the kind generally submitted to courts for decision and, hence, not
within the jurisdiction of the judicial branch.

On occasion, the Court has been obliged to decide issues more
or less directly connected with the elective process. In the 1950s
and 1960s, the Court addressed the apportionment of state legislatures in a series of decisions establishing the "one person–
one vote" principle: state legislative bodies must, as a matter of

principle, be apportioned so that voters have equal representation. Its most well-known decision in this area is *Baker v. Carr*, 369 U.S. 186 (1962), in which the Court determined that the Equal Protection Clause of the Fourteenth Amendment required that both Houses of the Tennessee Legislature be apportioned on the basis of population. The Court has also struck down statutes establishing discriminatory qualifications to vote or nominate candidates.

As a practical matter, this policy of avoidance of political questions has well served the court's institutional prestige. Recently, however, there have been signs that the Court may be entering a more highly politicized phase. A series of 5–4 decisions on important social issues, such as the authority of states to regulate abortion, have been aligned with the positions of the major political parties and associated with the political leanings of the respective justices. Appointments to the Court have become highly political events, and the process of confirmation by the Senate has generated tremendous political controversy. Although these developments are perhaps only an overt recognition of the Court's importance in the political governance of the nation, nonetheless the controversy may be undermining the Court's authority as an impartial constitutional umpire.

This greater politicization of the Court may also be reflected in its willingness to decide cases with overt political character. *Bush v. Gore*, 531 U.S. 98 (2000) has been criticized by many as a dangerous departure from the Court's long-established policy of restraint. In that case, the Court was called upon to review a judgment of the Florida Supreme Court ordering a partial recount of the votes cast in certain Florida counties in the 2000 U.S. presidential election. The case had arisen after the votes for President had been cast but before the results of the votes had been certified to the Electoral College for the official electoral vote for president. The Florida court had found that the machine-counting of paper punched ballots in those counties had failed in many cases properly to record voters' actual intentions as marked on the ballots. Persons conducting a manual recount were required to look at the individual ballots in order to ascertain the intention of the respective voters.

Candidate George W. Bush appealed this Florida decision to the U.S. Supreme Court. A principal ground for the appeal was that the "intention of the voter" standard of the Florida Supreme Court decision was too vague to produce a consistent count, thus depriving him of the Equal Protection of the Law in violation of the Fourteenth Amendment. A majority of the Court found the claim persuasive enough to support a stay of further proceedings in Florida. A few days later, a *per curiam* decision by seven of the nine justices sustained the Bush challenge on Equal Protection grounds. The intention of the voter of the Florida Supreme Court decision would allow different electoral officials to come to different conclusions from the same ballot. Hence, the standard deprived the candidates and the persons who intended to vote for them of the equal protection of the law.

The electoral time schedule did not allow time for further court proceedings or a recount that could satisfy requirements of the Supreme Court decision. George W. Bush was declared the winner of the Florida vote and thereby became forty-third President of the United States.

The Supreme Court's undertaking to decide a question of such obvious political character and the effect of its decision on the election of a United States President have seriously damaged its prestige in the opinion of many Americans. It remains to be seen whether the Court will weather these latest buffets to its role and its authority or whether its institutional role will continue to be burdened by political controversy and its decisions questioned as political rather than legal pronouncements.

## I. AMERICAN CONSTITUTIONAL LAW COMPARED

This book is far too brief to attempt a real comparison of the constitutional regime of the United States with the constitutional structures of other democracies of the modern world. A few words will have to suffice.

First, it must be stressed that in the United States, any court – state or federal – has the power to determine whether a state law, act of Congress, or federal or state administrative regulation or action violates the federal Constitution. For instance, the lowest state and federal criminal courts are frequently called on to determine whether searches and seizures by police officers have violated the Fourth Amendment or whether a confession was obtained in violation of the Fifth Amendment. Those courts are also competent to determine whether a state or federal law violates the federal Constitution in a case where such a determination is necessary to a decision in the case.

This apparently broad judicial power to examine the constitutionality of enactments and actions of the other branches of government is automatically constrained by the common law doctrine of *stare decisis* and the principle of the common law that a court's decision is binding only on the parties before it and on courts that are lower in the judicial hierarchy. Thus, a decision by a lower police court that a given criminal statute is unconstitutional may lead to abatement of the prosecution in which the point is raised but has no authority beyond the case in which it was rendered. By the same token, decisions of state supreme courts and federal circuit courts have wide authority within their respective jurisdictions, but they do not "invalidate" or otherwise displace the legislation in question.

What is more, judicial decisions are based on the facts of the cases in which they are rendered. Legislation is usually abstract. A decision that a law is unconstitutional may be limited by the facts of the case in which it was rendered. The law may be unconstitutional when applied to the facts of the case but may be perfectly valid and constitutional in other contexts.

The predominant model in many modern European and East Asian jurisdictions confers jurisdiction to consider constitutionality of legislation on a special "constitutional court" that has the authority to strike down or modify legislation based on the requirements of the constitution. For instance, the German Constitutional Court is the only German court empowered to declare national legislation invalid for repugnance to the German Constitution (Grundgesetz, Art. 100(1)). Other courts are required to assume that legislation is constitutional, although they can consider potential unconstitutionality when considering how to construe the legislation.

On the other hand, it can be argued that decisions of the European constitutional courts may be more wide-ranging than their American counterparts. Decisions of the German Constitutional Court have the status of legislation and can be abstracted to extend beyond the immediate parties and controversy before the court (BverfGG, Sec. 31(2)).

Once again, we can see how differing legal and political systems solve the same legal and political problems in somewhat different ways but ultimately implement these same basic values. The American system is generous in vesting its courts with jurisdiction to consider constitutional issues, but the constitutional decisions of these courts extend only as far as their decisions in other controversies. European systems tend to limit the courts that have power to declare legislation unconstitutional, but their special constitutional courts have power actually to invalidate a legislative enactment and to speak in a more generalized manner than even the U.S. Supreme Court would find appropriate.

Both European and American constitutional court judges are expected to represent a wider political, social, and economic perspective than their counterparts in the "ordinary courts." In most European systems, judges of the ordinary courts are appointed to lifetime careers under a judicial service system that provides for periodic review and promotion. This kind of system tends to produce a highly competent and professional judiciary, at the risk of also encouraging a degree of conformity and conventionality in judicial decision making. Constitutional court judges, on the other hand, are generally chosen by methods that permit the recruitment of talented jurists, even political figures and academics, with wider experience and perspective than can be generally found in the career judiciary. For instance, judges of the German Federal Constitutional Court are elected by the German Parliament (Grundgesetz, Article 94(1)) and serve for nonrenewable twelve-year terms (but not beyond the age of sixty-eight).

American judges, on the other hand, typically come from the bar and are chosen by processes that include substantial political elements. In many cases, this includes actual political election. In others, including the case of the U.S. Supreme Court, judges are nominated by executive leaders and confirmed by the legislature (in the case of the Supreme Court, the U.S. Senate). This kind of selection process automatically includes the kinds of inputs that have been consciously introduced into the methods of appointment of judges of European constitutional courts.

# 6

# American Civil Justice

THIS CHAPTER DOES NOT SEEK TO DESCRIBE FIRST-
instance American civil procedure in detail. Its purpose rather
is to discuss the role of civil justice in American political and economic society, to consider why the style of American civil procedure differs so greatly from the style of continental European
civil procedure, and then briefly to examine two controversial features of American civil justice: collective litigation in the form of
class actions and the availability of punitive as well as compensatory damages in certain types of tort claims. As will be seen,
the historical role of the jury is of central importance to most of
these questions. Some aspects of American jury trial are further
discussed in Chapter 8.

## A. THE ROLE OF CIVIL JUSTICE IN AMERICAN SOCIETY

Observers of the American political economy frequently express
some amazement at the prominent role of civil litigation in many
aspects of the American economy and society. American society is
somewhat exceptional not only in the frequency with which Americans resort to court to settle their disputes but, more significantly,
the scope and importance of social and economic issues that are
confided to the private litigation process. In the United States,

the civil justice system frequently performs functions that are discharged in other modern jurisdictions by other governmental institutions. This is true in the areas of compensation for personal injury, review and control of administrative and governmental action (or inaction), and in the area of regulation of business and moderation of the conflict between business and personal values.

For example, Americans rely on civil liability as the primary source of compensation and reimbursement of medical expenses for personal injuries sustained in a wide variety of circumstances. In many other modern economies, the existence of comprehensive health insurance and governmentally sponsored compensation programs mitigates the impact of accidentally caused injury and reduces the need to resort to litigation to seek substantial damage awards. By the same token, Americans' historical preference for jury determinations has developed into a litigation culture in which citizens with particularly appealing stories can be awarded levels of compensation that would not likely be available under comprehensive insurance or governmental compensation programs. Despite the comparatively high cost and inefficiency of the U.S. system, Americans may be reluctant to exchange a chance to win a compensation jackpot for a more efficient but more prosaic insurance-type system.

In the United States, judicial review of the actions of governmental agencies is within the purview of the ordinary courts and is accomplished through civil litigation. Unlike France and Germany, for instance, the United States has not developed any system of administrative courts to mediate the relationship of citizens and the administrative organs of government. For example, American parties and their lawyers bring civil cases in ordinary courts to desegregate schools, reform prisons and mental hospitals, seek recourse for police brutality, and review the actions of zoning boards. In some cases, these suits can seek damages awards; in many others, the remedy is limited to prospective corrective measures. Most of these cases are tried by judges rather than juries.

Finally, in the United States, many of the larger questions of the relationship of major elements of the economy with other such elements and with the ordinary citizenry are left to civil litigation in preference to detailed and active governmental regulation of the kind that might be found, for example, in the European Union. Although the state and federal governments enact and enforce a plethora of regulations of all forms of business and economic activity, it is generally conceded that the role of many American governmental agencies in business and economic regulation is somewhat less comprehensive and energetic than the role of their counterparts in other modern democracies. Some have suggested that this state of affairs may derive in part from the fragmented and diffuse nature of American politics in which political power is divided among state and federal governments and among the relatively independent legislative, executive, and judicial branches. Another reason for the relatively less robust governmental development may be the existence of the jury as an alternative institution with democratic attributes to mediate economic–social conflicts, such as product safety or environmental pollution, on a case-by-case basis.

Regardless of which came first, it appears clear that Americans have come to rely on civil litigation and, in many cases, the jury, to perform roles of conflict mediation on a number of levels that are performed by governmental, statutory, and political elements in other modern states. The relative merits of the respective approaches can be debated in several contexts and are subject to continuing comparison and discussion as the economy globalizes. What is important for the present inquiry, however, is that Americans' heavy reliance on civil litigation is not an entirely irrational peculiarity, but rather it is rooted in structural as well as historical aspects of the U. S. political and economic system.

## B. CIVIL PROCEDURE AND ADVERSARIAL LEGALISM

The preference of Americans to confide many issues of relatively broad political and economic significance to private litigation and determination by juries can be described as an aspect of "adversarial legalism" that characterizes the American legal–political system. As described by Donald Kagan in *Adversarial Legalism* (Harvard University Press, 2001), a fragmentation of authority and relatively weak hierarchical control in the United States have led to policy making and dispute resolution through formal legal contestation of individual cases initiated by active private litigants to an extent not known in other modern democracies. Americans seem to prefer to make policy on important social and economic issues by subjecting the issues to case-by-case decisions in litigated cases brought by private litigants.

Adversarial legalism may be rooted in America's political history, starting with the colonial experience and the American Revolution. The pre-Revolutionary remoteness of the British colonial administration and the subsequent distrust of all forms of central authority provided conditions favorable to decision of policy conflicts and lawmaking by local judges and juries. Late eighteenth-century notions of popular democracy lent legitimacy to decisions of common persons and supported the growth of the role of the common law jury. The common law tradition of lawmaking by accretion of individual judicial decisions gave adversarial legalism a vehicle for the development of law by contested case decisions. Conditions in the early United States permitted litigation at reasonable cost to private parties. The patchwork nature of the resulting doctrine and regulation was tolerable in the business and social conditions of the growing American national economy.

All of these factors contributed to a greater or lesser extent to the growth of a kind of adversarial legalism that pervades American political and legal institutions.

America's civil litigation systems and processes epitomize adversarial legalism. That is not to say that other litigation systems in England or the civil law world are not adversarial. Almost all systems of private civil litigation in the modern democratic world are more or less adversarial, in that parties generally initiate law suits, parties control the scope of the issues to be decided, parties proffer and identify the sources of factual proof to be received, and parties can terminate the litigation by agreement. However, the American litigation system stands at one extreme of the adversarial spectrum in the degree to which the conduct of civil litigation is entrusted to private parties and their lawyers. Private litigants are permitted to initiate legal proceedings based on minimal assertions of legal claims (notice pleading), they are given broad power to conduct factual inquiry and unearth evidence from each other and third parties with minimal court oversight (discovery), and they are given power and responsibility for the presentation of evidence and management of the trial process to such an extent that the roles of judge and jury are reduced largely to those of onlookers. As discussed herein, this allocation of roles is required to a large extent by the use of the jury to find facts in concentrated continuous oral proceedings. However, these attributes also have their root in an attitude toward decision making that nurtures both the use of the jury and the assignment of procedural roles primarily to private partisan, as opposed to public, neutral, litigation participants.

The qualifications and methods of selection of both judges and juries correspond to the enlarged policy-making role of civil litigation in American culture. American judges are appointed by politicians from the Executive Branch or are elected directly by the electorate. Jurors are generally chosen at random to represent the composition of the population at large. Both judges and juries have a kind of popular political legitimacy that is not generally associated with a highly professional judiciary as found in England as well as in most of the civil law world. Americans may well be more comfortable in entrusting the making of policy by litigation to judicial officers such as these, who bear some accountability, direct or indirect, to the political process.

## C. AMERICAN CIVIL PROCEDURE AND THE CONTINUOUS TRIAL

That there are significant differences between American civil procedure and the procedural systems of most civil law jurisdictions is apparent to even the casual observer. The large role of American lawyers in the preparation and presentation of civil cases, the time-consuming and expensive discovery process, the dramatic, concentrated trial – often before the jury as audience – all appear strange and foreign to a jurist from the civil law tradition. Although some of these differences may arise from other cultural or historical wellsprings, it is now clear that many of the salient characteristics of American civil procedure can be linked to its use of a concentrated and continuous trial rather than a discontinuous or sequential process for determination of factual disputes and, indeed, the entire case. Much of what may seem as unusual or even illogical to an outside observer can be explained as perfectly rational accommodations to the needs of a procedure that relies on a single continuous trial for all fact determinations.

The use of a continuous trial may in turn be linked to the historical use of the jury and a strong commitment to preservation of the role of the jury even as times have changed. The use of *ad hoc* lay juries and the confiding of all determinations of disputed fact to their decision mean that trial processes must be adapted to permit the jury to function as efficiently as possible under the circumstances. So, for example, it would not be realistic to expect a given group of six, eight, or twelve laypersons to convene and reconvene several times over a period of several months to hear the evidence in a civil case. Nor can one expect such a group to conduct a questioning of witnesses or draft a detailed opinion. The use of a fairly large group to hear the evidence and reach a decision means, as a practical matter, that the proceedings must be both concentrated and continuous for the institution to function at all.

The institution of the continuous trial is one that American civil procedure inherited from and continues to share with civil justice in Great Britain. Continuous civil trials continued to be the norm in nonequity cases in England long after the civil jury was abolished in 1917. Only recently, with the adoption of the Woolf reforms, has English civil procedure taken a step in the direction of continental European forms, including greater toleration for sequential conferences and hearings.

### 1. Fundamental Principles and Basic Institutional Arrangements

Before considering differences, a basic similarity of great importance should be remarked: American and Western European procedural systems all accept, in essence, the adversarial rather than the inquisitorial principle. Inquisitorial procedure assigns to officials the basic responsibility for gathering and presenting to the adjudicator the materials for decision. In addition, officials prosecute the cause, moving the case forward through the investigatory and decisional stages. Enforcement of legal rights is looked upon as a duty that rests on government and requires affirmative official action at every stage. Criminal procedure in most civil law jurisdictions can be said to be inquisitorial.

The adversarial principle, on the other hand, relies on party-prosecution. Each party controls and develops the preparation and presentation of its own cause; in essence, the enforcement of legal rights is left to the self-interest of those concerned. It is for them to prepare and prosecute the case and to move it forward through the investigatory and decisional stages.

No contemporary procedural system carries the adversarial principle to its logical extreme; too often, the assumption on which the principle rests – that parties, although not themselves equal in litigational ability, will be represented by counsel of roughly equal effectiveness – does not hold in practice. Accordingly, one expects – and finds – in every adversarial system elements that can be associated with the inquisitorial principle.

To the extent that departures from the adversarial model found in contemporary first-instance civil procedure in the United States and in Western Europe resulted from efforts to remove concerns respecting the relative representation available to parties, these systems should today be relatively similar in style. Their differences would flow from economic or sociological circumstances in different countries affecting the problem of ensuring reasonably comparable representation to the parties to a lawsuit. There is little reason, however, to assume that such considerations fully explain the significant differences that exist today.

The European and American procedural styles are very different. In the American system, the trial is concentrated in a single episode. Before trial, the lawyer for each side prepares with care the legal and factual issues that may arise. Discovery is had of the case materials available to the other side and prospective witnesses are insistently questioned. At the trial itself, the examination of witnesses is – subject to minor qualifications – conducted by the lawyers; the judge presides but is not responsible for the development of the case or for the questioning of witnesses.

On the other hand, in European systems such as that of the German Federal Republic, trials can be discontinuous. When the trial begins, the lawyer is not necessarily fully prepared on all legal and factual issues that may conceivably arise. Pretrial discovery is not available as such. Even when prospective witnesses have been identified, lawyers are not expected to question them in the course of preparation for trial lest their testimony seem to have been influenced by such contact. At the trial itself, the judge's role is central; the court has the basic responsibility for the questioning of witnesses as well as for developing the case to the point that it can be taken for decision.

## 2. The Significance for First-Instance Procedure of Concentrated Trials

How are these real and important differences between first-instance procedural arrangements in the United States on the one hand and in Germany on the other to be explained? Historical considerations, social and political values, and sociological and psychological assumptions are not without importance. However, an important cause for the characteristic features of each procedural style is arguably institutional in nature: the presence in one system of the concentrated – and, in the other, of the discontinuous – trial. Indeed, the particular difficulties generated for each system by the concentrated or discontinuous nature of the trial have affected that system's understanding and evaluation of the principles of party-presentation and party-prosecution. In the United States, the general effect has been to reinforce both principles. In Germany, on the other hand, these principles are less prominent and are complemented by stronger commitment of neutral public resources to ensure that justice is done. What particular consequences can be said to flow then in adversarial systems from a system's use of one rather than the other of these alternative forms of trial, the concentrated and discontinuous?

If justice is to be administered on an informed and rational basis, both parties must be able to thoroughly prepare and present their positions before the adjudicator takes the matter for decision.

Systems such as the American that combine the adversary principle with a concentrated trial have basically only two ways in which the foregoing can be ensured. One approach relies on the parties' pleadings; the other utilizes pretrial exchanges and investigations to frame the issues and to give notice of the evidence on which each party intends to rely.

If the avoidance of surprise is to be accomplished through the pleading process alone, the following are required: (1) each party's pleadings must not only state its position fully but also respond unequivocally to every position taken by the opposing party in its pleadings; (2) this exchange must continue until every point of agreement and disagreement between the parties has emerged; and (3) only the issues thus defined can be considered at trial.

For the most part, the old common law system of pleading exhibits these characteristics. However, all pleading approaches to the problem of surprise have certain serious disadvantages. In the case of common law pleading, some of the difficulties were contingent rather than inherent. In particular, pleadings had to be framed in terms of the common law forms of action, and these were in various respects remote from contemporary reality. Not only had the forms of action originally been framed for quite different economic and social circumstances but, over time, many fictitious allegations were introduced in order to modernize the substantive law. However, more fundamental difficulties inhered in the technique. An approach to issue-framing and notice-giving that depends essentially on the pleading process is inherently both complex and rigid. Even without the incubus of the forms of action, the pleading approach to the surprise problem seems too technical and arbitrary to be acceptable except on a *faute-de-mieux* basis.

In the United States, the pleading approach was supplanted by an approach that combines an abbreviated pleading process with arrangements that permit each party to familiarize itself before trial with details of the positions that the other party may advance when the controversy is ultimately presented to the adjudicator. This solution requires elaborate pretrial interrogatory and discovery procedures. The arbitrariness and abstractness that inhere in a full-blown pleading approach are avoided. Experience has shown that the pretrial procedures required can be cumbersome, extremely time-consuming, and very costly.

Approaches along the foregoing lines to the problem of surprise are open to procedural systems like the German that combine the adversary principle with a discontinuous trial. However, such systems have another choice as well; surprise at the trial stage can be avoided by the simple device of providing for further appearances before the court at a later date.

This third solution − continuance where needed to allow the development and presentation of new cause materials required in view of one's opponent's presentation − is utilized, in combination with an abbreviated but more detailed pleading process, in the modern period by such legal systems as the French and German.

Institutionally speaking, the French and German systems are free to adopt − or to dispense with − concentrated trials. In recent years, both systems have moved toward some concentration of hearings in an effort to deal with the problem of protraction of proceedings caused by scheduling several hearings. On the other hand, because of the jury, the American system is institutionally required to concentrate trials. Traditionally, courts of equity, which did not utilize juries, did not have concentrated trials. The presence of a jury makes a discontinuous trial impractical. Great administrative difficulty and personal inconvenience would be involved in reconvening the jury from time to time over an extended period. Moreover, at least until relatively modern times, material presented at widely separated points in time could not be preserved in a form that would have enabled the jury to refresh its recollection when it ultimately came to deliberate and render the verdict.

Both intuition and historical experience suggest that in the absence of an institutional imperative, such as results from the jury's presence in the common law, the problem of surprise is likely to be handled in adversarial systems through an abbreviated pleading process coupled with a discontinuous trial. At least for simpler cases, the German system has long had as its ideal the concentration of oral-argument, proof-taking, and final argument in a single session. However, this ideal has proved to be elusive; in German practice, the discontinuous trial is the norm in the more complicated cases. In the United Kingdom, where the jury has fallen into disuse in civil litigation, recent reforms restricting discovery have been accompanied by an increase in the participation of judicial personnel to guide the proceedings through a series of discontinuous hearings. There have been similar developments in administrative hearings in various countries. Frequently, arbitration proceedings make use of discontinuous hearings to deal with unexpected developments as the cases proceed.

This situation is understandable. If the trial is to consist of a single episode, pretrial procedures of one form or another must be developed to handle the surprise problem. But, such pretrial procedures – whether they take the form of extensive exchanges of detailed pleadings or of elaborate pretrial probing of the arguments of fact and law on which the other party proposes to rely – involve certain of the complications and costs previously described. The "chicken-egg" dilemma is encountered: Until a system makes available pretrial procedures that can effectively prevent surprise, the system can hardly insist on a concentrated trial. On the other hand, as long as a discontinuous trial is available, it is unlikely (for reasons suggested previously and further developed herein) that a procedural system will provide pretrial procedures designed to prevent surprise.

Yet another reason can be advanced to support the proposition that a legal system – given a free choice – is not likely to resort to trial concentration in order to solve the surprise problem. In view of the human tendency to procrastinate and the fact that at any given time at least one party to a lawsuit is likely to be interested in delay, the discontinuous procedure is, in a sense, natural. An adjudicator is not disposed to turn down plausible requests for postponements; indeed, to the extent that surprise is present, a refusal to grant a continuance may result in injustice. The stern discipline that concentration involves is, as a matter of human nature, unlikely to be imposed as long as, institutionally considered, the trial need not be a single episode.

### D. FURTHER PROCEDURAL CHARACTERISTICS ASSOCIATED WITH CONCENTRATED AND WITH DISCONTINUOUS TRIALS

The consequences that follow from the concentrated or discontinuous nature of the trial, respectively, are not limited to those discussed previously. Other procedural characteristics have a strong affinity for each form of trial.

The combination found in the contemporary American system of the single-episode trial with extensive pretrial procedures makes it necessary, in matters of any complexity, for lawyers to play an active role in gathering and analyzing evidence and in shaping the case in the period before trial. Where the responsibility for such full preparation rests on lawyers, it is unnatural and unreasonable to limit by legal rule or ethical canon their pretrial access to witnesses. Of course, such access involves appreciable risks that the witnesses' stories will be affected by pretrial contact with the perspectives brought to the case by the lawyers who interview and question them.

Because of his or her active role in the pretrial phase, the lawyer typically has, when presentation of the controversy begins at the trial, a greater understanding of the case than does the judge (or *a fortiori*, the jury). The adjudicator is hardly in a position to play a dominant role in the presentation of the case. It is, therefore, natural for the lawyers to handle the questioning of witnesses and the general presentation of the matter.

A concentrated trial thus inevitably reinforces the principles of party-presentation and party-prosecution and gives the lawyers a particular direction and expression.

Another characteristic of concentrated-trial systems is that the problem of delay arises at the pretrial rather than at the trial stage. Delay is unavoidable when the system is overburdened and cannot promptly provide the facilities required for conducting litigation. In all systems, the only remedy for this form of delay is to increase the system's capacity, by either providing more personnel or using existing facilities and personnel more efficiently.

Changes in either substantive or procedural law can result in more efficient use of existing facilities and personnel. For example, substantive-law rules that are clearcut and dispositive presumably reduce the range of potentially relevant evidence and make it possible as well for the adjudicator to decide with less analysis and reflection. And, a shift from collegial to single-judge courts renders the system more efficient in its use of judicial manpower. In this connection, it is interesting to note that French procedure (i.e., the *juge de la mise en état*, Arts. 763–781 of the Nouveau Code de Procédure Civile) as well as German procedure (i.e., the single-judge procedure, introduced in 1924, especially as modified by the 1974 and the 2002 amendments to Sections 348–350 of the ZPO) have, for first-instance proceedings, increasingly replaced the collegial court by a single judge.

Delay can also be caused, however, by one or both parties intentionally failing to proceed in a reasonably expeditious fashion. Where the trial is concentrated, such delay is found at the pretrial stage but is exceptional at the trial stage. Furthermore, to some extent, a party's willingness to seek and ability to obtain repeated time extensions at the pretrial stage are reduced by the ultimate concentration of the trial. The deadlines set for various steps to be taken during the pretrial stage will, by and large, involve substantial periods rather than driblets of time. Also, in courts with crowded dockets, postponing the time set for trial typically involves significant further delay. The court and any party interested in bringing the controversy to the stage of decision are thus aware of the serious consequences of postponement. If, despite these constraints, party procrastination remains a problem, the only remedy is presumably to increase the judge's involvement in the pretrial stage and enlarge his or her directive powers and responsibility. When this occurs, the principle of party-prosecution is correspondingly eroded.

Which further procedural characteristics are then typically exhibited by procedural systems that combine the adversarial principle with a discontinuous trial? As has already been remarked, in such systems, relatively little emphasis is placed on pretrial procedures. It follows that there is relatively little need – and often only limited possibilities – for lawyers to be active at the pretrial stage. Accordingly, these systems can – although they need not – advance certain policies that must be largely ignored by systems using a concentrated trial. Thus, even though the system accepts the principle of party-presentation, that principle may be qualified by discouraging – as the German and French systems do – pretrial contact between lawyer and witness. The rationale advanced is that fresh and unrehearsed testimony is inherently more reliable than testimony given by witnesses who have already discussed the case with one of the lawyers.

Where, as is typically the case, a system having the discontinuous trial does not make available techniques through which, before the trial begins, issues can be framed and the evidence upon which each side will rely made available to the opponent, extensive pretrial preparation by lawyers is both inhibited and hampered. Similar consequences flow from restrictions on the lawyer's contact with potential witnesses.

In these systems, lawyers thus often come to trial with little more understanding of the controversy than the adjudicator can have from the complaint and other documents filed with the court before trial. Accordingly, there is no built-in tendency for the lawyers to play a dominant role in the presentation of the controversy at the trial stage. As a result, the principle of party prosecution loses the support that it derives from the lawyer's pretrial preparation in systems such as the American.

Unlike systems that use the single-episode trial, in discontinuous systems the problem of delay centers, as far as procedure in first instance is concerned, on the trial phase rather than the pretrial phase. Even if the system is overburdened, relatively little difficulty need be encountered in bringing the controversy before a court because the first encounter in court can be perfunctory. The difficulty is rather to ensure that the cause is presented with reasonable promptness to the adjudicator.

Delay and inefficiency occur in these systems for one of two reasons. When the system is overburdened, the court may be compelled to apportion small amounts of time to each of the many matters that are before it rather than giving each matter as much time as it can effectively use. The only solution for the resulting delay – and inefficiency – is to increase the capacity of the system. Where the court of first instance is collegial, a system's capacity can be increased without increasing the size of the judicial establishment by reducing the size of a chamber for the purposes of decision and, in many cases, assigning responsibility for handling part or even all of the proceeding to a single member of the collegial panel. Other ways to increase capacity are to increase the size of the judicial establishment and streamline the procedure.

Another significant form of delay in these systems occurs, however, when one or both parties are not ready to proceed promptly and in full measure to each successive step in the episodic proceeding. In a discontinuous trial, each individual request for postponement or for further proceedings at a later date involves only a modest loss of time and typically invokes the need to avoid surprise. As a result, the other party (or its lawyer) may find persuasive opposition difficult, and the court is psychologically inclined to grant the request. The tendency to grant continuances freely is reinforced by the fact that, even in an overburdened system, there is comparatively little difficulty in setting a date in the relatively near future for another proceeding before the court. The session, directed to an aspect of the controversy rather than to the entire matter, typically need not be very time-consuming. Furthermore, if more time proves to be necessary than is available on the date first set, another postponement for a relatively short period can be granted.

Accordingly, adversarial systems using a discontinuous trial face a serious problem of delay at the trial stage, one that may be at least as serious as that encountered at the pretrial stage by adversarial systems using a concentrated trial. The only remedy ultimately available to discontinuous systems is to assign greater directive power to judges and to involve judges increasingly in management of the litigation at the trial stage. The delay problem thus sets in motion forces that profoundly affect the principle of party-prosecution. The marked tendency in the twentieth century of continental European adversarial systems to emphasize the judges' directive role and increase their directive powers is, in this perspective, a natural and predictable phenomenon just as the absence of a comparable trend in the American system is.

## E. CIVIL JUSTICE AS PUNISHMENT?

Many foreign observers of American civil justice are surprised by the fact that in virtually all American jurisdictions, damage awards can be made for the purpose of punishing the defendant for wrongdoing in distinction to compensating the victim of the wrongdoing. Conventional jurisprudence in most civil law jurisdictions limits the role of civil damages to compensation for harm caused by the defendant's tortious conduct. Punishment is strictly a matter for criminal and administrative proceedings instituted by public authorities.

Punitive damages have a long and generally honored place in American legal culture. Once again, the practice came from England. At the time of the American Revolution, English common law recognized the right of juries to award punitive damages, in addition to compensatory damages, in certain cases of aggravated misconduct such as assault or malicious libel.

Over two centuries of American legal culture, the law of punitive damages has developed variously and unevenly in the American jurisdictions. Every American state jurisdiction permits punitive damages in some extreme circumstances. Beyond that, however, there is great variation among the American states as to the circumstances under which punitive damages may be awarded, the degree of egregiousness of conduct required, the permissible size of an award in the context of the nature of the wrongdoing or the net worth of the defendant, and the rigorousness of appellate review of punitive damages awards. This variation makes generalization difficult and risky beyond the most basic of observations.

First, in practically all American jurisdictions, punitive damages only come into play in cases of egregious tortious conduct. Ordinary negligence or strict liability does not implicate punitive damages. Misconduct greater than ordinary fault is universally required – ranging from "gross negligence" to deliberate wrongdoing – before a punitive award can be considered. In most jurisdictions, deliberate tortious misconduct such as fraud, assault, or deliberate conversion of the property of others can support an award of damages to punish the tortfeasor. In recent years, some states have raised the minimum standard for punitive awards from gross negligence to deliberate, or at least wanton, misconduct.

Traditionally, the prospect of punitive damages was regarded as an incentive to potential plaintiffs to seek civil redress of serious breaches of the peace. The windfall nature of such awards has led some American states in recent years to enact reforms requiring part or all of punitive damages awards to be paid to the state, usually after payment of any contingent compensation due the lawyer who prosecuted the case.

The theory behind punitive damages is one of deterrence. Sometimes referred to as "smart money," a punitive damages award is supposed to be calculated in an amount that will make the guilty defendant feel the pain of his misdeeds and to deter him and others from similar misconduct. For this reason, the financial capacity of the defendant, legally irrelevant to other issues in most civil cases, is of prime relevance in the determination of punitive damages. The larger the financial capacity of the defendant, the more the jury should award in order to get its attention. Presumably, poorer defendants can be made to "smart" by a smaller award.

Recently, the U. S. Supreme Court has ruled that there may be constitutional limits on the size of punitive damages awards. Rejecting the notion that punitive damages are unconstitutional per se, the Court ruled in *BMW v. Gore*, 517 U.S. 559 (1996), that an award of $2 million in punitive damages based on misconduct resulting in no more than $4,000 in actual damages was so excessive as to implicate the Eighth Amendment prohibition on "excessive fines or cruel and unusual punishment." In particular, the Court cautioned states from magnifying punitive damages awards based on the effects of defendants' misconduct in other jurisdictions.

In *State Farm Mutual Auto Insurance Co. v. Campbell*, 530 U.S. 408 (2003), the Court set aside another multimillion-dollar punitive damages award and suggested that a certain proportionality between the amount of actual harm caused and the amount of punitive damages awarded has constitutional dimensions.

The two recent punitive damages cases in the U. S. Supreme Court represent only a small fraction of the many cases in which American appellate courts have reduced or set aside what they regarded as excessive punitive damages awards. The degree to which appellate courts feel free to revise punitive damages awards varies somewhat among states. Some state appellate courts are relatively ready to revise an apparently excessive punitive damages award in the interests of overall justice. Other courts are more deferential to the decision of the jury and will set aside or reduce a punitive award only in rare circumstances. Across the judicial landscape, though, it is fair to say that the really large punitive awards that make notice in the international press are almost always reduced or set aside on appeal and are very rarely paid by the parties against whom they are levied.

The legal and policy justification for punitive damages relates to the greater role American society expects its litigants to bear in the maintenance of the legal order. A relatively weak public apparatus for regulation by detailed administrative norms and for investigation and prosecution of crime is complemented by motivated private litigants and their lawyers. Safeguards are provided through the structure of legal rules enforced by the trial judge and the appellate process. The citizen jury provides the democratic legitimation that is provided by prosecuting officials in many other regimes.

It can be debated whether entrusting the enforcement of public norms and deterring violations to private litigants and their lawyers is the most cost-efficient and effective way to implement public policy.

## F. COLLECTIVE LITIGATION

The United States enjoys the distinction (or notoriety) of hosting the currently most extreme development of collective civil litigation in the modern legal world: the "opt out" class action. The Federal Rules of Civil Procedure and numerous state counterparts permit representative plaintiffs to bring civil actions in behalf of any number of similarly situated persons or entities as long as "common questions of fact and law" predominate and the class action is the best and most efficient way to assert the common claims. The results of such representative actions both benefit and bind all members of the defined class, whether or not they took part in or were even aware of the litigation, unless they choose to "opt out" of the defined class at the time the class action is "certified" by the trial judge.

The American form of class action has historical roots. It was exported to the New World in the form of English equity practice, which permitted representative proceedings in certain matters affecting numerous potential litigants. Class actions of the "opt-in" kind, where each member of the class has to agree to the class representation, were provided for by the 1938 Federal Rules of Civil Procedure. Those Rules were amended in 1966 to greatly strengthen the class action remedy. One of the changes was to make the default class action an opt-out proceeding. Under this arrangement, potential class members would be notified of the action. Those who did not evidence their desire to leave the class would be automatically included and bound by the result.

An essential feature of the American class action is the control by the court over key aspects of the case, notably "class certification" and settlement. If a party or group of parties files a case that purports to be a class action, the court must make an express determination of whether the requirements of Rule 23 are met early in the litigation. Are there common questions of law or fact that apply the same way to all members of the plaintiff class? Do these questions predominate? At one time, American courts applied a high threshold to these determinations. Only claims in which all elements, including damages, were virtually identical could satisfy this prerequisite. Traditionally, this requirement excluded most cases of mass tort, in which damages suffered by the injured were deemed too individualized to be susceptible to collective adjudication. More recently, courts have taken a more pragmatic approach and cases have been certified as class actions based on common questions of liability, with the determination of damages to occur individually following decision of the common issues.

Class certification also requires a preliminary determination that the named plaintiffs are, in fact, fairly representative of the other members of the described class and that they and their counsel are competent to represent the interests of the class. Often a single-mass default results in the commencement of several more or less simultaneous class actions. When potential classes overlap, the cases are generally consolidated before a single judge for the purpose of class certification and all further proceedings. Counsel for the respective representative plaintiffs vie to be named "lead counsel" for whatever classes will be certified in the consolidated litigation. To the extent that rational case management had previously been hindered by American federalism, which allows class actions to be brought in either state or federal court, a recent statutory amendment has diverted all the larger class actions to federal court where they can be managed in a consistent manner.

Once a class action is certified, all potential class members are notified and given the opportunity to opt out of the class if they wish to do so. Notification can be by mail, when practicable; otherwise, by publication in mass media, by television, by e-mail, and even by Web sites on the Internet. Members can opt out by completing and returning a simple form or by otherwise indicating their desire not to be included in the class. If a member opts out, he is not entitled to the benefit of any class settlement but is also not bound by any adverse disposition of the class litigation. If the member fails to opt out within the time specified in the notice, he or she is automatically included in the class and entitled to the benefit and bound by the burden of any judgment or settlement obtained by the class action.

American civil litigation is characterized by the high percentage of cases that settle before trial – easily more than 90 percent. The proportion of class actions that are resolved by settlement is even higher. In fact, trial and judgment in a class action is the rare exception rather than the rule. The process of settlement of a class action once again involves participation of the court. No class action can be settled unless the settlement is examined and approved by the court as fair and equitable to all members of the class.

Although the representative parties are nominally responsible for direction of class litigation undertaken in their name for the benefit of themselves and their fellow class members, as a practical matter, the lawyers representing the class have the deciding voice. Typically, class actions are taken on contingency fees by specialized law firms with the expertise and financial resources to manage and fund what are sometimes massive and cumbersome legal enterprises. The representative plaintiffs have no downside risk. They are not asked to bear the considerable expenses of getting a class action certified and the members duly notified. The class lawyers, on the other hand, invest huge amounts of professional effort and make substantial out-of-pocket disbursements in getting the class certified and in prosecuting the action to settlement or judgment. This inversion in the amount at risk between lawyer and client means that the lawyer-client relationship is also inverted. The lawyer makes decisions for the class with little regard for the views of the nominal plaintiff he or she represents.

The recent history of American class-action litigation has included several developments that are regarded as greater or lesser abuses by all but the most dedicated class-action aficionado. Entrepreneurial lawyers organize class actions to vindicate rights of which the class members were not even aware, and then settle those class actions on terms that concretely benefit the lawyers but which provide little measurable benefit to the class represented. Defendants have incentives to collude with plaintiffs' lawyers to generate class-action settlements that will provide universal absolution against potential liability. Plaintiffs' lawyers utilize the leverage of class actions to increase the stakes to such a level that all but the most hardy defendants will settle almost any claim for something to avoid the risk of a horrendous jury verdict. American judges, accustomed to the passive role of litigation referee, are poorly situated to make proactive investigations of the reasonableness and fairness of settlements proposed by colluding representative parties.

These abuses have been and continue to be met with corrective legislation. The Private Securities Litigation Reform Act of 1995 set higher thresholds for class action pleadings to screen out securities class actions of little merit. The Class Action Reform Act of 2005 addresses some of the abuses perpetrated by a handful of class-action-friendly state courts by permitting removal of all but the most insignificant class actions from state to federal court based on a relaxed standard of diversity of citizenship. Additional legislative measures are currently under consideration.

Jurists from civil law backgrounds sometimes view the opt-out class action as an unacceptable compromise of the principle of the autonomy of the individual litigant. How can a party be bound by a legal proceeding in which he or she did not voluntarily appear and take part or at least have notice and the opportunity to do so?

However, the American class action must be regarded in the context of the large assignment given to private civil justice in the American political economy. Many functions of law enforcement and compensation that are collectivized by government regulation, legislation, and administrative or criminal proceedings in European or East Asian jurisdictions are left to private litigants to pursue in civil courts in the United States. The relatively high cost and expense of American legal proceedings means that, absent some collective processes, many legally cognizable injuries would go unreimbursed and much law would go unenforced. The fear of a class action may well impose standards of care and restraint on large economic actors in the United States that are the subject of detailed government regulation in other modern jurisdictions.

Even as the United States is attempting to reform its class-action process to eliminate serious shortcomings and abuses that have become evident over the years, civil law jurisdictions in Europe and East Asia are studying ways in which their civil processes can be collectivized in order to deal more efficiently with mass defaults in today's global economy. The expansion of representative actions in consumer, environmental, and securities cases in such traditionally class-action- unfriendly jurisdictions as Germany suggests that the future will see a greater use of collective remedies in major civil matters worldwide. An example of this development is the enactment of the *Kapitalanleger-Musterverfahrensgesetz* (Act on Model Proceedings in Capital Market Disputes) as of November 1, 2005, introducing new means of collective litigation for capital-market disputes in Germany.

## 7

# American Criminal Justice

C RIMINAL LAW IN THE UNITED STATES PRESENTS A
diversity and complexity that is not encountered in any other
modern legal system. This chapter addresses only a few significant
aspects of American criminal law that resonate with some of the
noteworthy characteristics of the American legal system in general, such as American federalism, American constitutionalism,
and American systems of court procedures.

At the outset, it should be noted that criminal law, like virtually
all American public law, is now completely statutory. This was
not, however, always the case. In the early years of the American
republic, the elements of many crimes were defined by prior judicial decisions, as was the law of criminal evidence and procedure.
For instance, the first criminal case brought before the newly constituted District Court for the District of Maine in 1790 was a
common law prosecution of an individual who had seized a small
sailing ship and murdered the captain. The defendant was prosecuted under the federal common law of piracy, which the court
discerned from tradition and reports of prior judicial decisions,
largely in England. Based on this case law, the defendant was
convicted by a jury and duly hanged.

The common law of crimes remained viable in the United
States until the mid or later part of the nineteenth century.
Even as American states commenced to identify crimes and

punishments by statute, the common law continued to play a major role in fleshing out the legislation. For instance, in *Common-wealth v. Webster*, 59 Mass. 295, 303–304 (1850), a mid-nineteenth-century murder case that has since been studied by genera-tions of American law students, the Supreme Judicial Court of Massachusetts noted:

> In seeking for the sources of our law upon this subject, it is proper to say, that whilst the statute law of the commonwealth declares (Rev. Sts. *c.* 125, § 1,) that "Every person who shall commit the crime of murder shall suffer the punishment of death for the same"; yet it nowhere defines the crimes of murder or manslaughter, with all their minute and carefully-considered distinctions and qual-ifications. For these, we resort to that great repository of rules, principles, and forms, the common law. This we commonly desig-nate as the common law of England; but it might now be properly called the common law of Massachusetts. It was adopted when our ancestors first settled here, by general consent. It was adopted and confirmed by an early act of the provincial government, and was formally confirmed by the provision of the constitution (ch. 6, art. 6,) declaring that all the laws which had theretofore been adopted, used, and approved, in the province or state of Massachusetts bay, and usually practised on in the courts of law, should still remain and be in full force until altered or repealed by the legislature. So far, therefore, as the rules and principles of the common law are applicable to the administration of criminal law, and have not been altered and modified by acts of the colonial or provincial govern-ment or by the state legislature, they have the same force and effect as laws formally enacted.

Gradually, during the nineteenth century, the various American jurisdictions made their criminal laws statutory and the role of the common law was reduced. Several states even referred to their compilations of criminal law as "codes," although such codes do not exhibit the abstract and coherent structure of most European codifications. More recently, the ALI's Model Penal Code and similar model legislation sponsored by other study groups have led to improvement in the organization and coherence of the criminal law in many states.

## A. AMERICAN FEDERALISM AND CRIMINAL LAW

From the earliest days of the nation, criminal law has been primarily law of the individual states. Each state possesses a fully developed law of crimes. Each state also has its own prosecutorial competence and facilities as well as a complete court system to process criminal cases and a penal system to punish the offenders. However, the federal government has always possessed the power to define and punish crimes against the federal order within areas of federal competence. As noted previously, as early as 1790, federal courts were entertaining common law prosecutions for such crimes as piracy on the high seas. Prosecutions for violations of federal criminal law are brought in the federal courts by federal prosecutors, and persons sentenced to confinement are accommodated in federal penal facilities.

In more recent years, there has been a great increase in federal criminal law. Misdeeds that have long been crimes under the law of the various states have been made federal crimes to the extent that they may involve interstate commerce or some other federal area of concern. *U.S. v. Lopez*, 514 U.S. 549 (1995), discussed in Chapter 4, is an example of an attempt by Congress to "federalize" the formerly purely state law crime of possession of a firearm at school. Many antisocial actions are now crimes subject to the authority of one or more states and simultaneously subject to the criminal authority of the federal government.

The fragmentation of criminal law among the fifty states and overlapping jurisdiction of the federal government have many consequences for American criminal prosecutions. First, much criminal conduct may involve more than one state. Such crimes can involve intricate choice of law problems and, in some cases, can be prosecuted and punished by more than one state. The authority of state law, state police, and state criminal prosecutors extends only to the borders of the respective states. This can hamper state prosecutions of criminal activity that covers more than one state. Although interstate compacts for sharing of information and mutual assistance have mitigated this problem to some extent, each state is jealous of its sovereignty. Thus, for instance, the return of fugitives who have fled to other states requires extradition proceedings similar to those that take place between sovereign nations.

Federal criminal jurisdiction, on the other hand, is nationwide, and federal law enforcement authorities such as the Federal Bureau of Investigation (FBI) function on a nationwide basis. For this reason, criminal activity that involves more than one state is likely to be subject to a federal criminal statute that can support federal law enforcement activity and federal prosecution. For instance, the practice of stealing automobiles and then driving them to other states to impede prosecution long ago led to federal legislation criminalizing interstate transportation of stolen motor vehicles. Based on this legislation, federal authorities effectively prosecuted car-theft rings for many years.

Another consequence of overlapping state and federal criminal jurisdiction is the potential of multiple criminal prosecutions and punishments for a single criminal act. The Double Jeopardy Clause of the Fifth Amendment of the U.S. Constitution (and similar provisions in most state constitutions) prohibits the federal government (or the state, as the case may be) as sovereign from subjecting a person accused of a crime to multiple prosecutions and punishments for the same operative facts. However, this clause does not prevent two sovereigns (i.e., two states, or a state and the federal government) from prosecuting a person whose single act has simultaneously violated their respective laws.

Also, the result in one prosecution has no preclusive effect on the other. Conviction or acquittal in state court has no effect on a subsequent prosecution in federal court for violation of a federal crime based on the same alleged conduct and vice versa. At the discretion of the respective courts, the punishments levied can overlap or cumulate.

This consequence of American federalism combined with the degree of discretion allowed to state and federal prosecutorial authorities results in sometimes unseemly competition or cooperation among state and federal authorities. In 2004, various states and the federal government vied for the right to prosecute two individuals accused of random shootings that killed several individuals in states surrounding Washington, DC. Ultimately, the prosecuting authorities agreed that the duo should be first prosecuted in Virginia on the grounds that the Virginia courts could impose the death penalty and had the facilities and system to bring the defendants most rapidly to face that ultimate punishment.

## B. CRIMINAL CONSTITUTIONAL REVIEW

As discussed in Chapter 5, an important body of American constitutional law concerns the limits placed on the activities of police and prosecutors and the conduct of criminal trials by the U.S. Constitution, mainly the Bill of Rights and the Fourteenth Amendment. Constitutional issues can be raised at any stage of a criminal prosecution. For instance, asserted violations of the Fourth Amendment by unlawful searches and seizures may be raised by motions to suppress evidence in the first-instance trial of the crime charged. Some constitutional guarantees such as the privilege against self-incrimination (Fifth Amendment) and the right to confront adverse witnesses (Sixth Amendment) are asserted by evidentiary objections before or during trial. And, as was the case in *Lopez*, a criminal prosecution can be the vehicle to test the constitutionality of the very statute on which it is based.

State criminal prosecutions are subject to rights and guarantees contained in state constitutions as well as many of the most important federal guarantees. The latter are imported to govern state proceedings by the Due Process Clause of the Fourteenth Amendment of the U.S. Constitution.

Judges of the ordinary state and federal trial and appellate courts are expected to rule on these constitutional claims in the course of the litigation and any appeals. Decisions of the state courts of last resort are final on questions of state constitutional law. However, claims of deprivation of rights guaranteed by the federal Constitution can support a petition for *certiorari* from the highest court of a state to the U.S. Supreme Court.

A person convicted and punished for violation of state law can also raise constitutional issues not finally adjudicated in the regular appeals process by petitions for post-conviction relief in the state courts. The common law writ of *habeas corpus* permitted a confined person to challenge the legality of his confinement by requiring the confining authority to "produce the body" and justify continued confinement. This traditional remedy has been supplanted in most jurisdictions by various forms of statutory postconviction review processes.

Federal and state postconviction review procedures permit persons convicted of crime to challenge the constitutionality of their convictions based on issues that could not be finally adjudicated in the criminal trial itself. Under these procedures, state prisoners can petition federal district courts based on claimed denials of rights guaranteed by the Fourteenth Amendment of the Constitution. Even though the state courts may have already ruled on these claims, there is no preclusive effect unless the state court rulings have been expressly affirmed by the U.S. Supreme Court. The federal court of first instance is free to consider the constitutional claim anew, subject to appeal to within the federal court system potentially to the U.S. Supreme Court.

Thus, for example, Stillman Wilbur's claim that Maine's murder statute violated the Fifth Amendment of the federal Constitution because it, in effect, cast the burden of proving his state of mind on the defendant, was rejected by the Maine Supreme Court. That did not stop Wilbur from asserting the same claim on postconviction review in the federal courts. He convinced the U.S. District Court sitting in Maine that the Maine statute under which he was convicted was unconstitutional, thereby winning an order from the federal court that the State of Maine must provide Wilbur with a new trial under a constitutional standard. On this federal constitutional issue, the decision of the federal court of first instance effectively overruled the contrary decision of Maine's highest appellate tribunal. The district court decision was ultimately affirmed by the U.S. Supreme Court in *Mullaney v. Wilbur*, 421 U.S. 684 (1975) and Stillman Wilbur's Maine murder conviction was vacated, subject to retrial based on the constitutional standard. In recent years, state and federal governments have sought to restrict the number and scope of review of postconviction remedies in the interest of more rapidly reaching final criminal dispositions.

The 1960s and early 1970s saw a considerable expansion of procedural rights of criminal defendants. Under the leadership of Chief Justice Earl Warren, the U.S. Supreme Court construed the Fourth, Fifth, and Sixth Amendments and the Due Process Clause of the Fourteenth Amendment of the U.S. Constitution to require states to provide free defense counsel for indigent defendants (*Gideon*, 1963), to mandate that state police give pre-interrogation warnings (*Miranda*, 1966), to prohibit state prosecutions based on coerced confessions (*Escobedo*, 1965), and to bar admission in state criminal prosecutions of evidence obtained from unlawful searches and seizures (*Mapp*, 1960). The frequent result of this constitutional doctrine was the exclusion of reliable evidence obtained in violation of the constitutional norms. Without expressly repudiating the jurisprudence of the Warren era, the current Court has adopted a more conservative and prosecution-friendly construction of the same constitutional provisions.

## C. THE ADVERSARY CRIMINAL JUSTICE SYSTEM

American criminal justice remains adversarial to an extent that may seem extreme when compared to the standards of most other modern jurisdictions. The essential issue in any American criminal prosecution is not whether the defendant in fact committed the criminal act of which he or she is charged but rather whether the prosecution has proved, beyond a reasonable doubt, that he or she committed that act. The fact finder is instructed to focus on the evidence proffered and admitted. Does that evidence lead to a conclusion of guilt beyond a reasonable doubt? If it does not, the defendant is entitled to acquittal regardless of the fact finder's reasonable belief or conviction of guilt.

In this sense, criminal trials are considered as contests between prosecution and defense rather than investigations into whether a crime has been committed and who committed it. Although this standard and approach may be thought to favor criminal defendants, as a practical matter, it has several consequences.

First, the adversarial model of American criminal justice affects the role of the public prosecutor and law enforcement officials. American prosecutors are generally authorized to commence and maintain criminal prosecutions if there is evidence of "probable cause" that the defendant may have committed the crime, regardless of their own level of belief or lack of belief in guilt or innocence. Although prosecutors are constitutionally required to make exculpatory evidence available to a defendant or his or her lawyers, they are under no general duty to make sure that such evidence is presented to the court or otherwise to look out for the rights or interests of the person charged. The American trial judge plays a passive role in the fact-development part of the criminal process, so the criminal defendant cannot look for much help from from the judge.

This extreme adversarialism in criminal process means that much depends on the skill and effectiveness of the criminal defense lawyer to secure just treatment for his or her client. The importance of effective legal representation has been recognized by the U.S. Supreme Court, which ruled in *Gideon v. Wainwright*, 372 U.S. 335 (1963) that persons accused of all but the most trivial of crimes are entitled to publicly provided legal representation if they cannot afford to hire lawyers on their own. Persons with means can hire highly skilled criminal defense advocates, whose energy and ability can sometimes improve their chances of acquittal at trial or other more favorable treatment from the criminal justice system.

Another feature of American criminal justice that can be derived from its partisan and adversarial character is the "plea bargain," a process whereby a prosecutor and a criminal defendant can negotiate charges and dispositions of pending and anticipated criminal proceedings. Although the agreed-upon dispositions do not bind the court in its sentencing role, the court is scarcely in a position to challenge what has been agreed on by the parties to the case before it. In some cases, the plea bargain process can result in guilty pleas to factually inapposite charges as well as dismissal of fully founded ones, all in an effort to reach a "bottom line" disposition acceptable to both sides. Although it has been criticized as undermining the legitimacy of the law of crimes and punishments itself, the plea bargain is a practical necessity in a criminal justice system overflowing with business yet staffed and funded on a minimal basis.

## D. THE PROSECUTION FUNCTION

Although the role and function of public prosecutors in American jurisdiction roughly correspond to those of their counterparts in other modern democracies, there are some aspects of the charging function that deserve comment.

First, American prosecutors are usually chosen by some form of political process. In most states, local district attorneys are elected to two- or four-year terms of office by popular election by the voters of the locality they serve. Attorneys General of the respective states are in most cases elected to similar terms on statewide ballots. In some states, the Attorney General is chosen by the legislature or appointed by the Governor. Federal prosecutors for each federal judicial district are political appointees of the President. In all cases, prosecutors are more or less directly politically accountable for their performance in office. The mode by which they are chosen and their short terms of office means that American prosecutors have a degree of political sensitivity that can influence the kinds of cases they prosecute and the manner in which they prosecute them.

American prosecutors also enjoy a degree of prosecutorial discretion that may seem extreme to jurists from many civil law systems. In most states, the prosecutor is the only official that can initiate a serious criminal prosecution. There is no appeal or judicial review of a prosecutor's decision to initiate or not to initiate a criminal prosecution. Sovereign immunity protects prosecutors from civil claims based on alleged wrongful prosecution or failure to prosecute. In general, the decision of whether to prosecute and the charges on which the prosecution will be based is solely that of the prosecutor untrammeled by oversight by higher authority.

The power of the prosecutor to initiate criminal prosecution is subject to the constitutional requirement that prosecutions for serious federal crimes be commenced by grand-jury indictment. The institution of the grand jury was exported to the American colonies by eighteenth-century British justice. Springing from the same roots as the trial, or petit, jury, grand juries were originally convened as inquests in various localities as the King's justices rode circuit throughout England. Their function was to determine whether any crimes had been committed that warranted prosecution. The grand jurors acted on the basis of their own knowledge as well as information placed before them by citizens and officials. Their concurrence by majority vote was required before a prosecution could be commenced. Once a prosecution was commenced, the trial would take place before a petit jury of twelve individuals who had not served on the grand jury in connection with the charge.

At the time of the American Revolution, the grand jury was perceived as a safeguard against unjustified criminal prosecutions and was incorporated into most state constitutions as well as the Fifth Amendment of the Federal Constitution. In their current forms, grand juries typically consist of between twelve and twenty-three members. Grand jurors usually serve for a period of several months, during which they are called together periodically to consider evidence of criminal activity and issue indictments.

Grand-jury proceedings are secret and *ex parte*. The jurors meet solely with the prosecutors. The potential defendants are not entitled to know of the existence of the grand-jury proceedings or to be there. The prosecutor discloses to the grand jury evidence of conduct that he or she considers criminal and requests that the grand jury indict the persons involved of specific crimes. The rules of evidence that govern proof at a trial do not generally apply at grand-jury proceedings. Evidence may be presented by live witnesses or by documents. If a majority of the grand jurors present vote in favor of the charge, an indictment issues. The indictment names the person charged, identifies the conduct on which the charge is based, and specifies the crime charged. If a majority of the grand jurors present vote against the charge, a "no bill" is returned. A no bill does not prevent the prosecutor from returning to the grand jury to seek another indictment if he or she finds additional evidence that might support charging a crime.

Although once considered a safeguard against unjustified criminal accusations and a restraint on abuses of prosecutorial discretion, current prevailing opinion views the grand jury as a "rubber stamp" for the prosecution. There are increasingly common calls to discontinue its use in favor of some better means to control prosecutorial zeal and protect the citizens from unjust prosecution.

The introduction of "sentencing guidelines" and other forms of specificity in criminal punishments has resulted in augmentation of prosecutors' powers. Traditionally, a criminal statute would provide a range of potential punishments for a particular crime. The judge had a large measure of discretion in fashioning a sentence within this wide range. Starting in the early 1980s, Congress adopted sentencing guidelines providing for specified levels of punishments for every federal crime based on a number of identified factors. The statutory factors included the defendant's criminal record, whether the crime was outrageous or unusually cruel, whether the defendant acknowledged responsibility for his or her conduct, and similar considerations. Many of the guideline sentences are harsh in comparison to sentences that were routinely given at the time the guidelines were adopted. The guidelines typically provide that sentences for defendants who plead guilty and incriminate others are considerably more lenient than dispositions for defendants who insist on their right to be tried by jury and face proof beyond a reasonable doubt. On the federal level, practice under the guidelines has led to a noticeable reduction in trials and an increase in plea bargaining. These guidelines since have been imitated in several states.

As originally conceived, once a defendant had been convicted of a particular criminal charge, the judge had the responsibility to make the additional factual determinations necessary for the application of the guidelines. Based on these factual findings, the judge would apply the guidelines and determine the sentence.

In a series of recent cases, this aspect of the guidelines was successfully challenged as an infringement of the defendant's right to jury trial. Because the guidelines are in actuality statutes that attach penal consequences to potentially disputed facts (e.g., the degree of cruelty with which a criminal act was committed), a defendant has the right that such fact-finding be made by a jury. In the case of *U.S. v. Booker*, 543 U.S. 220 (2005), the U.S. Supreme Court ruled that preservation of the defendant's right to trial by jury requires that the formerly mandatory federal guidelines be considered as only recommendations that would not be legally binding on the judge in sentencing for specific crimes. It is anticipated that the guidelines will maintain a strongly influential role in determining criminal sentences even though they are no longer mandatory. In a previous case, *Blakeley v. Washington*, 542 U.S. 296 (2004), the Court had invalidated state guidelines sentences based on nonjury fact-finding as violative of the Fourteenth Amendment Due Process Clause.

Under the guidelines, mandatory or suggested, the prosecutor can determine the likely severity of the punishment that the defendant will undergo by choosing among available charges. Judges can be expected to depart from the disposition indicated by the guidelines only in rare circumstances. Thus, in bargaining a plea or deciding to face trial, the defendant must contend with the charges (and punishments) picked by the prosecution and has little effective recourse to the judge in the event of a conviction.

The wide scope of discretion afforded American prosecutors, their political sensitivity, and the tremendous pressure that the extreme adversarial system can bring to bear on a criminal defendant mean that persons accused of crime must rely heavily on their defense counsel to make sure that their rights are protected and that they are fairly treated in the criminal trial process. Much depends on the skill, zeal, and energy of criminal defense lawyers to make the American system "work." Defendants who lack the financial resources to employ such counsel must depend on the ability and commitment of public defenders and appointed lawyers to safeguard even their most basic constitutional rights.

## E. CRIMINAL JUSTICE AND JURY TRIAL

A central feature of American criminal justice is the determination of guilt or innocence by trial to a jury of laypersons. The modern American criminal jury has descended from its English ancestor with remarkably little change. Every American state, as well as the federal courts, provides jury trial in all serious criminal cases.

A criminal defendant's right to have his or her guilt or innocence determined by a jury is so fundamental to American notions of justice and fair play that it has been incorporated as in the Fifth Amendment to the federal Constitution and in the state constitutions of all the states. Indeed, any attempt by a state to abridge or abolish this right would risk violating the Fourteenth Amendment of the U.S. Constitution, which has been construed to require jury trial in all serious criminal prosecutions, state as well as federal, as an element of "due process of law."

Traditionally twelve in number, the trial jurors are generally selected by more or less random processes to reflect a rough cross section of the community. The jurors deliberate independently from the judge, whose decisional role is limited to instructing the jurors in the law that they are supposed to apply to the facts as they find them.

Criminal juries are instructed as a matter of law that they can only convict a criminal defendant if they find that each and every element of the crime charged has been proven "beyond a reasonable doubt." This is considered the highest standard of certainty that can be applied in a judicial proceeding and is contrasted with the "preponderance of evidence" standard that applies in most civil cases. There have been many efforts to formulate and explain the "reasonable doubt" standard by prosecutors, defense lawyers, judges, and even academics. Ultimately, these efforts seem to be little more than substitutions of words.

Criminal jury deliberations are secret, and the result of the deliberations is usually a general verdict of "guilty" or "not guilty" of the offense or offenses charged. A criminal jury's verdict of acquittal is not subject to challenge for factual inaccuracy and is virtually immune from appeal.

The independence of the jury, its exclusive jurisdiction to find the facts and apply the law to those facts, the generality and opacity of its decisions, and the practical finality of its judgments mean that there is no practical way to require the jury to maintain any particular standard of factual accuracy or regular application of law in its decision-making process. As a practical matter, a jury can acquit a criminal defendant for whatever reason it chooses, and its decision will be final.

This degree of power and autonomy of the American criminal jury has led in some cases to verdicts of acquittal that seem to be directly contrary to the evidence and the law as instructed by the judge. In the years immediately preceding the American Revolution, colonial juries often refused to convict their fellow colonists of violations of laws that were unpopular in the community. The ability of a trial jury to nullify a criminal prosecution by returning a verdict of acquittal means that there is opportunity for the voice of the community to be heard not only in the enactment of criminal laws but also in every individual criminal case. "Jury nullification" means that a criminal defendant has an opportunity to appeal to community values that may transcend an unjust law or argue exceptional facts of a particular case that relate to the policy behind a law rather than its actual provisions. A jury's untrammeled power to acquit can also be exercised based on the prejudices and biases of the community. An example of this darker side of jury nullification is exemplified by an all-white jury's acquittals of white police officers of assault on an African American in the *Rodney King* case even though the event was recorded on videotape.

## F. THE DEATH PENALTY IN THE UNITED STATES

One feature of American criminal justice that is alien not only to many foreign observers but to many Americans as well is the continued maintenance of the death penalty by the federal government and many states. Capital punishment came to the American colonies from England, where hanging was the prescribed form of punishment for most serious crimes at the time. Abolition of capital punishment was no part of the American Constitutional debate, and all of the early American states adopted the practice.

The nineteenth century saw increased moral and social concern about the legitimacy and value of the death penalty. Several American states (e.g., Michigan, 1863; Maine, 1873; Oregon 1914) abolished capital punishment and some of the newer states (e.g., Hawaii) never adopted it.

The mid-twentieth century saw renewed doubt about the death penalty and increased agitation to dispense with what had come to be regarded as an immoral, barbaric, and ineffective form of punishment. Constitutional objections to the death penalty were grounded on the Eighth Amendment to the U.S. Constitution, which prohibits "cruel or unusual punishments," on the Sixth and Fourteenth Amendment Due Process clauses because of the apparent capriciousness of the ultimate penalty, and the Equal

Protection Clause of the Fourteenth Amendment based on a perceived tendency of death sentences to fall unevenly on minority groups and particular classes of defendants, such as black men accused of sexual assault on white victims.

The constitutionality of death sentences came to the U.S. Supreme Court in *Furman v. Georgia*, 408 U.S. 238 (1972). In that case, a majority of the Supreme Court invalidated death sentences in Georgia and Texas on the grounds that "the imposition and carrying out of the death penalty in these cases constitute cruel and unusual punishment in violation of the Eighth and Fourteenth Amendments." The brief *per curiam* opinion did not identify a rationale for the Court as a whole. Groups of justices filed concurring opinions identifying invidious discrimination in the administration of the death penalty, characterizing it as "offensive to human dignity," and focusing on an intolerable capriciousness in its application "in the same way that being struck by lightning is cruel and unusual" as the individual bases for the collective majority decision.

The seemingly broad scope of the Supreme Court's reasoning in *Furman v. Georgia* brought the death penalty to a halt nationwide. Over time, however, individual jurisdictions sought to amend their capital punishment legislation and procedures to meet criticisms suggested by *Furman* and other Supreme Court death-penalty cases. Although some of these attempts were in turn struck down, those death-penalty schemes that conferred the death-sentencing function on the jury, which was to apply specific standards in a separate process following the determination of guilt, began to pass constitutional muster.

By the early 1990s, capital punishment was once again available in a majority of states and by the federal government, although actual utilization has varied greatly. Some states, such as Texas and Florida, have been aggressive in sentencing and executing convicted offenders, whereas other states have maintained the death penalty "on the books" without actually making use of it. In some former death-penalty states such as Massachusetts, post-*Furman* efforts at reinstatement have failed to gain legislative approval. In recent years, the Supreme Court has refused to permit execution of certain categories of offenders, such as children and severely mentally retarded individuals, and has restricted the use of capital punishment to homicides committed under seriously aggravated circumstances.

Most recently, death-penalty challenges have been raised based on concerns about the accuracy of the criminal process in general and the risk of irrevocable injustice in the event of the erroneous conviction of an innocent defendant. In a number of cases, DNA analysis has cast serious doubt on the guilt of individuals under sentences of death for a variety of aggravated homicides. Concern about the possibility of executing an innocent person led the Governor of Illinois to suspend executions in 1998 and ultimately to commute the sentences of 145 death-row inmates just before he left office. States are now reexamining their procedures for capital prosecutions to set higher thresholds of certainty and develop processes for assuring that only the truly guilty will pay the ultimate penalty. Reforming current adversarial criminal jury trial processes to generate that level of certainty is proving to be a serious challenge to lawmakers and political leaders.

It must be stressed that there is a wide diversity of opinion on the death penalty in America, and that by no means do all states embrace this institution or support its continuance. A few states have never authorized capital punishment and in several others, capital punishment remains a bad memory since the mid-nineteenth century. Even among those states that have adopted post-*Furman* death-penalty legislation, there are many that do not actively implement capital prosecutions or sentencing. Americans are politically divided on the issue, and there are many who continue to hold capital punishment as immoral, unjust, and ineffective and who continue to work for its abolition. Awareness of world human rights opinion condemning capital punishment, concern about the certainty of criminal judgments, and worry about continuing disparity in death-penalty sentencing may be now combining to prepare the way for the end to the era of capital punishment in American criminal justice.

# 8

# American Trial by Jury

O NE OF THE SALIENT CHARACTERISTICS OF AMERICAN
civil and criminal justice, which causes and explains many
other significant structural and procedural differences from corresponding civil law institutions, is the use of a lay jury to decide
disputes of fact in civil and criminal cases. It can be fairly said that
the role of the jury in civil and criminal trials is central not only to
the structure of the proceeding and functions of its participants but
also to the fundamental values that the civil and criminal justice
system protect and promote.

## A. HISTORICAL BACKGROUND OF AMERICAN
JURY TRIAL

Trial by jury developed in England and was exported to the
American colonies along with the other features of English civil
and criminal justice. The Anglo-American jury has its roots in the
Middle Ages, when English judges assembled groups of knowl-
edgeable citizens from the locality where a crime was committed to
assist in the determination of the identity of the wrongdoer. Over
the centuries, this early inquest jury evolved into two subforms:
the grand jury and the petit or trial jury.

Grand juries have the responsibility of determining whether the
facts relating to a particular event justify the lodging of a criminal

charge, or indictment, against a particular person. In this sense, they are investigative in nature. Grand juries function *ex parte* and in secret. Generally, they hear only the prosecution's evidence, although grand juries have been known to subpoena evidence *sua sponte*. Composed of between twelve and twenty-three members, grand juries act by majority vote. The result of their deliberations is either an indictment charging a particular person with a particular offense or a "no bill" declaring that on the evidence considered, no indictment will be returned.

As of the time of the American Revolution, grand juries were considered as safeguards of the citizenry against harassment by unjustified criminal prosecutions. Thus, both the federal and most state constitutions required that serious criminal prosecutions be instituted by proceedings before grand juries. Over the years, the value of grand juries as meaningful screens of criminal prosecutions has come into question. As of the start of the new millennium, grand juries are increasingly regarded as "rubber stamps" for prosecutors and, hence, as unnecessary procedural formalities in the criminal justice system.

The trial or petit jury had developed pretty much to its present form and composition by the time the American colonies broke loose from England. As of that time, in every colony practically all serious crimes and significant civil cases at law were tried to petit juries of twelve persons. Juries heard cases under the oversight of judges but deliberated separately and in secret. Their verdicts were subject to very limited oversight on appeal.

The independence of trial juries and their decision making from control by judges had been established in England well before the American Revolution. In *Bushell's Case*, Vaughn 135, 124 Eng. Rep. 1006 (C.P. 1670), an exasperated English judge attempted to punish the foreman of a jury that had refused to return a guilty verdict in a prosecution of William Penn for violating laws prohibiting the practice of the Quaker religion. The English House of Lords sustained Bushell's appeal, holding that no juror could be punished for returning a "wrong" verdict.

The independence of juries played a key role in the events leading up to the American Revolution. In many cases, colonial juries refused to return guilty verdicts in prosecutions of their fellow colonists for violations of regulatory laws enacted by the English Parliament in the 1760s and early 1770s. This power of the jury in effect to nullify prosecutions with which the jurors did not agree came to be regarded as an important guarantee of freedom from official oppression. Guarantees of jury trial for citizens accused of crime were written into every one of the constitutions of the first states and into the Fifth Amendment of the federal Constitution.

By the early nineteenth century, jury trial was well established in all jurisdictions of the new nation. De Tocqueville remarked at length on the institution and practice of jury trial in the American states. He placed emphasis on the jury trial as a political institution[1]:

> Each American citizen is elector, eligible [for office], and juror. The system of the jury, as it is understood in America, appears to me as direct and as extreme a consequence of the dogma of the sovereignty of the people as universal suffrage.

As new American states were created throughout the nineteenth century, jury trial became similarly incorporated into their civil and criminal justice systems. At present, jury trial is available as of right to persons accused of serious crimes in all of the fifty American states and in the federal justice system. Similarly, in every state, litigants in most civil cases of the kind traditionally denominated as "legal" (as opposed to "equitable") have the right to trial by jury,

[1] Alexis de Tocqueville, *Democracy in America*, 261 (Harvey C. Mansfield & Delba Winthrop, eds., Chicago, 2000).

although the precise scope and contours of this institution vary somewhat among states.

Historically, the number of members of a petit or trial jury has been twelve. Exactly how this number became established in England long before the American Revolution has never been convincingly demonstrated. Suggestions that the number is linked to the number of disciples of Christ or that it came from the mystical significance of the number 12 in prehistorical Druidic culture all seem of equal plausibility. Certainly, early Americans considered the size of juries to be of significance in the role of the jury as a guarantor of individual rights.

In more recent times, investigation by psychologists of the dynamics of group decision making have disclosed that groups of ten to fourteen persons interact in a particularly felicitous manner when addressing questions of the kind raised by legal cases. Such groups give individual members good opportunity for participation in discussion, while reducing the risk that a single juror will dominate the debate or the resulting decision.

## B. THE JURY AS FACT FINDER AND CASE DECIDER

### 1. Selection and Composition of Juries

Although juries of the Middle Ages were composed of individuals who had actual knowledge of the particular events that they were investigating, modern-day jurors are expected to come to their duties equipped with their general knowledge and experience of the world but without specific knowledge of the matter they are to decide. Currently, jurors are carefully screened to make sure that they do not possess specific individual knowledge of the facts they are to hear.

In highly publicized criminal cases, this policy against extraneous information sometimes means that it is difficult to find qualified jurors who do not have at least some knowledge of the event in question. In 1806, after questioning scores of potential jurors for a trial of Aaron Burr for treason, Chief Justice Marshall was unable to find twelve persons who had not heard something about Burr's alleged plot to seize the Western territories and set up a new state. Out of necessity, Marshall was compelled to accept the jurors' assurances that what they had heard would not influence their appraisal of the evidence placed before them in court. This solution is still employed in selecting juries in sensational cases in the age of television and pervasive media.

Although historically jury service was reserved for persons of property, for those who had political connections, and for men, currently every effort is made to select juries from pools that represent the population generally. Most jurisdictions use voter registration lists or lists of licensed drivers as the source of potential jurors. In some jurisdictions, the inclusiveness of these lists is compromised by exemptions or excuses based on occupations and personal circumstances. For instance, in many jurisdictions, doctors, teachers, lawyers, judges, public officials, mothers with young children, and a number of other defined categories are exempt from jury service or may be excused on request. These numerous excepted categories can result in juries composed disproportionately of retired and unemployed persons.

A few jurisdictions have developed the "one day – one trial" method for trial jury selection. In these jurisdictions, there are practically no exemptions, and personal circumstances can affect the timing but not the obligation to perform jury service. Each individual juror is required to serve for one day or, if she or he is selected for a jury that day, for the duration of the trial for which she or he is selected. Under these programs, even lawyers, law professors, and judges serve on juries. Experience to date has not substantiated early concerns about disproportionate influence of these "super jurors," and the quality and credibility of the resulting juries may have improved.

Typically, a number of jurors are notified to appear at the courthouse on the date one or more trials are expected to start. After some general orientation by video media as well as by judicial personnel, a group of potential jurors is brought to the courtroom where the trial is to be held. After being given an idea of what the case is about and who are the parties, the potential jurors are then questioned, sometimes as a group and sometimes individually, about any potential individual knowledge about the case or any interest that might affect their suitability for service. Jurors who disclose relationships with parties, counsel, or the issues under consideration that could trammel their judgment are excused. The actual jury that is to try the case is then drawn from the remaining members of the pool.

One feature of American jury trial that currently arouses some controversy is the long-established practice of allowing the parties a limited number of "peremptory challenges" or "strikes," by which each party can disqualify a certain number of selected jurors without giving any cause. Typically, the number of such strikes is small, often three per side in a civil case, sometimes more in a criminal prosecution. The idea is that a party has a degree of latitude to eliminate from the jury persons whom he or she may perceive as likely to be unsympathetic without having to show grounds for disqualification for bias.

The difficulty with peremptory challenges arises when the basis for exercising them is the race or gender of the potential jurors. Prosecutors have been known to use their strikes to remove persons of the defendant's race from criminal trial juries. On the other hand, defense counsel sometimes tries to strike young women from juries hearing prosecutions for sexual assault. Efforts to manipulate the racial or gender composition of the jury in this manner have been condemned by the U.S. Supreme Court. In *Batson v. Kentucky*, 479 U.S. 79 (1986), the Court ruled that exercise of peremptory challenges by the prosecution based solely on race is a violation of the defendant's right to due process of law. In practice, the *Batson* doctrine has been difficult to apply. If the prosecution has any plausible reason to disqualify a potential juror other than race, the prosecution is free to act. And there is no constraint on the ability of the defense to exercise peremptory challenges for any reason, including race or gender. For these reasons, some reformers have called for the abolition of peremptory challenges.

One of the principal justifications for the use of the jury in civil and criminal cases is that it is supposed to represent the parties' community and to bring to the proceeding community values and the collective community experience. Recent reforms to jury-selection practices have sought to effectuate this policy. Egregious failure of jury-selection procedures to include a wide sample of the community can have constitutional consequences. For instance, the U.S. Supreme Court has held that systematic exclusion of African Americans from a pool of potential jurors can be a deprivation of due process or equal protection of the laws protected by the Sixth and Fourteenth Amendments.

Although the Constitution requires that pools of potential jurors more or less fairly represent the composition of the community as a whole, there is no constitutional guarantee that a randomly chosen jury in an individual case will have any particular gender or racial composition. As long as the pool is fairly constituted and as long as selection from the pool is random, the actual composition of the jury need not bear any particular resemblance to the racial or gender composition of the community or to the race or gender of the parties.

## 2. Function of the Jury at Trial

Traditionally, the Anglo-American jury has functioned as a passive audience in its reception of information and finding of facts at trial. The mode of procedure is highly oral, visual, and forensic. All proceedings are conducted by the parties' attorneys, who present the evidence to be considered through witnesses and exhibits and make direct appeals to the jurors' shared knowledge of the real world. The jury does not have the power to guide the inquiry or control any aspect of the proceedings. The jurors sit in a "jury box," generally located at one side of the courtroom, and look and listen.

Historically, almost all meaningful communication with the jury by either lawyers or judge was oral. Presumably, this reflected the fact that at the time jury trial reached its current stage of development, not all jurors could be counted on as able to read or write. By the same token, jurors were traditionally not allowed to take notes of the trial.

Reliance on purely oral communication limits the amount and complexity of material that can be communicated, tends to protract proceedings, and may jeopardize the retention by the jurors of complex details. For this reason, some courts have recently begun to experiment with allowing jurors to take notes during long or complex proceedings.

Communication with jurors during trial is also one-way communication. The jurors are not permitted to talk with the lawyers or to ask questions themselves of lawyers or witnesses. The model juror is expected to sit like a sphinx and listen to the testimony and argumentation without betraying any reaction or indication of how she or he is receiving the material. Although astute trial lawyers claim the ability to "read" the thoughts of jurors, the lack of real two-way communication has long been seen as a drawback to jury process.

Recent reforms in some jurisdictions provide juries with the ability to pose written questions to be submitted to the judge who can then determine whether they are proper to be posed to a lawyer or witness. So far, there has been little use of this procedure in practice. Formulating questions collectively can be cumbersome. The requirement that the question be vetted by the judge means that there can be a long interval between the time a question may arise in the mind of a juror and the time the question is posed to the witness.

Subject to these structural limitations, the ability of jurors to absorb and retain information presented to them in court has been demonstrated to be impressive. Studies have shown that the collective memory of twelve ordinary citizens and their collective experience with the world can be powerful tools for the analysis and determination of factual disputes. Both anecdotal and empirical evidence have repeatedly established that where the subject matter is within the realm of ordinary human experience, the jury is a reliable and effective fact finder and decision maker. Juries are particularly effective in evaluating arguments based on known traits of human behavior or known phenomena of the real world. In this context, there is real basis for the saying that "Twelve heads are better than one."

Fact-finding by juries comes under greater strain with increasing complexity of the material presented and when the material presented does not resonate directly with the jurors' real-life experiences. Cases involving large volumes of abstract material are difficult to present to juries. The oral method of presentation is far too slow for masses of abstract information, which in real life is generally transmitted and received in writing. The jury process is not well adapted to the receipt and assimilation of volumes of written material. Although written exhibits are often presented in court, there is no time for the jurors to read any significant volume of written information. Exhibits are useful for significant kernels that can be pointed out by the lawyers, not for transmission of data to be absorbed in mass. Anyone who has attempted to read written material by committee knows the frustrations and inefficiencies of this kind of exercise.

These limitations on oral proceedings were early recognized in England, where proceedings such as extensive accountings involving volumes of written information were handled solely by judges sitting in equity. Some courts in the United States have suggested that in highly complex cases, the jury's limitations on reception and assimilation of complex and voluminous abstract information may implicate the Due Process Clause of the Constitution, creating a "complexity exception" to the constitutional guarantees of jury trial. Many commentators continue to argue that juries are inherently not qualified to deal with complex and voluminous abstract information and that cases involving such information should be decided by judges.

The jury's strength in matters resonating with the jurors' collective life experience may mask limitations on its ability to deal with matters that are not within the realm of ordinary human knowledge and activities. As technology continues to burgeon and life becomes ever more complex, the likelihood increases that a particular case will involve issues that are entirely foreign to the personal knowledge and experience of all of the jurors. By now, almost every case involves some issue so far outside of general knowledge that at least one "expert witness" is required to explain the matter to the fact finder and opine on the correct resolution of one or more specialized issues in dispute. Antitrust cases with sophisticated issues of economics, patent cases with difficult questions of science or technology, medical malpractice cases involving disputes about proper medical or surgical procedure, product and medical liability claims with competing contentions of science, statistics, and causation are the kind of cases that are increasingly raising doubts about the jury's competence as a fact finder and decision maker.

How can individual laypersons make reasonable decisions about subject matters totally foreign to them? How can a juror decide whether the gibberish of one expert witness is to be believed in preference to the gibberish of another?

Questions about the objective competence of the jury in cases involving specialized issues have overlapped with concerns about a relative handful of cases in which jurors have reached results that seemed somewhat extreme. Some have argued that in cases where the subject matter is outside ordinary human experiences, jurors are deprived of the anchors of their own life knowledge and are subject to exaggerated influence by secondary factors or oversimplified and distorted images served up to them by the lawyers. This has led to a widespread suspicion of the jury system by potential corporate defendants and to calls for reform of either the jury system or of the substantive law that the jury is asked to apply.

## 3. Rules of Evidentiary Admissibility

A corollary of the Anglo-American jury trial tradition is an intricate body of law defining and limiting the kinds and form of evidence that can be submitted and considered by the jury in its role as fact finder in civil and criminal cases. These rules are designed to ensure that the jury will base its decisions on information that is reliable, that is subject to fair opportunity for testing and evaluation by the trial process, that is reasonably related to the rules of law that are supposed to be applied, and that is unlikely to encourage a decision on some basis other than the proper application of the legal rules to the facts objectively found. Because of the opacity of jury decisions, the rules are applied as "rules of admissibility." They determine what information can be learned by the jury at all. The theory is that if the jury is given only information of a particular level of quality and fairness, its decision can be presumed to be fairly reached and properly grounded. This means that questions about admissibility must be determined before the jury hears or sees the evidence. If a particular item or kind of information is deemed "inadmissible," it will not be imparted to the jury or referred to at all.

One of the most well known of the rules of evidence is the "hearsay rule." This rule is designed to prevent admissibility in evidence of statements made outside the courtroom when their relevance depends on their truth. So, for instance, a statement by a witness to a crime or accident would not be admitted unless the witness appeared in court and were subject to cross examination.

The hearsay rule is based on issues of both reliability and fairness in presentation. Statements made in real life may or may not be reliable depending on their circumstances and the motive and character of the person making them. At least some infirmities in a witness's testimony can be addressed by cross-examination in the presence of the fact finders who are to evaluate the testimony. The opportunity to confront witnesses in court and cross-examine them in front of the jury is deemed to be so important in American procedure that it is constitutionally guaranteed in criminal cases by the Confrontation Clause of the Sixth Amendment to the U.S. Constitution. Out-of-court statements covered by the hearsay rule may not be admitted in evidence and may not be considered by the jury.

The hearsay rule's apparent wholesale ban on admissibility and consideration of secondhand evidence is compromised by several limitations on its applicability and by myriad exceptions for particular kinds of statements or statements made under particular circumstances. For instance, if a statement is relevant merely for the fact that the statement was made, regardless of whether or not it is true, the statement is not considered to be hearsay. Thus, contract terms, conveyances, warnings, notifications, and the like are generally not banned. Out-of-court statements by an opposing party can be offered as "admissions" and are not barred by the hearsay rule. Business records, official reports, spontaneous excited utterances, and statements of intention are among the various statements excepted from the hearsay rule because of presumed reliability or necessity.

Although the hearsay rule adds complexity and perplexity to American jury trial proceedings, in final analysis there is little evidence of consequence that is totally filtered out. The unnecessary procedural wrangling caused by this rule has led some commentators to question whether it continues to be necessary.

Evidentiary questions are decided by the judge as the overseeing monitor of the jury trial. They are supposed to be raised in such a manner as to allow decision before the information reaches the jury. Thus, lawyers are required to ask questions of the witness in a form so that the subject matter of the answer is more or less discernable from the question. This allows the opponent to raise an objection to a question that is likely to elicit information inadmissible in evidence before the witness has opportunity to answer. This is traditionally done by counsel rising from a seated position at counsel table and simultaneously stating "Objection!" right after the question and before the answer. The judge can then sustain or overrule the objection, sometimes after argument by counsel, usually at a corner of the judge's bench outside the hearing of the jury. If a lawyer knows in advance that the opponent is likely to elicit a particularly important bit of potentially inadmissible evidence, he can file an advance "*motion in limine*" that the evidence be excluded.

Evidentiary objections and rulings add to the interest and excitement of American trial proceedings. Whether the evidentiary screen retains an important function in the quality of American civil and criminal justice may be subject to some question.

4. The Application of the Law in Jury Proceedings

Although the jury is given the responsibility for determining the facts in American civil and criminal jury proceedings, the determination of the law is the exclusive province of the judge. Since most cases require that the law be applied to disputed fact scenarios, these divided functions must somehow be brought together to make the final fact-law determination.

Theoretically, there are two ways by which a judge–jury partnership could apply law to disputed facts. One approach would be for the jury to consider only questions of fact and to render a report of the facts found to the judge, who would then apply the legal rules to the facts reported by the jury and issue the final judgment. This approach is used relatively rarely in complex civil cases, such as patent matters. The jury is given a questionnaire, or "special interrogatories," asking for key factual determinations. The answers to the special interrogatories are then used by the judge as the basis for application of the relevant law and the rendition of the final judgment. Special interrogatories are almost never used in criminal matters.

The predominant method by which the law is applied to facts found in jury trial process is through the judge's instruction of the jury in the applicable law. Once the jury has heard the evidence of the facts in dispute, the judge then instructs or "teaches" the jury the law that would be applicable to the facts as the jury might find them. Traditionally, the judge's "charge" to the jury was orally delivered by the judge at the end of the evidence just before the commencement of deliberations. The length and complexity of some jury charges have led observers to wonder how lay jury members can possibly remember, let alone apply, a mass of abstract legal doctrine delivered to them orally. Concerns about the effectiveness of oral charges have led some courts to permit part or all of the judge's charge on the law to be delivered to the jury in writing so that the jurors can refer to the applicable law during the course of their deliberations.

The perceived advantages of giving the jury the applicable law in a charge and allowing the jury to apply the law to the facts are twofold. First, in days past, the use of any written media to communicate with jurors of limited or varying reading ability has been seen as bringing an added burden and risk of error. Second, the charge method gives the jury greater latitude to reach decisions on the ultimate outcome of the case in a more holistic manner and reduces the significance of potential disagreements about individual facts. As indicated herein, the ability of a jury to approach a case holistically and decide it based on the jurors collective sense of right and justice, sometimes regardless of the niceties of the law, has long been considered an important safeguard for individual litigants and an opportunity for court judgments to reflect the values of the community.

## 5. Jury Deliberations

American trial juries deliberate in secret and outside the presence of the judge. Once the presentation of evidence is completed, the lawyers have argued their cases, and the judge has rendered his or her charge, the jurors are brought to a jury room where they can conduct their deliberations. A traditional jury room contains a long table, twelve chairs, and an adjoining bathroom, thus permitting the jury to be self-sufficient for enough time to allow useful discourse and decision making. In the older courthouses, one sees jury rooms with doubled doors to ensure soundproofing and discourage eavesdropping.

Before the jury retires, the trial judge generally appoints one of the members "foreperson." The job of the foreperson is to conduct the deliberations and render the verdict in the name of the entire jury. A jury foreperson has no more voting power than any other juror and is supposed to serve as a facilitator of discussion rather than a leader with an agenda.

The format of jury deliberations is left to each individual jury. The only requirement is that the jurors attempt to come to a consensus on the issue or issues submitted to them for decision. Usually the process consists of discussion and successive votes. Although in most cases jury deliberations are orderly, there are reports of sharp, even physical conflict among jurors where there are strongly held and divided views.

For centuries, trial or petit juries acted only by unanimous consensus of the members. A single "holdout" could result in a "hung jury" and prevent the rendition of a verdict. This requirement of unanimity has been regarded by many as an important safeguard for criminal defendants. A single juror maintaining a reasonable doubt can prevent a criminal conviction. Although unanimity continues to be the rule for criminal trials, in many states civil juries may speak based on super-majorities such as 9–3 or 5–1. In a criminal case, a "hung jury" is not the equivalent of an acquittal but rather leads to a retrial of the case before a different jury.

Jury deliberations have long been a subject of great interest among jurists, social scientists, and even writers and film directors. Predicting and second-guessing jury determinations have long been a popular preoccupation not only among lawyers but also for the public at large. In recent years, social scientists have studied the jury function extensively, both through interviews with actual jurors and the creation of "mock juries" to hear real and simulated cases. G. K. Chesterton, the British essayist, wrote in "The Twelve Men" of his experience serving as a juror in a criminal case at the Old Bailey in London at the turn of the twentieth century. He likened the deliberations of the jurors to a mystical or religious experience. More recently, the American film, *Twelve Angry Men*, consists entirely of a jury deliberation and portrays the psychological interplay among the jury members as they decide a serious criminal case.

## C. ACCOUNTABILITY OF THE JURY AND REVIEW OF JURY DETERMINATIONS

The jury's fact-finding process and the fact determinations that result from that process enjoy a near immunity from scrutiny or review by the trial judge or higher courts on appeal. In civil cases, to be sure, if the pleadings and discovery disclose no genuine issue of material fact, the trial judge can bypass the jury and render summary judgment based on the undisputed facts. Similarly, if the facts as proven at trial admit of only one legal outcome, the judge can withdraw the case from the jury's consideration by "directing a verdict." However, if there is any conceivable basis for different fact conclusions, the trial judge may not interfere, but must entrust the case to the jury for consideration and resolution. In criminal cases, there is no summary judgment and a verdict may be directed only in favor of the defendant.

Most jury verdicts are stated in general terms such as "Guilty" or "Not Guilty" or, in civil cases, "For the plaintiff in the amount of . . . " or "For the defendant" without more. Such verdicts disclose nothing of the jury's reasoning. There is no requirement or expectation that the jury will explain its reasons for reaching any particular result. Those are locked up forever in the secrecy of the jury room.

When one considers the history and composition of the jury, this opacity of reasoning is not surprising. In the early days of jury practice in England, many jurors were unable to read or write. The difficulty of trying to get twelve persons to agree on a precise path of reasoning and the words to explain it makes clear why juries cannot really be expected to justify their decisions.

Both as a matter of policy and practical necessity, appellate courts are deferential to fact-finding by juries. To set aside a jury verdict based on error of fact, the appellate court must be convinced that no reasonable jury could have possibly found the necessary facts to sustain the judgment based on the evidence presented at trial. This deference is incorporated into the Seventh Amendment of the U.S. Constitution, which provides that in civil cases "no fact tried by a jury, shall be otherwise re-examined in any Court of the United States, than according to the rules of the common law." Similar guarantees can be found in the constitutions of many of the states. This means that claims of factual error by juries are seldom given much attention on appeal.

The jury has often been compared to a "black box." The inputs can be controlled, but the process that takes place within the box cannot be controlled or even observed. The only guarantee that the output will be of high quality is to control the inputs and hope that the jury will function as it should. Appellate scrutiny of jury process, therefore, focuses on these inputs in the form of the trial judge's rulings on evidence and on the trial judge's communication of the applicable law in his or her charge. Errors in either of these inputs can lead to invalidation of a jury verdict if the appellate court concludes that the error could likely have influenced the outcome. However, the question of what actually influenced the outcome will forever remain unanswered.

The process by which a jury reaches its verdict is also largely beyond scrutiny. As long as the inputs to the jury are not inappropriate, what the jury does with these inputs and how it conducts itself during deliberations are its own business. Oversight of the jury's decision-making process is limited to whether the jury received any unauthorized external inputs. Thus, communications by parties or others with the jury about the subject matter of the case, or even acquisition of specific knowledge by the jurors' own spontaneous investigations, will cause verdicts to be set aside. However, no inquiry is allowed into matters of the jury's internal deliberations. For example, in *U.S. v. Tanner*, 483 U.S. 107 (1987), the U.S. Supreme Court refused to allow inquiry into the function of a criminal jury in the presence of evidence that jurors were drinking and ingesting marijuana and cocaine during their deliberations.

### D. THE ROLE OF THE JUDGE IN JURY TRIAL

As discussed in Chapter 6 with respect to civil cases, the use of juries to find facts imposes some structural constraints on the role of judges in the conduct of jury cases. American law's extreme solicitude for the jury's fact-finding role means that judges are required to bend over backward to avoid trammeling the jury or impinging on it by trial-management measures affecting the finding of the facts.

In civil cases, if the facts legally relevant to determination of an issue are truly beyond dispute, the trial judge can bypass the jury and render summary judgment with respect to that issue. Otherwise, however, all fact determinations must be preserved for the jury. Nor may the trial judge manage the trial-preparation process in a way that influences the jury's fact-finding function or constrains either party from developing and presenting evidence relevant to fact determinations.

The result of these constraints is that American trial judges have a limited role with respect to fact development and presentation of facts to juries. The judge sits as a kind of neutral umpire over the process, scrupulously refraining from giving any indication of his or her own reaction to the evidence or of his or her views on the facts. Although American judges have the theoretical power to ask their own questions of witnesses, they rarely make use of it for fear of inappropriately influencing the jury's fact-finding function.

The primary role of the judge during jury trial is to enforce the rules of evidence and procedure that screen the fact inputs to the jury and then, at the end of the proceeding, to instruct the jury on the law that the jury will apply to the facts found. Although a trial judge can act *sua sponte* on evidentiary issues, he or she generally will refrain from doing so, again to avoid an impression that he or she has an agenda on the facts. Thus, the burden is on the respective lawyers to invoke the rules of evidence by proffers of evidence on the one hand and objections, or motions *in limine*, on the other.

The American trial judge views the fact development of a case with a certain detachment, as a spectator of a process rather than a responsible participant. As long as the rules of evidence are observed, the trial judge has no responsibility to process the facts or to reach conclusions from the facts as a whole. In fact, it is generally better if judges reach no fact conclusions of their own that might affect their umpireal neutrality. The facts are the province of the jury.

Thus, the strength and power of American judges with respect to the development of common law doctrine and in the area of constitutional judicial review is complemented by a relatively shrunken role in fact development in jury cases. Moreover, the judicial passivity that is functionally required when juries find the facts has carried over as a matter of practice to the many cases in which judges are required to find the facts themselves. Judges in jury-waived cases, in nonjury cases formerly considered "equity," and in the many cases in lower civil and criminal courts where jury trial has never been available, tend to manage and conduct fact-finding in a manner similar to the way they run jury trials. They sit as passive audiences for the lawyers' presentations. Fact determinations are reserved for the end of the proceedings, and generally the judges do not interfere other than to apply and enforce the rules of evidence.

Although the primary justification of the rules of evidence – namely, to legitimate the jury's otherwise inscrutable fact-findings by controlling the inputs – does not apply to nonjury proceedings, the rules still generally apply. Because the judge must often hear the disputed evidence in order to rule on its admissibility, the objective efficacy of the evidence regimen can be doubted. Indeed, many judges "relax" the rules of evidence in nonjury proceedings in the interest of speed and efficiency in presentation.

## E. THE ROLE OF LAWYERS IN JURY TRIAL

One of the practical consequences of committing the fact-finding process to a lay jury brought together for a relatively brief trial is that the role of lawyers in the trial process is greatly augmented. The jury is not in a position to render any significant work in the management of fact-finding or the development of the facts themselves. The judge holds back in order to avoid any appearance of interfering with the jury's prerogative or seeking to influence the outcome of the jury deliberations. This leaves the lawyers with the biggest part of the necessary work.

As in most litigation systems, the parties' lawyers must determine whether facts exist that will sustain a particular claim or defense. However, the American trial advocate must also then develop those facts and package them in a form that will be intelligible and persuasive to a lay jury and then present them in a very short interval of time. This requirement explains and justifies the Anglo-American practice of preparing witnesses, even "coaching" them. Without advance preparation, it is difficult to conceive that lay witnesses will be able to make cogent, persuasive, and concise presentations to the jury at trial. Any loss in witness credibility arising from the lawyer's preparation is outweighed by the need simply to get the witness ready to perform in a high-stress environment.

The process of fact presentation at trial has developed to a high art in the American legal culture. Lawyers who can make fact presentations that convince juries are considered the elite in the world of litigation. The importance of the lawyer's role in case presentation, the substantial scope allowed lawyers in fulfilling their responsibilities, and the concomitantly limited roles of judges in trial presentations combine to support the perception that the skill and energy of the presenting lawyers have a great influence in litigation outcomes. This reality results in both great pressures on trial lawyers to make presentations that win for their clients and in substantial rewards for those who are able to use their talents and energy effectively to produce those wins. This state of affairs resonates positively with libertarian notions of individual choice and freedom – let the best person win – but may raise questions of fairness and objective justice in cases of disparity of presentation talent or the means to hire it.

## F. THE FUTURE OF AMERICAN TRIAL BY JURY

Although American jury trial flourished in the United States throughout the nineteenth and most of the twentieth centuries, recently there are signs that the actual use of juries to hear and determine civil and criminal cases has greatly diminished. Stories and anecdotes about the increasing rarity of jury trials have gradually been substantiated by objective empirical research. This research has documented that the frequency of jury trial as a means of resolving civil disputes and adjudging criminal charges has dropped precipitately both absolutely and relatively from the level of utilization in the first half of the twentieth century. Although both civil and criminal parties retain their constitutional rights to jury trial in all of the American states and under the federal Constitution, litigants now seem to be "voting with their feet" by choosing methods of resolving their disputes other than submitting them to juries. The tremendous growth of plea bargaining, stimulated in part by federal sentencing guidelines that strongly reward acknowledgment of guilt, has resulted in fewer criminal jury trials. In civil cases, the increasing use of arbitration in contract matters and the high rate of case settlement before trial have reduced the proportion of cases filed that actually go to juries to less than 1 or 2 percent in almost all American jurisdictions.

The reasons for this trend away from an institution that has been seen as the core of the American justice system are not totally clear. It is evident that a major share of the responsibility for the current state of jury trial disuse is borne by the tremendous costs imposed on private litigants in order to make the jury system work. The large case-presentation roles of the litigants and their lawyers and the opportunity to strongly influence case outcomes by superior presentations cause litigating parties to expend huge sums in discovery and case preparation. There is almost no end to what can be justified in terms of time and money in hopes of getting a good outcome before the jury. It is easy for litigation costs to become a large percentage of the amount or interest in dispute, despite every effort by parties and lawyers to hold them in check.

Another factor that may cause some parties to avoid jury trial is the potential unpredictability of outcome and the difficulty in securing judicial review of fact determinations by juries. Although jury trial has shown itself a reliable and accurate means of judging facts over many cases, the degree of variability in individual cases can be high. In those cases where the jury's determination may be extreme, there may be no effective review on appeal.

These considerations suggest that civil jury trial, at any rate, will largely disappear as a means of resolving ordinary civil disputes, if it has not already done so. Will jury trial continue to have a role in civil cases at all in the future? There is some suggestion that civil jury trial, despite its relative costliness and unpredictability, will continue to play a viable social – political role in resolving civil conflicts that embody fundamental collisions of major elements in the social political and economic order. As indicated in Chapter 6, in the United States civil jury trial functions as a kind of regulator of the conduct of major elements of the national economy. In the absence of detailed governmental regulation, business enterprises' conduct vis-à-vis the public can be subject to the *ex post facto* scrutiny of a semidemocratic institution of the community. The jury can apply community values in resolving these conflicts and redressing the harms resulting therefrom.

Drug companies, environmental actors, and manufacturers of products that affect the public must subject their own balancing of competing interests of public safety and private gain to second-guessing by the community in the form of the jury. For instance, the design of a small snowplow widely sold in the northeastern United States includes a semipermanent frame that is bolted to the front of small trucks and large automobiles. The plow itself can be easily attached to this frame when needed for plowing. When the plow is not attached, the frame can be seen as an increased hazard to occupants of other automobiles in the event of collision. There is no particular government regulation that prescribes what kind of frames may be attached to vehicles under these circumstances. Instead, contentions that the design of the frame unreasonably jeopardizes other motorists are submitted to juries in cases brought by persons injured by the frame for *ex post facto* determination. Careful manufacturers heed the possibility that their products may be judged in this manner. Thus, the jury functions as a mode of regulation even in the absence of detailed or specific regulatory rules or standards.

Therefore, the civil jury may well continue to play a valid role in determining what cigarette companies can do to promote the sale of their products, how careful a drug company must be before it releases a new drug to the public, and/or what kind of training a company must provide to its employees to minimize the risk of sexual harassment. The expense of jury proceedings will of necessity limit this kind of social and regulatory function to those areas where the stakes are high enough to justify it. However, it can be expected that there will continue to be cases in which the value of this kind of determination justifies the cost of civil jury proceedings.

The future of jury trial in criminal cases is somewhat brighter. Although greatly diminished in frequency from the early part of the twentieth century, criminal jury trial still appears to be the method of choice to decide serious criminal prosecutions. In fact, recent U.S. Supreme Court judgments have tended to give the jury more responsibility rather than less. For instance, in *Ring v. Arizona*, 536 U.S. 584 (2002), the Court held that decisions of whether to impose the death penalty in a criminal case must be made by juries, even though such decisions were traditionally within the purview of trial judges. On the other hand, in ordinary criminal cases, the cost of jury trial for both the public and the criminal defendant will continue as a pressure in favor of resolution by other means.

# 9

# Choice of Law, International Civil Jurisdiction, and Recognition of Judgments in the United States

## A. INTRODUCTION

The broad discipline of conflict of laws – or, to use the nomenclature preferred in Europe, private international law – deals with legal problems that have significant connections with more than one politically organized society. Basically, three distinct although interrelated questions are posed: (1) in what circumstances is it appropriate for a legal order to charge its juridical institutions with the adjudication of interstate or international controversies; (2) from what source or sources are to be derived the rules and principles to regulate such controversies; and (3) in what circumstances and to what extent should a legal order accord respect locally to adjudications given in an interstate or international controversy by the juridical institutions of another sovereign? These problems are addressed by the three branches of private international law: adjudicatory jurisdiction, choice of law, and recognition and enforcement of foreign judgments. This chapter considers some important recent developments in these three areas in the United States.

The experience of the United States with conflict of laws is particularly rich because conflictual problems arise with respect to interstate as well as international situations. Generally speaking, for the most part, each state of the United States is sovereign in private-law matters. Chapter 4 discussed the federal and state court systems whose work and responsibilities overlap and interrelate in various and complex ways. State courts can apply federal law and federal courts can apply state law. Each state – subject to any applicable treaty provisions and to certain controls based on provisions of the Constitution of the United States (in particular, the Due Process Clause of the Fourteenth Amendment and the Full Faith and Credit Clause of Article IV) – has its own system of procedure, substantive law, and private international law.

In the areas of choice of law and recognition and enforcement of foreign judgments, a given state may approach interstate and international cases somewhat differently. Such differences are more likely to arise with respect to recognition issues than choice-of-law issues because interstate recognition practice is largely controlled by federal standards developed under the Full Faith and Credit Clause, a constitutional provision that does not apply internationally to foreign judgments. Little if any federal control exists over state choice-of-law practice, whether interstate or international.

On the other hand, in interstate and international situations alike, claims of adjudicatory jurisdiction can be tested under the Due Process Clauses of the Constitution. It follows that at least in this field, interstate and international practices must converge. In recent years, there appears to be a tendency in choice-of-law and recognition-and-enforcement practice to approach international and interstate cases on the same terms and to reach comparable results.

Against this general background, some of the high points in the recent history of choice of law, adjudicatory jurisdiction, and recognition and enforcement of foreign judgments are considered herein. The discussion begins with choice of law, touches briefly on recognition and enforcement, and concludes with adjudicatory jurisdiction, the area that has seen the greatest change and development in the last decade or so.

## B. CHOICE OF LAW

Choice-of-law theories have traditionally focused on a single element of a situation or transaction in order to relate or allocate – "connect" – the case to a single legal community. Thus, issues characterized as contractual might be referred to the place of contracting. Issues sounding in tort can be associated to either the place of the wrongful conduct or of the injury. Descent and distribution problems could be assigned to the decedent's domicile at death. Regardless of the connecting elements preferred, traditional choice-of-law methods that seize upon a single aspect of a situation or transaction to determine the applicable law emphasize simplicity, convenience, and uniformity of result.

An entirely different approach to choice of law is also possible. Rather than emphasizing a single aspect or element of a given situation or transaction, all its significant elements can be analyzed and the governing law determined by rationally elaborating and applying the policies and purposes underlying the particular legal rules that come into question and by considering as well the needs of interstate or international intercourse. These instrumental or functional approaches rest on the premise that – as propositions of law are designed to advance policies and purposes – a given rule has no reason to apply unless the particular situation implicates the policy or purpose the rule is intended to advance. Such a method tends to accept that cases involving "true" conflicts may be governed by different laws depending on the forum in which the litigation proceeds. This skepticism regarding the possibility of achieving "decisional harmony" leads multiple-aspect methods to give greater weight to achieving appropriate results in particular cases than do more traditional approaches.

In the late 1950s, a great debate began in the United States between proponents of traditional approaches to choice of law by a single-aspect, jurisdiction-selecting method, and innovators who advocated a multiple-aspect method reasoning from the policies that informed the possibly applicable rules of law to determine which should be applied. By the early 1960s, what the Europeans call the "American Revolution" was well underway. In 1963, the New York Court of Appeals decided the seminal case of *Babcock v. Jackson*, 12 N.Y. 2d 473 (1963). By the end of the decade, the new approach had gained broad acceptance among courts and scholars.

The Restatement Second, Conflict of Laws 2d, adopted and promulgated by the American Law Institute in May 1969, for the most part reflects the new methodology. In its Section 6 – Choice of Law Principles – the Restatement accepts *dépéçage* and sets out a number of factors that are to be considered in choosing the law applicable to a particular issue in both interstate and international matters. These include the following:

(a) the needs of the interstate and international systems
(b) the relevant policies of the forum
(c) the relevant policies of other interested states and the relative interests of those states in the determination of the particular issue
(d) the protection of justified expectations
(e) the basic policies underlying the particular field of law
(f) the certainty, predictability, and uniformity of result
(g) the ease in the determination and application of the law to be applied.

By the early 1970s, the new approach was well launched in the United States. During this decade, the new method became firmly established in the courts. However, the euphoria felt by many scholars in the 1960s respecting choice-of-law theory and method has subsided. Today, as in the late 1970s,

[t]hose who work in the field of choice of law are, at times, discouraged by the apparently intractable nature of the problems

with which they must grapple. Intricate and subtle analyses are undertaken; ambiguities and uncertainties are painfully resolved. Ultimately, a result is reached, yet the solution is too frequently neither entirely satisfying nor fully convincing.[1]

Policy-based analysis has made American jurists aware, often painfully so, of the true complexity and difficulty of the choice-of-law problem. An enormous effort has been – and continues to be – made to understand the problem fully and to meet, rather than to conceal, its difficulties. It remains true, however, that in some situations, the new methodology continues to encounter difficulty in determining the purposes of internal-law rules and in giving principled solutions to "true conflicts."

It is difficult to imagine a return to the single-aspect, jurisdiction-selecting method that was displaced in the 1960s. Yet, it is by no means clear that the new method always works well. Some choice-of-law problems seem so inherently difficult and complicated that generally satisfying solutions cannot be achieved.

The 1981 decision of the U.S. Supreme Court in *Allstate Insurance Co. v. Hague*, 449 U.S. 3021 (1981), reflects the difficulties and complexities of contemporary American choice-of-law analysis.

Hague, a resident and domiciliary of Wisconsin, died of injuries suffered when a motorcycle on which he was a passenger was struck from behind by an automobile. The accident occurred in Wisconsin, immediately across the border from Red Wing, Minnesota, where Hague had been employed for the past fifteen years and to which on the day of the accident he was commuting from his Wisconsin home. The operators of both vehicles were Wisconsin residents; neither carried insurance. Hague did have uninsured motorist coverage of $15,000 per person for each of his three cars. The policy contained a provision that placed a ceiling of

---

[1] A. von Mehren, "Choice of Law and the Problem of Justice," [1977] *Law & Contemporary Problems* 27.

$15,000 on recovery for any accident and thus forbade aggregation or "stacking" of his three uninsured-motorist coverages.

After the accident but before the litigation began, Hague's widow moved to Red Wing, Minnesota. Subsequently, she married a Minnesota resident and lived with him in Minnesota. As personal representative for the estate, Hague's widow brought an action against the insurance company in the Minnesota courts to recover $45,000, representing an aggregation of the three $15,000 coverages in Hague's policy.

Under Wisconsin law but not under Minnesota law, a clause prohibiting such aggregation or "stacking" of uninsured-motorist coverages was permissible. The Minnesota courts applied the Minnesota rule that prohibited the anti-stacking clause and thus allowed a recovery up to the $45,000 total of the three policies. The U.S. Supreme Court granted *certiorari* and, in due course, affirmed the Minnesota judgment, concluding that the choice of Minnesota law did not violate any provision of the U.S. Constitution.

Many commentators considered the result reached by the Minnesota Supreme Court plainly wrong although perhaps not constitutionally infirm. A detailed examination of the three opinions in the U.S. Supreme Court cannot be undertaken here. An explanation of the *Hague* decision is the extreme reluctance of the Court to exercise constitutional control – which could be grounded on the due process requirement – over choice of law even where the correct result seems plain.

This reluctance to control state choice-of-law practices under the Due Process Clause has long been clear and is understandable. The reluctance, based in considerable measure on a desire to avoid the heavy burdens that involvement with this intractable subject matter would entail, has become greater as functional or instrumental methods have replaced more mechanical approaches to choice-of-law issues. The *Hague* result can best be explained as a reflection of the methodological difficulties that inhere in the policy-based, multiple-aspect method that is now dominant in the United States.

## C. RECOGNITION AND ENFORCEMENT OF
## FOREIGN JUDGMENTS

The area of recognition and enforcement of foreign judgments has not seen developments in recent decades comparable in importance to those in either choice-of-law or adjudicatory jurisdiction.

Traditionally, questions of recognition and enforcement of foreign judgments were a matter of the autonomous law of each of the fifty American states or of federal law in cases brought in the federal courts. As discussed herein, recognition and enforcement of judgments of sister states of the United States is regulated to some extent by the Full Faith and Credit Clause of the U.S. Constitution. However, traditionally, there was no corresponding control over state courts with respect to recognition and enforcement of judgments of the courts of foreign nations.

In the 1970s, for the first time in its history, the United States entered into negotiations for a bilateral convention comprehensively regulating a broad area of recognition and enforcement practice. Discussions were begun with the United Kingdom of Great Britain and Northern Ireland on a Convention Providing for the Reciprocal Recognition and Enforcement of Judgments in Civil Matters between the United States and the United Kingdom. Although the convention ultimately was rejected by the British government, the effort to negotiate this convention was an important step in departing from the tradition of leaving international recognition and enforcement practice within the province of state rather than federal law. In view of its foreign-relations power under the Constitution, the federal government can clearly regulate the subject. For a long time, political considerations stood in the way of using in this field the foreign-relations power.

The first major assertion of federal power over recognition and enforcement of internationally foreign adjudications was the ratification by the United States in 1966 of the 1958 United Nations Convention on the Recognition and Enforcement of Foreign Arbitral Awards (the New York Convention). The worldwide success of this convention means that even now in many jurisdictions, foreign international arbitral awards may be more easily enforceable than the judgments of foreign national courts.

Over the years, the United States has gradually showed a willingness to participate in more international agreements regulating the international aspects of civil justice. An example of the United States' greater willingness to use federal power to handle conflictual problems in the international arena is its participation in the work of the Hague Conference on Private International Law.

The United States sent observers to the Conference's Eighth (1956) and Ninth (1960) Sessions. Since the Tenth Session (1964), the United States has participated as a Member in the Conference's work. To date, the Convention on the Service Abroad of Judicial and Extrajudicial Documents in Civil or Commercial Matters, the Convention on the Taking of Evidence Abroad in Civil or Commercial Matters, the Convention Abolishing the Requirement of Legalisation for Foreign Public Documents, and the Convention on the Civil Aspects of International Child Abduction have been ratified by the United States.

In the 1990s, the Hague Conference undertook the challenge of international jurisdiction and recognition of foreign judgments on a worldwide scale. European nations had achieved consensus in this area via the Brussels and Lugano Conventions, later codified as the Brussels Regulation of the European Union. It was hoped that this major regional success could be a springboard for a comprehensive international solution to a series of problems that the explosion of international trade and commerce was making ever more urgent of solution.

A near decade of drafts, meetings, consultations, and debates failed to produce any real consensus on both sides of the Atlantic. By 2002, it had become clear that a convention governing international jurisdiction and recognition was unlikely and the Conference decided to restrict the scope of the project to a convention governing the validity and applicability of private agreements as to jurisdiction and choice of law. This very limited convention was ultimately initialed in June 2005 and awaits ratification by the U.S. Senate and the ratifying bodies of the other foreign signatories.

The failure of the Hague Conference on International Jurisdiction and Recognition and Enforcement of Foreign Judgments was a great disappointment to American and foreign jurists who have long sought greater harmony in this crucial area. It reflected continuing transatlantic differences in the treatment of several crucial issues in jurisdiction and the strength and obduracy of important interests with stakes in the divergent rules. However, the impasse in The Hague was the starting signal for the work on a federal statute dealing with the recognition and enforcement of foreign judgments. In 2000, the ALI undertook a project to develop a proposed federal statute on recognition and enforcement of foreign-country judgments. The Proposed Final Draft of such a statute, along with Comments and Reporter's Notes, was approved at the ALI May 2005 Annual Meeting. Thus, at the beginning of the twenty-first century, at least within the United States, potential uniform rules are emerging.

In sharp contrast to the situation internationally, recognition and enforcement within the United States of sister-state judgments is determined by federal law deriving from the Full Faith and Credit Clause of Article IV of the Constitution of the United States. The last development of truly fundamental importance in this area was arguably *Sherrer v. Sherrer*, 334 U.S. 343 (1948). By the beginning of the twentieth century, it was established that a state could not invoke public policy (*ordre public*) to refuse recognition to a sister-state judgment. (The public policy exception, of course, can be invoked with respect to an international foreign judgment.) As the century progressed, the full-faith-and-credit mandate became still stricter. *Sherrer* extended the mandate to findings of jurisdictional facts made in contested proceedings; today, the situations are limited in which a sister-state judgment resulting from a contested proceeding can be denied effect. Sister-state default judgments are more vulnerable because the court addressed can review jurisdictional findings. In other respects, however, default judgments are assimilated to contested judgments for full-faith-and-credit purposes.

From time to time, there have been suggestions that, where the state-addressed concern for the matter regulated by the sister-state judgment is strong, recognition should not be required. *Thomas v. Washington Gas Light Co.*, 448 U.S. 261, 285–286 (1980), may give some limited support for this view. The case involved the issue of whether the obligation of the District of Columbia to give full faith and credit to a Virginia award of disability benefits under the Virginia Workmen's Compensation Act barred a supplemental award under the District's Compensation Act. A plurality of the Court adopted a broad theory to put aside full-faith-and-credit objections to the District of Columbia's supplemental award:

> Of course, it is for each State to formulate its own policy whether to grant supplementary awards according to its perception of its own interests. We simply conclude that the substantial interests of the second State in these circumstances should not be overridden by another State through an unnecessarily aggressive application of the Full Faith and Credit Clause. . . .

We therefore would hold that a State has no legitimate interest within the context of our federal system in preventing another State from granting a supplemental compensation award when that second State would have the power to apply its workmen's compensation law in the first instance. . . .

It remains to be seen whether the *Thomas* decision and the plurality's rationale for it will be confined to the field of workers compensation, where special considerations are present, or will be adopted with respect to sister-state judgments generally. If the rationale is not confined, the *Thomas* case will mark a significant change in interstate recognition practice in the United States. It seems unlikely, however, that the rationale will be given a broad application.

### D. JURISDICTION TO ADJUDICATE

The last area that requires consideration is adjudicatory jurisdiction. Here, the latter decades of the twentieth century saw dramatic changes of great theoretical and practical significance.

In the United States, assertions of adjudicatory jurisdiction have traditionally been rationalized in terms of power. As Justice Holmes put it in a famous aphorism: "The foundation of jurisdiction is physical power. . . ."[2] This power rationale crystallized in the famous decision of the U.S. Supreme Court in *Pennoyer v. Neff,* 95 U.S. 714 (1878), and received perhaps its most extensive application in *Harris v. Balk,* 198 U.S. 215 (1905). In the latter case, the state in which Balk's debtor was physically present was allowed, despite due-process objections, to assert jurisdiction over Balk by personally serving his debtor. As the power rationale requires, the jurisdiction thus established over Balk was limited to the amount of the debt owed him. In these decisions,

---

[2] *McDonald v. Mabee,* 243 U.S. 90, 91 (1917).

the U.S. Supreme Court embraced the proposition that the due process requirements of the Fifth and Fourteenth Amendments to the U.S. Constitution are satisfied if – and to the extent that – the legal order asserting jurisdiction has physical power over the defendant's person or property.

In time, a competing rationale emerged in the United States. It came to be recognized that considerations of convenience, fairness, and justice could also ground assertions of adjudicatory jurisdiction. This alternative to the power theory first decisively emerged in *International Shoe Co. v. Washington*, 326 U.S. 310, 316 (1945). The State of Washington sued in its courts a Delaware corporation to recover unpaid contributions to the state unemployment compensation fund. The corporation contested jurisdiction, arguing "that its activities within the state were not sufficient to manifest its 'presence' there" so that the assertion of jurisdiction was a violation of due process as guaranteed by the Fourteenth Amendment of the U.S. Constitution. The U.S. Supreme Court upheld the State of Washington's assertion of adjudicatory jurisdiction and advanced a new rationale on which jurisdictional claims could be based:

> [D]ue process requires only that in order to subject a defendant to a judgment *in personam*, if he be not present within the territory of the forum, he have certain minimum contacts with it such that the maintenance of the suit does not offend "traditional notions of fair play and substantial justice." . . .

For nearly three decades, despite obvious tension, the *Pennoyer* and the *International Shoe* rationales coexisted as apparent equals. This theoretical ambivalence was reduced by the Supreme Court's decision in *Shaffer v. Heitner*, 433 U.S. 186, 196, 212 (1977). Heitner, a nonresident of Delaware, sued in the Delaware courts various present or former officers or directors of the Greyhound Corporation, a Delaware corporation, and its wholly owned subsidiary, Greyhound Lines, a California corporation. Heitner alleged that the individual defendants had violated their duties to Greyhound by causing it and its subsidiary to engage in actions that resulted in the corporations being held liable for substantial damages in a private antitrust suit and a large fine in a criminal contempt action. The activities that led to these penalties took place in Oregon.

Jurisdiction was established over the individual defendants by sequestering stock and options to purchase stock belonging to them. The certificates representing the stock were not physically present in Delaware but, under Delaware law, the *situs* of ownership of all stock in Delaware corporations is Delaware.

The individual defendants challenged the assertion of jurisdiction over them on several grounds, including that under the rule of *International Shoe Co. v. Washington*, they did not have sufficient contacts with Delaware to sustain the jurisdiction of that state's courts. The Delaware Supreme Court took the position that jurisdiction can be based *either* on considerations of fairness *or* on considerations of power. The jurisdiction asserted by Heitner plainly rested on the latter theory and satisfied the constitutional standards traditionally applicable where that theory is invoked. As noted in the Court's opinion in *Shaffer*, "[t]his... analysis assumes the continued soundness of the conceptual structure founded on the century-old case of *Pennoyer v. Neff*...." The Court went on, however, to conclude:

> [t]he fiction that an assertion of jurisdiction over property is anything but an assertion of jurisdiction over the owner of the property supports an ancient form without substantial modern justification. Its continued acceptance would only serve to allow state-court jurisdiction that is fundamentally unfair to the defendant.
>
> We therefore conclude that all assertions of state-court jurisdiction must be evaluated according to the standards set forth in *International Shoe* and its progeny.

Delaware's assertion of jurisdiction over the individual defendants' appellants was inconsistent with that constitutional limitation on state power, and the judgment of the Delaware Supreme Court was reversed.

The great importance of *Shaffer* does not lie in justifying new bases for the assertion of adjudicatory jurisdiction; in this respect, *Shaffer* does nothing more than reinforce *International Shoe*. *Shaffer's* significance lies rather in the fact that its theoretical premise requires the repudiation of various rationales that were traditionally taken to satisfy the due-process requirement. *Harris v. Balk* was overruled and the well-established institution of limited general jurisdiction based on the presence of assets belonging to the defendant thus disappeared from the American scene. Moreover, jurisdiction based on personal service alone without additional connections of the defendant with the forum state, although not expressly considered by the *Shaffer* court, is clearly called into question. In general terms, *Shaffer* reduces the possibilities for asserting general jurisdiction – that is, of claiming the power to litigate any kind of claim against the defendant. Perhaps the only bases of general jurisdiction that will survive are the defendant's habitual residence and a legal person's place of incorporation and principal place of business. The decline of general jurisdiction will encourage the development of new bases of specific jurisdiction; jurisdictional claims will have to be justified in terms of the convenience, fairness, and justice of the legal system in question adjudicating the particular controversy.

*Shaffer v. Heitner* was a case of jurisdiction of the courts of one American state over a resident of another American state. The U.S. Supreme Court addressed limitations of American courts' jurisdiction over international defendants a few years later in *Helicopteors Nacionales de Colombia, S.A. v. Hall*, 466 U.S. 408, 415, 418 (1984). The court disposed of a case that had been brought in the Texas state courts by survivors of four Americans (but non-Texans) who were killed when a helicopter crashed in Peru. The only connection between the defendant, a Colombian helicopter transportation provider, and Texas consisted of purchases of helicopters and equipment from a Texas manufacturer and relating training trips. At the U.S. Supreme Court level, the parties conceded the lack of specific jurisdiction and that "the claims against Helicol did not 'arise out of,' and are not related to, Helicol's activities within Texas." Thus, the Court explored whether the business contacts to Texas constituted general jurisdiction. It rejected that and concluded that Texas's assertion of general jurisdiction was unconstitutional:

> [P]urchases, even if occurring at regular intervals, are not enough to warrant a State's assertion of in personam jurisdiction over a nonresident corporation in a cause of action not related to those purchase transactions. Nor can we conclude that the fact that Helicol sent personnel into Texas for training in connection with the purchase of helicopters and equipment in that State in any way enhanced the nature of Helicol's contacts with Texas. The training was a part of the package of goods and services purchased by Helicol . . . We hold that Helicol's contacts with the State of Texas were insufficient to satisfy the requirements of the Due Process Clause of the Fourteenth Amendment.

The *Helicopteors* case has been controversial not only for its specific – general jurisdiction dichotomy – but also for its failure to address the issue of relatedness for specific jurisdiction. Today, American doctrine on jurisdiction as it affects potential defendants from other countries continues to be somewhat troublesome to foreigners who do business or have any form of presence in the United States. In default of an authoritative U.S. Supreme Court ruling on the subject, American plaintiffs' attorneys continue to assert jurisdiction over foreign defendants based on theories of general jurisdiction and even "tag jurisdiction" (based solely on service of process during a defendant's temporary presence within the United States). Such jurisdictions are frequently upheld by lower courts under broad readings of *International Shoe Co. v. Washington* and *Helicopteors*. Assertion of American jurisdiction under these circumstances is frequently seen as exorbitant and onerous to those foreign defendants who become subject to such jurisdiction, particularly when their own legal regimes or the Brussels Regulation would not support jurisdiction under like circumstances. Unfortunately, the hope that such jurisdictional dissonance would be harmonized at The Hague has proven to be ill-founded. New ways to resolve these differences will have to be found. In the meantime, parties who have the opportunity to do so are resorting increasingly to international commercial arbitration to protect themselves from what they consider exorbitant jurisdiction of American courts.

### E. EUROPEAN–AMERICAN PROBLEMS OF DISCOVERY AND TAKING OF EVIDENCE ABROAD

As indicated previously, the United States became a party to the 1970 Hague Evidence Convention on the Taking of Evidence Abroad. This convention was created to facilitate the reception of evidence in civil law judicial proceedings as well as the presentation of evidence at Anglo-American "trials." It was not apparently designed to assist American-style pretrial discovery proceedings. Pretrial discovery, as it is known in the United States, is not a characteristic feature of the civil procedure regime of most foreign nations and, in some cases, can contravene their public policy concerning the privacy of individuals and their business and personal affairs. Indeed, Article 23 of the Hague Evidence Convention gives individual signatory states the option to opt out of the convention with respect to requests to obtain pretrial discovery of documents as known in common law states.

Most of the civil law signatories of the convention have opted under Article 23 to deny or limit the use of the convention by American litigants seeking document discovery. However, contrary to the expectations of some of the European parties to the convention, American litigants have been able in many cases to directly obtain pretrial discovery of documents and other evidence abroad through the discovery procedures of American courts.

Foreigners forced to litigate in the United States, either as plaintiff or defendant, are subject to the procedural regimen of the American court in which they find themselves. American courts assert the authority to require litigants to cooperate with discovery requests regardless of where the evidence sought may be found. Thus, a foreign corporation that is party to a case in a United States court may be required to accede to depositions of its employees in its home country and to make production of documents or other evidence under its control in its home country, even though such procedures would be unavailable in domestic litigation under its national procedural system. A foreign litigant may even be required to disclose information that is privileged under its own law but not protected under the law of the American jurisdiction that is the forum of the controversy. Noncompliance may result in discovery sanctions such as issue preclusion, costs awards, dismissal or default on claims, or, in some cases, contempt.

The claim that pretrial discovery of documents and witness evidence abroad should take place solely under the Hague Evidence Convention was rejected by the U.S. Supreme Court in *Societe Nationale Industrielle Aérospatiale v. U.S. District Court*, 482 U.S. 522 (1987). There, the U.S. Supreme Court stated that American litigants are not relegated to the Hague Convention as the sole or even first means of obtaining evidence abroad. According to *Aérospatiale*, they can make use of other techniques to compel foreign litigants and persons subject to the jurisdiction of American courts to provide discovery that cannot be had under the auspices of the Convention. The trial court must determine on a case-by-case basis whether a discovery measure would affront international comity or unfairly burden a foreign national or institution.

This assertion of the "hegemony of American law" has caused European jurisdictions to consider retaliatory measures such as "blocking statutes" aimed at preventing their citizens from cooperating with American discovery in an effort to curb or frustrate the extraterritorial effect of discovery measures in U.S. litigation. Some commentators, however, suggest a less confrontational approach based on a possible amendment of the Hague Evidence Convention or some bilateral agreement to restrict extraterritorial discovery of evidence and documents in the hands of persons or entities not parties to the litigation, although recognizing the reality that the actual parties to a case in the United States civil justice system will be required to abide by the rules of that system.

This is another area in which the differences in the role allocations and structures of procedural regimens cause friction when they interact internationally. Contracting parties can often reduce these kinds of frictions by agreeing to international commercial arbitration under which they can choose the type of tribunal that will resolve any disputes that may arise. There remains a need for law harmonization for those litigants (chiefly, tort claimants and defendants) who are unable to choose their tribunal in advance.

# 10

# The American Legal Profession

T HE SIZE AND ORGANIZATION OF THE BAR, THE LAWYER'S conception of his or her role, and the general style of legal education in a society reflect the historic position of the lawyer and the society's traditional conception of law. This chapter begins with a discussion of American legal education because its style and approach are closely related both to the importance of decisional law in common law legal systems and to the problem of maintaining legal unity in the American federal system.

Before considering educational arrangements, some remarks are in order respecting American legal philosophy. Speaking generally, the schools that have flourished in the United States parallel those found in Great Britain and on the continent of Europe. Liberalism, utilitarianism, natural-law theories, sociological jurisprudence, conceptualism, functionalism, interest analysis, legal realism, economic analysis, and logical positivism are among the conceptual and intellectual systems that have influenced American legal thinking.

Historically, a rough parallelism exists between philosophical movements in American and European legal thinking. In the late nineteenth and early twentieth centuries, when a conceptual and formal jurisprudence (*Begriffsjurisprudenz*) based on the premise that the law was logically complete (*die logische Geschlossenheit des Rechts*) was widespread in Europe, the same assumption of a complete body of pre-existent law supported a mechanical jurisprudence in the United States.

In time, sociological jurisprudence and legal realism challenged this premise in the United States just as did such theories as *Interessenjurisprudenz* in Germany and Geny's *libre recherche scientifique* in France. Oliver Wendell Holmes, Jr., legal scholar and later Associate Justice of the U.S. Supreme Court in the first third of the twentieth century, is generally credited with being the founder of the school of thought known as American Legal Realism. His seminal work was *The Common Law*, published in 1882. Holmes maintained that the law is not inherent in the order of the cosmos, but reflects the social and economic views of the judges who "find" or "make" it as the case may be. Common law judges are ultimately legislators, applying their views of the world in the limited compasses of the cases that they decide.

Today, there is widespread agreement in the United States that a formal or conceptual theory of law is inadequate; however, no single school or theory is universally accepted. Indeed, in recent years, the rise of critical legal studies and of economic analysis of legal rules has resulted in sharper divisions within American legal thinking than have been known since the days of legal realism in the 1920s and 1930s. At least some of those who form part of the critical movement reject the utility – and, indeed, the possibility – of giving an intellectual structure to law. Most scholars do not accept this view and believe that, although law is ultimately much more than a purely formal system, principled solutions to legal problems are possible and desirable. Accordingly, these scholars – unlike at least some adherents to critical legal studies – both respect the doctrinal aspects of law and seek to adapt rules and principles to changed or new circumstances in such a way as to maintain a significant degree of continuity, predictability, and legal security.

The American Legal Profession

## A. AMERICAN LEGAL EDUCATION

Historically, the education and training of lawyers in the United States has been the purview of the Bar rather than the university. In continental Europe, law faculties were established at major universities starting in the twelfth century. These faculties have trained the jurists who have become the lawyers, judges, and legal academics of the civil law system ever since.

The American colonies, on the other hand, took over the English method of training law professionals. In England, lawyers were trained by lawyers. No university education was required. Qualification to practice law was based on a kind of apprenticeship, whereby the candidate "read" law for several years in the offices or "chambers" of a practicing member of the bar, and lodged at "Inns of Court" where they absorbed law by social interaction with experienced colleagues and later by more formal exercises, moot courts, and lectures.

The role of the bar in training and developing jurists was carried over to the new American states. Throughout the nineteenth century, the dominant methods of learning the law and qualifying to practice in the various American states were various forms of apprenticeship followed by comprehensive oral and written bar examinations, all administered by the legal profession without any connection to the formal university establishment.

Universities came relatively late to the education of lawyers in America. Although Harvard University was chartered in 1636, it did not have a law faculty until 1817. The earliest law schools in the United States were founded by lawyers, who supplemented their practice incomes by giving lectures to law aspirants. Gradually during the nineteenth century, most of the major private and public universities founded their own law schools, which have ultimately become the dominant form of legal education. There remain, however, several "free-standing" law schools not affiliated with any university. Currently, all American states require a law-school education as a prerequisite for admission to practice law, and the former practice of law apprenticeship has died out.

An important characteristic of American legal education is its post-graduate character; previous university study – usually leading to a B.A. or a B.S. – is normally required before a person can begin the study of law. Accordingly, American students rarely begin legal studies before the age of twenty-two or twenty-three, and many are older. In recent years, it has become more common for persons considering legal careers to work for one or more years between college and law school, in part to make sure that their choice is a considered one based on reality.

### i. The American Law School

Reflecting the federal structure of the American polity, there are no national universities – and, hence, no official national law schools. Education at all levels remains essentially a state or – especially in the eastern United States – a private responsibility. Such federal control as exists is essentially indirect through grants-in-aid to which strings may be attached. But, because legal education receives relatively little financial support from the federal government, this form of indirect federal control is relatively unimportant.

The lack of central control, coupled with the importance of privately endowed universities such as Chicago, Columbia, Harvard, Stanford, and Yale – to name only five, all of which have distinguished law schools – results in some diversity in such matters as curriculum and teaching practices. To ensure that minimum standards are maintained, the American Bar Association (ABA) – a private organization – has established basic requirements. The vast majority of law schools meet these requirements. At least two-thirds of the American law schools also meet the stricter standards required for membership in the Association of American Law Schools, also a private organization. Many American states require a degree from an ABA accredited law school as a prerequisite for admission to the bar.

A further distinction is useful in discussing American law schools. Historically, legal training focused on the law of the American state in which the aspirant hoped to practice. Many of the early law schools were similarly "local" in that they focused on the law of the state in which they were located. Although some of these local schools are still in existence, the trend for some time has been in favor of "national" law schools. These schools draw students from all parts of the country and prepare them for practice in any state. Obviously, national law schools do not teach the law of a specific jurisdiction; they seek to present an overall view. General approaches to problems are considered and the range of possible solutions is analyzed. Legal education thus gives greater attention to reasons and policies than to doctrinal propositions and black-letter rules. The adaptive capacity of law is emphasized, even at the expense of dogmatic certainty. Examination of the foundations on which legal rules and principles rest often assists in maintaining the underlying unity of the common law tradition in the face of state control of private law.

American law schools vary considerably in prestige and in the perceived quality of their legal educational products. Graduation from one of the most highly esteemed law schools opens career doors and ensures membership in a professional elite that can greatly further a legal career. Admission to almost all law schools is competitive, based on scores on the national Law School Aptitude Test required by almost all law schools, plus undergraduate academic record, prior work achievement, and other intangible considerations of "character." In recent years, news media have maintained informal but highly influential ranking systems under which all American private and public law schools are assigned to four "tiers" in descending order of prestige. Competition for admission to first- and even second-tier law schools can be extremely keen.

Selective admissions based on performance criteria mean that there is not likely to be a great deal of difference in intellectual capacity or performance capability among the members of any particular student body. The fact that the students are generally intellectual peers may facilitate the kind of instruction by discussion that is the traditional hallmark of American legal education.

There is one more attribute of American legal education that has an important influence on the profession as a whole. Over the last half of the twentieth century, American legal education has become very expensive. Private American law schools charge substantial tuition and fees for the instruction that they provide. As of the writing of this edition, the annual student budget for a year at a major American private law school was more than $55,000. Even state university law schools typically charge substantial tuition, presumably on the theory that they are preparing students for lucrative careers and, hence, can expect to be compensated for it.

Students often defray these large sums for tuition, fees, and support during law school by government-guaranteed loans. Other forms of financial aid may also be available but are typically limited. The result is that many American jurists commence their careers in the law burdened by massive debts. The pressure of these debts is seen by many as a reason why virtually all students who have the opportunity to do so choose to start their careers in large law firms that pay the highest compensation.

## 2. The Law School Curriculum

Since about 1900, the first degree in law – originally called the LL.B. but today usually denominated the J.D. – has required three years of instruction. Over the decades, the courses taught, the style of teaching, and the degree of student choice have undergone significant variations. Since 1829, when Justice Story began to reorganize the curriculum of the then-young Harvard Law School – the school was established in 1817 – legal education has been traditionally professional in its orientation. Students are assumed to have acquired a basic liberal education before they enter law school. The typical law student is reasonably mature and the great majority seek to prepare themselves for a legal career rather than to acquire a general education.

Recent years have seen some perceptible movement toward the theoretical and academic in American legal education. Younger colleagues come to law teaching with advanced degrees in related subjects such as history, economics, or political science and often little notion of any form of real-life law practice. Courses are presented more as academic inquiries than as preparations for professional endeavor. The result of this movement may be to cast more of the responsibility for practical preparation of legal professionals on their future employers or the bar in general.

Today, the first-year curriculum is largely – or entirely – prescribed. The bulk of the program consists of common law courses: contracts, property, and tort. Instruction is also given in civil procedure, usually taking the federal rules of civil procedure as the basis for instruction, and criminal law, including relevant constitutional protections. Some schools offer a general constitutional law course in the first year. Others give students in the second half of the year a choice among a variety of subjects such as constitutional law, legal philosophy, and administrative law. Classroom instruction is typically supplemented by work in legal writing and analysis, taught in relatively small groups. Most schools have a moot-court competition in which first-year students are given the opportunity to brief and argue a case before a court constituted of older students and teachers.

After the first year, students are largely free to select the courses they wish to study. A course in the ethics of the profession is required in all American law schools. A fairly substantial piece of legal writing – the third-year paper – must usually be completed before the student can graduate. Of course, certain optional subject matters are taken by most students. These include constitutional law (where it is not prescribed), commercial law (essentially a study of the Uniform Commercial Code), corporation law, anti-trust law (a study of legal restraints on monopolistic practices), evidence, federal taxation (state taxation is of less importance and is only infrequently studied in law school), administrative law, labor law, and private international law ("conflict of laws" in American parlance). The range of course offerings, however, goes far beyond these staples. There are advanced common law subjects such as restitution and trusts, as well as family law and the law of inheritance. Special areas – for example, insurance and maritime law – are covered. Instruction is available in legal history, comparative law, and public international law. Courses in criminology, legal philosophy, church and state, corporate finance, economics and the law, international business problems, and international commercial arbitration suggest the range of courses offered. More recently, law school curricula have been embellished by courses on "internet law," "law and the mind," and similar topics. Various clinical and practical skills courses are also available.


### 3. American Legal Pedagogy

Originally, instruction at American law schools proceeded along lines similar to those traditional in Europe. The subject was presented *ex cathedra*. A great change in method began in 1871 when Dean Christopher Columbus Langdell of the Harvard Law School published his casebook on contracts, an ordered collection of cases – largely appellate court opinions – for the instruction of students. Langdell drew an analogy between natural science and legal science. For him, the decided cases constituted the materials that, upon analysis, would yield rules and principles. Once case books were available to the students, the next step was to abandon the traditional lecture method and to analyze with the students the cases that they had – at least in theory – read before each class. The discussion – or, as it is sometimes called, Socratic – method inevitably emphasized technique and analysis rather than systematic statements of rules and principles. With its progression from the particular to the general, the case method of instruction is deemed to be closer to the genius of the common law than is the lecture method. The emphasis on analysis rather than prescriptive formulation was reinforced by the nature of the material studied. At national law schools, the material was naturally drawn from many different jurisdictions, including England; accordingly, the material presented on a given topic was typically not completely consistent either in analysis or result. A comparative dimension, with its liberating effect, became inescapable in American legal education.

The case or discussion method has evolved and changed in many ways since Langdell's day. Course books are no longer composed exclusively of decisions. Statutory materials, administrative regulations, and extracts from articles and treatises are now extensively quoted. Editors increasingly supply their own commentaries and expositions. Indeed, many contemporary course books are, in reality, unwritten treatises.

Equally pervasive and significant changes have occurred in the classroom. Especially after the first year, many instructors depart significantly from the discussion method to economize on time and to broaden and deepen the student's exposure to materials and ideas that are important for a full understanding and appreciation of the legal order. The basic justification for use of the case method remains that it can, when skillfully employed, give students an understanding of how legal rules and principles emerge, develop, and are ultimately reshaped or discarded. The case method is uniquely suited to the task of developing in students an understanding of legal relevance and the capacity to state, analyze, evaluate, and compare concrete fact situations. Students learn to employ sources as they are used by lawyers and judges and then to formulate, on their own responsibility, both results and the propositions on which these results rest.

This capacity and understanding are no doubt the most important lessons that a law student can learn in law school, but their acquisition may not require three years. Moreover, exclusive reliance on a discussion method may leave the student uncertain about – or even unaware of – important legal rules, practices, and institutions. Much of what is required for a full legal culture can probably be more quickly and easily obtained by reading – or hearing – systematic presentations. Finally, the discussion method – perhaps because it is seen as less fruitful in the more advanced stages of legal education – may after the first year come to bore students and teachers alike.

For these reasons, among others, recent decades have witnessed a decline in popularity of the case method, especially in the second and third years. Some of the innovations encountered can be looked upon as variations on the method. For example, problems may be used to supplement or replace cases. But, the traditional lecture method has also regained some of its former popularity.

## 4. Clinical Legal Education and Law Reviews

Some of the most interesting and dramatic changes in law pedagogy during the last thirty years of the twentieth century have been seen in the development of clinical legal education. Clinical legal education currently takes two forms. In one, students are presented with a simulated factual situation and asked to develop evidence, give counsel, and take appropriate procedural steps. The basic effort is to expose students to the realities of law practice in a controlled context so that they will learn both by doing and by criticism of what they do. Currently, many law schools offer simulated workshop courses in trial advocacy, negotiation, federal litigation, and similar practice-oriented skills. In these workshops, often given intensively over short intervals, the students practice their skills and receive critique, often from experienced practitioners who assist in the instruction on a part-time or volunteer basis.

The other form taken by clinical legal education is less structured. Students engage in actual law practice, usually representing indigent clients in domestic relations, housing, benefits, and other contested matters, under the supervision of experienced lawyers who serve as clinical instructors. This approach has the advantage, of course, of actuality and realism. A challenge to this form of clinical legal education stems from the fact that life rarely consistently presents itself in the guise best suited to pedagogical purposes. It is difficult to achieve consistency in experience or exposure for each individual student.

Since the 1970s, when clinical legal education began to become a part of American law school curricula, considerable progress has been made in achieving high quality of instruction and consistency of experience. Although controversial at the beginning, now it is difficult to imagine an American law school curriculum without several clinical offerings. As legal education in general becomes more theoretical, and in the absence of formal programs for skills development and transition into the profession, clinical legal education may be seen as young jurists' best opportunity to gain the practical skills and professional self-confidence to launch their legal careers.

One further aspect of American legal education is worth noting. A substantial part of the legal education of many American law students is acquired in student activities that occur outside the formal course of study. This is particularly true for those students who work on a school's law review.

The oldest American law review is that at Harvard, established by students in 1877. Today, more or less similar publications are found at almost all law schools. Indeed, more specialized journals have sprung up at many schools. In almost all cases, the editing is done entirely by law students, free from faculty control. The lead articles in these journals are selected by the student editors from among manuscripts submitted by legal scholars and lawyers. Each issue also includes student writing, usually taking the form of either a treatment of an area of the law or a sharply focused discussion of a recent decision or a recent piece of legislation. These student-edited journals have long been the most important American professional legal periodicals.

## 5. Examinations and Grading

A word is in order with respect to the examination and grading system in American law schools. Examinations are written; there is no counterpart to the oral examination known on the continent of Europe. Usually the instructor sets questions that require the student to analyze and handle several sets of more or less complicated facts from the perspective, depending on how the question is put, of a lawyer, a judge, or a legislator drafting a law. For most subject matters, essay questions, as such, are only infrequently set by the examiner. Students are examined at the end of each course by the course instructor who sets, reads, and grades the examination. There are no external examiners.

Grading is today done on an anonymous basis. Over the decades, there have been many changes in the form in which grades are given. At some law schools, formerly all grades were numerical and the class was ranked in order from top to bottom. In most law schools, class rankings have been dropped and letter grades have been substituted for numerical grades. Some schools have gone further and use a pass-fail system. Usually such systems amount to a pass system; today, very few American law students fail regardless of the grading system utilized.

## 6. Transitions to Law Practice

Today, a significant number of law students obtain legal work in law firms or in governmental law offices after their first year of law school. Following their second year, most law students spend most of the summer vacation in legal work. American law firms use summer job offers to get an impression of potential future employees and to attract students in whom they are interested to their practices. Summer experiences give students some insight into law practice and thus provide a better basis for the important career choice that students normally make in the course of their third year of school.

In the final year of law school, the students interview with law firms and other employers of lawyers whose work, geographical location, size, and other characteristics are attractive. Students whose academic performance has been outstanding and whose personality is well fitted to legal practice are likely to receive a number of attractive offers.

Students with high academic records may seek to serve for one or two years as law clerk to a federal judge or to a judge on a high state appellate court. Especially desired are clerkships with Justices of the U.S. Supreme Court. The clerkship experience is valued in part because of the insight that close contact with a judge can give into the working of the legal process. Generally speaking, graduates with records of moderate distinction from good law schools obtain satisfying employment upon graduation. Starting salaries – especially in large firms in metropolitan centers – remain very attractive.

## 7. Admission to the Bar

Before the law school graduate can practice law in the full sense, he or she must obtain admission to a state bar. As the federal nature of the American legal system would suggest, regulation of the legal profession is the concern of the states, each of which has its own requirements for admission to practice. All applicants for admission are required to take a written examination that usually lasts two to three days.

The examination is typically largely administered by the bar of the state in question under the supervision of the highest state court. In recent years, all states have adopted a national "multistate" examination as a part of their own state bar examinations. The non-multistate portions of each state's bar examinations usually concentrate on the laws of the particular state where bar admission is being sought. Accordingly, before attempting a state's bar examination, graduates of national law schools typically spend two to three months studying in an intense "bar review course" to familiarize themselves thoroughly with the particularities of that state's law – particularities that often were not considered in law school. A significant percentage of those who sit for the bar examination do not succeed on their first try; most of them pass on a later attempt.

Once the hurdle of the bar examination has been surmounted and the ethics committee satisfied as to the character of the applicant, in most states the young lawyer immediately becomes a full-fledged member of the state bar. There is no "Referendariat" or clerkship period. One is a qualified member of the legal profession upon passage of the bar exam and admission to practice by the highest court of a state.

## B. THE AMERICAN LEGAL PROFESSION

In discussing the structure and characteristics of the legal profession, it is important to bear in mind that the profession is a unitary one; a distinction between *avocats, avoués,* and *notaires* is unknown in the United States; and the English distinction between solicitor and barrister does not exist. Of course, specialization occurs. For example, some American lawyers devote most of their time to the presentation of cases in court. Others spend almost all of their time in office work and counseling. However, these specializations reflect personal predilections and are not required.

Lawyers have played important roles in national and local politics since the early days of the American republic. Over half of the signers of the American Constitution were lawyers. Both the national and state legislatures are typically well-seeded with members of the bars. Of America's forty-three presidents, twenty-five have been lawyers.

The prominence of lawyers in political life may be related to the relative importance of the legal practitioner in America's systems of civil and criminal justice and the importance of legally informed private initiatives in all American political and regulatory institutions. The American systems require that private attorneys play major roles in the initiative and resolution of litigation, in the structuring and documentation of all kinds of transactions, and in the protection of their clients' from one another and from unwarranted government intrusion in their affairs. This social – political emphasis on private, as opposed to governmental, legal initiative and defense means that private lawyers occupy a rather more central role in the overall political and governmental structure than is the case in many other modern democracies. Another result is that America has developed an enormous cadre of legal practitioners, nearly one million as of the writing of this edition. This is the largest absolute number of lawyers as well as the highest number of lawyers per capita of the general population of any nation in the world. The United States as a whole sports one fully trained and licensed lawyer for every three hundred persons.

There is no distinct judicial or prosecutorial career in the United States. Judges are typically recruited from among mature lawyers who have distinguished themselves in the practice of law, in government service, or in academic life; the state attorney-general and staff are recruited largely from lawyers in private practice and, in due course, these functionaries often return to private practice.

Another characteristic of the American legal profession is that many lawyers spend a part of their careers in government service; shifts between public employment and private practice are frequent. Of course, some lawyers have their entire career in government service. But many – and among them are often the most influential – combine periods of public service with periods of private practice. Something similar occurs with respect to house or corporate counsels – salaried lawyers in the employ of private business concerns. Many of these are recruited from among lawyers with substantial experience in private practice. However, it is rather rare for a lawyer, once employed as a house counsel, to return to private practice.

## 1. Private Law Firms

Private practice can be carried on by a single lawyer practicing alone; however, many lawyers, especially in cities, practice in firms or partnerships. Law firms come in every size, from small partnerships of two or three lawyers to large multinational enterprises with thousands of legal professionals. The traditional law-firm structure was a general partnership consisting of a number of partners and a group of younger employed lawyers, usually called "associates." Currently, law firms operate as partnerships, limited partnerships, professional service corporations, and limited liability companies.

Regardless of the formal structure of the firm, in each case the younger associates hope ultimately to become partners or principals in the firm and thereby entitled to share in the direction and the profits of the enterprise. In larger firms, only a small fraction of those initially hired as associates will ultimately succeed to the senior status; most will not. Those who do not have various courses open to them. Some, for example, become house counsel for private business corporations, others go into government service, still others continue private practice either alone or in another firm. The emergence of large law firms is a relatively recent phenomenon of the second half of the twentieth century. It appears to have been, in large part, a response to the growing complexity of modern law. Single practitioners and small law partnerships simply could not give the range of advice necessary to structure important business deals or effectively staff long and complex litigation.

## 2. Bar Associations and Regulation of the Bar

As indicated previously, under America's particular form of federalism, lawyers are regulated almost exclusively by the respective states. Each state determines for itself the qualifications for legal practice. Each state has its own apparatus to license and discipline members of the bar. In some states, the bar is considered to be a part of the "judicial branch" of government and, as such, is regulated by the state's highest court, acting in an administrative and even legislative capacity. In these states, court-promulgated rules govern the bar, and a court-sponsored agency enforces the standards of lawyer conduct. In other states, the bar is regulated by statute law adopted by the legislature or by a mixture of court rules and statutes.

In every state, there is a bar association. These associations generally promote the interests of lawyers within the state and are also concerned with maintaining professional and ethical standards. In a few states, the bar association is a quasi-public institution, membership is required of all lawyers, and the "unified bar association" is entrusted with the enforcement of professional standards. Regardless of exact form of the system, each state sanctions unprofessional conduct by reprimand, suspension, or disbarment.

In addition to state bar associations, there is a national bar association founded late in the nineteenth century. The American Bar Association is the largest professional organization in the United States or, for that matter, the world. With nearly three-quarters of a million members, it is active in many areas: law reform, professional responsibility, law-school accreditation, and continuing legal education, to name only a few.

### 3. Legal Aid and Access to Justice

A legal system that relies heavily on the private initiative of parties and their lawyers for the assertion or defense of legally protected interests poses real problems for people who are unable to afford to pay the cost of legal services. Traditionally, the bar recognized an ethical obligation to provide legal services to indigent parties in certain classes of cases. Indeed, in serious criminal matters, an accused is constitutionally entitled to legal representation.

In recent years, it has become clear that the legal needs of indigent Americans cannot be met by the voluntary efforts of the bar alone. Both state and federal governments have been required to expand the scope and availability of legal aid. For example, in many metropolitan and rural areas, legal service offices – financed by federal, state, and local sources – provide legal assistance for such matters as landlord–tenant and family-law controversies. In some areas, volunteer lawyers' projects coordinate the provision of services by lawyers on a voluntary basis. In recent decades, many law firms have increased the amount of legal aid they furnish on a *pro bono publico* basis.

All states and the federal government provide indigent criminal defendants with defense counsel for all criminal prosecutions in which imprisonment or a substantial fine can be imposed. Sometimes, particularly in urban areas, criminal defense services are provided by "public defenders," generally staff attorneys of a defense services organization. In more rural areas, private practitioners are assigned to defend indigent criminal defendants and paid modestly for their services from public funds.

Despite steady increases in the resources and programs devoted to providing legal services to indigent persons, the present perception is that the need for such services is now greater than it ever has been. The increasing complexity of social and political institutions make legal assistance a necessity even for relatively simple and basic matters, such as applying for public assistance. Increasing costs for many legal services are beginning to price the availability of legal help beyond the means of most Americans other than the most wealthy persons and concerns.

These developments are leading the bar and political leaders to consider more fundamental reforms to the American legal establishment. Some of these include support for litigants to appear and litigate "pro se" without lawyers, simplification of legal procedures and forms to require less legal assistance, authorizing the providing of "unbundled" legal services short of full representation to parties who cannot afford traditional lawyer representation, and reinforcement of government-supported neutral institutions to reduce the burden on parties and their counsel in legal activities. Some of these necessity-driven measures may ultimately lead to significant restructuring of the American legal system.

## 4. Lawyers' Fees and Compensation

The American system of lawyer compensation has several features that differ from practices in other parts of the world. In litigation, the English and German practice of placing ultimate responsibility for attorney's fees on the losing party is not followed in the United States. According to the "American Rule," each side bears its own litigation costs except for certain relatively minor court costs of an administrative nature. In certain kinds of cases, a litigant who successfully challenges the legality of governmental action can recover reasonable legal fees as approved by the court. This principle has been extended to a few categories of purely private claims, such as certain claims for employment discrimination.

Critics of the American Rule note that a defendant who defeats the plaintiff's claim is nonetheless burdened with the cost of doing so and that a successful plaintiff receives compromised compensation. On the other hand, the risk of having to pay the other party's fee if unsuccessful might deter plaintiffs of modest means from initiating meritorious litigation. Lawyers' heavy responsibility for successful outcomes in American litigation and the lack of a fee table or firm practice limiting potential fees also militate in favor of restricting liability for lawyers' fees to the party that retained the lawyer.

Fees are, for the most part, agreed upon between lawyer and client. The fee-table system, found in many European countries, is not used in the United States. An extreme result of this form of contractual freedom in the area of lawyer compensation is the "contingency fee," legal in every American state. Under a contingency fee arrangement, a plaintiff's lawyer can agree that he or she will only charge a fee if the plaintiff is awarded compensation in the litigation. If there is no recovery, there is no fee. On the other hand, if the case succeeds, the fee will typically be calculated as a percentage of the recovery. Percentages of 33 percent or even 40 percent of the amount recovered are typical, depending on the complexity of the case and the size of the potential recovery.

Contingency-fee arrangements are strictly regulated in most states, and the amount of compensation payable in individual cases is subject to court review for egregious unreasonableness. Contingent fees are especially frequent in personal-injury actions where these arrangements permit persons without means to litigate cases that their lawyers think are likely enough to produce recoveries and, hence, fees to justify the investment of their time and energy on a contingent basis.

## 5. The American Judiciary

A discussion of the American legal profession should not close without mention of the American judiciary because the judiciary springs from and is closely connected with the profession – perhaps more so than in many other legal systems.

The federal structure of the American judiciary and the division of jurisdiction and judicial function among the states and federal government were discussed in Chapter 4. The discussion herein focuses more on how judges are trained and selected and how their careers develop.

Although there is considerable diversity among the American jurisdictions in the selection and tenure of judges, in all cases, judges are chosen from the ranks of mature legal practitioners. There is no separate track for judicial aspirants after law school. A person who ultimately wants to be a judge generally will try to acquire practice seasoning and experience and place him- or herself in a position to eventually participate in the applicable selection process. Traditionally, in most states, leading practitioners would be eligible to serve on the bench after many years of law practice or mixed practice and government service. More recent years have seen a trend in some states toward younger judges who ascend the bench after relatively few years in practice, generally in a state prosecutor's office, and who then hope to be named to higher courts later on.

The manner of selection of judges and their tenure varies greatly among the American states. All federal "Article 3" judges, from the various district courts to the U.S. Supreme Court, are appointed by the President, confirmed by the U.S. Senate, and serve for life. Federal administrative and magistrate judges may be appointed by other agencies and serve for terms of years, with statutory protection against arbitrary removal.

Many states follow the federal model of appointment of judges, usually by the governor subject to legislative confirmation. In some states, such as Maine, judicial appointment is for a seven-year terms, with expectation of reappointment in the absence of serious misconduct.

In a number of American states, judges of some or all courts are popularly elected. Elected judges are more prevalent in the Midwest and the South and are the product of populist legislation from the nineteenth century. Elected judges typically serve for limited terms and are subject to reelection. The effect of electoral politics and the will of the populace on judicial independence (and, in some cases, judicial quality) have been demonstrated often enough to raise calls for reform that have been repeated over the years. In recent years, the growth of contributions and expenditures in some judicial campaigns has reemphasized some of the most trenchant criticisms of this system.

In some formerly elective states, compromise arrangements have been instituted, such as the Missouri Plan, under which judges are initially appointed but then subject to a popular review vote after a relatively short period of service. These reforms have mitigated the worst abuses that formerly prevailed in the states that have enacted them. However, in some states, the election of judges remains a popular political institution that has resisted all efforts at change or reform. Occasional scandal or question about the quality of some incumbents has not yet been able to force meaningful change of this anachronistic American institution.

In almost all jurisdictions, whether appointive or elective, eligibility for judgeships is frequently connected with politics. Political leaders such as presidents and governors tend to appoint judges with whom they have been politically associated. Judicial elections are political events. In recent years, there have been efforts to reduce the role of politics in judicial selection and to encourage merit candidates. In several jurisdictions, appointing officials have constituted advisory and screening panels to solicit qualified candidates and to review the qualifications of potential appointees. In some states, a judicial aspirant without political connection can apply for consideration via one of these panels.

Judicial tenure also varies from life tenure at the federal level and in some states to relatively short terms subject to political reelection. There is no particular system for judges to be professionally evaluated and considered for promotion to higher courts. Judges with life or appointive term tenure need only render a minimum performance to escape discipline or nonrenewal of their appointments. Elected judges need only to please the electorate that retains them in office. Thus, the mix of judicial independence and susceptibility to influence varies a good deal. What is generally absent, though, is any systemic oversight to reward good performance and motivate improvement within the judicial establishment.

American judges have traditionally shown strengths based on their relative maturity and their prior experiences as lawyers at the bar. They are seen as representative of the legal and political community rather than as a remote professional elite. On the other hand, the political dimension with popular election at its extreme must be seen as a severe drawback. Another limitation of the American system is the lack of any particular organized method of rewarding judicial competence by promotion within state or federal judiciaries.

# 11

# The United States and the Global
# Legal Community

AMERICAN LAW ACADEMICS SHOULD SPEAK AND WRITE
about the role and influence of the American legal system in
the modern legal world with some diffidence. In a sense, this is an
issue that is better addressed from the outside. Foreign jurists, who
experience the American legal system from the outside, are likely
to be in a much better position to gauge the effect and influence
of American legal institutions on the world legal order than is an
American academic or practitioner.

On the other hand, as the end of what some have called "the
American Century" has come and gone, the issue of America's
relationship with the other great and small lands, jurisdictions,
economic and political systems, and cultures of the modern world
has come very much to the fore. Questions that were often muted
during the long years of the Cold War are now fueling public
debate in the stark new world following the fall of the Berlin Wall,
September 11, 2001, and the American invasion of Iraq. This is a
time to talk and write frankly in the hope that honest dialogue will
increase understanding and enable us to work better together to
make the world a better place for all our grandchildren.

This chapter focuses on three main themes. The initial part
discusses the various structural and political conditions and circumstances that define and affect the relationship of American
law and the American legal system with the global legal order.

The second theme addresses the expansive role of American private law and the role of private litigants vis-à-vis the global legal order. The third part touches rather briefly on American restraint with respect to global legal institutions. It concludes with a few remarks on the potential role of American law in the world of the future.

## A. THE AMERICAN LEGAL SYSTEM IN WORLD CONTEXT

Unlike Roman law, which exerted influence over the world's legal systems for nearly two millennia, or even English, French, or German law, which spread to much of the then-civilized world during the nineteenth and early twentieth centuries, American law and legal institutions were not given much cognizance by other countries until the middle of the twentieth century. This was largely because (1) in contrast to the major European powers, America did not found many colonies abroad; (2) America's early economic activity was focused on developing its own vast territory; (3) American law was not in a form that encouraged export and emulation: and (4) the international language of discussion and exchange was French, and in scientific matters, German. America's language was widely spoken only within the empire of its motherland and cultural competitor, Great Britain.

The first two of these circumstances are matters of history that are generally known and do not bear further discussion. However, it may be worthwhile to consider why American law has traditionally not been susceptible to easy export and emulation abroad. The answer may lie in two particular features of the American system: the uncodified common law form of much of American private law, particularly during the nineteenth and early twentieth centuries, and the peculiar and extreme form of American federalism.

American private law in the basic fields of contract and tort began as common law inherited from England. Unlike codified civil law, which predominates in most of the world, common law was created by the decisions of judges. Published judicial decisions of innumerable individual cases, knitted together by the rule of *stare decisis*, gradually produced rules of decision that can be finely attuned to differences in operative fact. Americans, as well as Britons, point with pride to the judicial creativity represented by accretions of case law centuries old that gradually have evolved and adapted to the changing requirements of a modern economy and society.

The problem is that common law is difficult to export except to a colony of the mother country that can use the mother country's body of decided case law to serve as a reservoir of doctrine until the offspring system has built up a system of case law of its own. To take an actual example, when Japan decided to modernize its economy and political institutions and looked for a body of doctrine and procedural law, it could scarcely be expected to have adopted some thousands of preexisting decisions of English or American courts, have translated them into Japanese, and then asked Japanese lawyers and judges to use this mass of case law as the source of legal principles for the reformed Japanese legal system. It is not at all surprising that Japan adopted German codified civil law and civil procedure law in the late nineteenth century. The codified doctrines of civil law in Europe were and continue to be much more susceptible to comparative study and adaptation by foreign nations seeking to improve their legal systems than the case-law solutions of the Anglo-American world.

Moreover, America's unique history as a collection of British colonies that banded together to break free from the mother country and form a new federal state has resulted in a fragmentation of most private law and considerable public law among the fifty states. In most private law questions, American law is the law of a particular state, such as New York, California, or Maine. This was even more the case in the nineteenth and early twentieth century before the movement toward uniform law and the growth of federal economic legislation resulted in some coherence in certain areas. Back in the "old days," an observer from abroad would be hard put to determine what was the American law on any given social or political issue and would be required to look at legal resolutions of particular states as well as the central government through the lens of a complex federalism. Again, it is not surprising that countries seeking to modernize their legal systems would turn more readily to the national private-law regimes of the legal systems of Europe than attempt this kind of an exercise.

Very likely, language also played a part in the early days, when French was the language of diplomacy and German the language of science. In the nineteenth and early twentieth centuries, persons interested in studying American law would have had to be conversant in English, common enough in the British Empire but elsewhere scarcely a language of first resort. The influence of this language factor has become much more important, and in the other direction, in the world of the third millennium.

Indeed, a survey of the worldwide influence of modern legal systems as of the beginning of the twentieth century would have disclosed that German procedural and substantive law enjoyed far greater worldwide credibility and attention than did the law of any of the then forty-eight American states or of its federal government. The influence of German law on such future economic and political giants as Japan, Korea, and China at the end of the nineteenth and beginning of the twentieth centuries means that even as of today, more people live in countries with German-influenced legal systems than in lands that have followed the American model. German influence even appears in America's own Uniform

Commercial Code, which was originally conceived and long brought forward by Karl Lewellan, who received his early legal education at the University of Rostock, Germany.

Some of this changed at the end of World War II. The political and economic strength of the United States following the war and during the latter half of the twentieth century have inevitably led to export of American public- and private-law doctrine in several forms. For instance, the concept of written national constitutions interpreted by the judicial branch of government, refined and developed over a century and a half in the United States, took rapid root in post-war Europe, especially the Federal Republic of Germany. Over the last fifty years, European constitutionalism has developed its own special character from which Americans can now in turn learn new ideas and approaches. Most would agree, however, that its modern-day roots were derived from the American experience, adapted to Europe in the late 1940s and 1950s.

Other ways in which American law has extended its influence in the post–World War II world have been more indirect. The case law format and American federalism have continued to be significant hurdles to widespread adoption of private-law doctrine and procedural law. By and large, Europe, as well as those countries in the rest of the world that were influenced by European law and legal systems in the late nineteenth and early twentieth centuries, have tended to stick with their forms of civil and criminal procedure in favor of wholesale adoption of American models. Basic civil and criminal law doctrine has also been pretty much unaffected by American solutions.

On the other hand, it is also true that in many important areas of present-day law giving and law practice, American influence is profound and ongoing. This is true both in private and public national law and in public international law, although in opposite directions.

## B. AMERICAN PRIVATE LAW IN THE MODERN WORLD

Although there has been no widespread adoption in Europe or elsewhere of American state contract and tort law by foreign legal systems, nonetheless most present-day lawyers who practice international transactional law and engage in international litigation would be relatively helpless without a real knowledge of American substantive and procedural legal institutions. This is not because of any concerted governmental activity on either side of the Atlantic or Pacific. Rather, the current worldwide influence of American law and legal institutions is the result of (1) private negotiations in which American law is chosen to govern major transactions; (2) the role of international financial institutions, funded in part by the United States that condition financing participation on American-style legal arrangements; and (3) a more diffuse but not less effective transmission via educational and cultural means.

Probably the most significant expansion of the role of American private law has been to govern major financial transactions involving foreign entities. The almost universal rule that parties to transactions can pick the law to govern their relationship has permitted American banks, investment banks, major corporations, and other financially significant actors on the world economic stage to require that American law apply to transactions in which they participate. This has partly been out of necessity – from the American side. Many Americans have been and continue to be unfamiliar with any foreign languages. American lawyers, by and large, have little familiarity with the civil-law–based systems that govern most of the world. It is no wonder that they insist on application of the American law with which they are familiar when their client's economic power enables them to do so.

This kind of economically based law export does not necessarily reflect the relative objective merits of the American model compared with other legal regimens that could have come into

consideration. Many European lawyers have expressed bemuse-
ment at the awkward constructs needed to create binding contractual obligations because of the Anglo-American requirement
of consideration. Frequently, the extremely detailed form of
American contracts and financing instruments have seemed odd to
Europeans, who can document transactions with simpler instruments because of a more robust doctrine of good faith and commercial reasonableness.

American private law began to become relevant in London,
Frankfurt, and Paris because of increasing internationalization of
major American enterprises. For the reasons suggested previously,
American firms doing business abroad, merging with foreign entities, and forming foreign subsidiaries tended to prefer to be subject
to American law wherever possible. American law firms formed
branches abroad to provide these clients with American law support and to help manage their relationships with the foreign legal
environments in which they were doing business. It is significant
that, up to very recent times, many of these American branch
offices abroad tended to provide most of their legal services to
American clients and, to a large degree, on questions of American
law.

This export of American private law to protect American economic actors has been intertwined by a form of law export that is
connected with the kinds of economic and financial transactions
themselves. The economic expansion of the post–World War II era
has seen the development of many kinds of capital and financing
transactions that were unknown beforehand. Such major elements
of the modern commercial economy as equipment leasing and
financial derivatives were first brought to commercial significance
in the United States based on the structures and institutions of
American law. American lawyers and law firms developed a high
level of expertise in these new kinds of commercial transactions
and instruments. These kinds of transactions came to the world

economy not through the writings and teaching of academics but rather through their practical use by American lawyers in international transactions. As these kinds of transactions became commonplace in the international arena, it is not surprising that American law and legal forms would continue to be applied wherever they could and that there would be a degree of foreign adoption of American legal structures to govern foreign counterparts of these new elements of the commercial financing world.

Another example in this general area is the American law of bankruptcy reorganization. The concept of corporate reorganization had been a part of American bankruptcy law since before World War II, but was brought to a new level of sophistication and utility in the Bankruptcy Reform Act of 1976. This may have been an example of an idea whose time had come. In other parts of the world, it was becoming evident that traditional liquidation and apportionment bankruptcy regimes could result in unnecessary losses when corporate enterprises experienced financial difficulties. The American solution was at hand. It is not surprising that other governments found it a useful model and patterned their own reorganization legislation, to some extent, on it.

Another vehicle for the dissemination of American legal doctrine and institutions has been the activity of certain international financing organizations, particularly the International Monetary Fund (IMF) and the World Bank. The major role of the United States since World War II in the financing and operation of both of these organizations has resulted in a degree of law export by virtue of the requirements laid down by them as preconditions for loans or grants. For instance, following the fall of the Berlin Wall and the opening of the economies of Eastern Europe in the early 1990s, the World Bank provided loans to many foreign governments to update elements of their public economies, from transportation equipment to computers. However, those loans were only granted if the grantee nation had in place government procurement laws and other legal institutions that would give reasonable assurance that the grant monies would not be frittered away or diverted in corrupt transactions. The laws and legal institutions proposed to the grantee governments were typically American in form and drafted by American jurists. Often, they were translated and adopted rather uncritically to facilitate the desired grant or loan.

A similar form of law export has been connected with the activities of the World Trade Organization (WTO). Membership in the WTO requires a domestic legal system that protects many forms of property, including intellectual property. Although the law of intellectual property is old and developed in many nations, the United States has been very ready to insist that the local law of members of the global trading club must protect intellectual property to an extent similar to such protection in the United States.

The dismantlement of the Soviet Union resulted in a need in Eastern Europe and Central Asia for modernization and improvement of law and legal institutions to facilitate democratization and the functioning of market economies. It is not surprising that many of the Eastern European and Central Asian nations turned to American models to regulate their new private-enterprise economies. The U.S. State Department, in cooperation with the American Bar Association, has been active in providing consulting assistance and training for lawyers and judges to governments interested in American-style legal and governmental institutions. This effort has met with some success in such areas as stock market, bank, and utilities regulation. However, more idiosyncratic American institutions such as civil jury trial have not met with widespread acceptance. Instead, most of these lands rejuvenated and modernized their pre-Soviet civil law systems, many of which were based on the German model.

Taken together, this expansion of American law that is linked with America's strong position in the world economy cannot fail to affect the legal regimens of every developed and undeveloped economy that does business with American interests. This is the primary reason why large law firms in every country of the world need jurists who are familiar with American law to advise their major domestic clients.

## C. AMERICAN LITIGATION ABROAD

Another area in which American law has made itself felt abroad, sometimes to an inordinate extent, is the field of civil litigation. A certain expansiveness in American concepts of international jurisdiction has brought peculiar features of American tort law to the doorsteps of the rest of the world, where it is not always very welcome. Again, the bulk of this development has occurred since World War II, more specifically in the last thirty years of the twentieth century.

American law of international jurisdiction has been historically informed by its law of interstate jurisdiction. The United States is a union of independent states, each exercising its own civil and criminal jurisdiction. From the nation's beginnings, it has been vital that the rules of interstate jurisdiction not unduly burden interstate commerce or fracture the unity of the American economy. Such concepts of general jurisdiction, minimum contacts, tag jurisdiction, and the effects doctrine grew out of the need to foster interstate economic activity. Such generosity in interstate jurisdiction was not particularly problematical considering the relative similarity of the American states and continually improving means of communication among them.

America may have been a bit naive in applying such generous jurisdictional concepts to international civil jurisdiction as well. Legal doctrine, social priorities, economic conditions, and cultural values differ to a much greater degree among nations than among

American states. Respect for national sovereignty and differences in language are also important. America's generosity in recognition of foreign judgments is little compensation for a civil jurisdiction that is seen by many foreigners as onerously expansive.

Part of the expansiveness of American civil jurisdiction is undoubtedly fueled by the economic conditions that gave rise to the spread of American transactional law abroad. The multifarious activities of American economic elements in all the world may have made it seem easier to expand the reach of American courts as well.

The unwelcome expansiveness of American civil jurisdiction is complemented by American choice of law doctrine that sometimes causes American legal norms to be applied to circumstances and transactions that seem much more closely related to the legal and social priorities of another modern jurisdiction. Should the question of what duty is owed to a passenger on a ski lift in Austria turn on whether the passenger was an American or a German?

Finally, the expansive American civil jurisdiction sometimes brings to foreign actors legal liabilities and responsibilities to which they have not consented. In the commercial transactions realm at least, it can be said that American law is generally applied with the consent of the foreign party. In the field of tort law, however, American procedural and sometimes substantive law can be foisted on a foreign enterprise that has certainly not bargained for it. That makes it all the more onerous in the experience.

Two areas may serve as examples. American substantive as well as procedural law have been applied to products liability claims filed against foreign enterprises for injuries sustained by both American and foreign consumers. In the human-rights area, American courts recently were the theaters of several major efforts to secure compensation for various groups of victims of the Nazi regime and World War II, most of whom lived in Europe. Similar suits have been filed by victims of apartheid and of totalitarian regimes in the Philippines and other parts of the world.

These latter suits may seem somewhat ironic in view of human-rights issues over American treatment of persons in detention at Guantánamo Bay and in Iraq. However, American courts are open to these persons as well, some suits are pending, and when called on to do so, American courts have provided relief.

Parties abroad who become embroiled in American civil litigation are also offended by American discovery procedures, which often result in incredible costs and sometimes invade the realm of information considered confidential by foreign enterprises. Foreign responses to the expansiveness of American civil justice have not been effective to ease the friction. To be sure, American judgments for punitive damages will not be enforced in Germany. However, that does not help the German firm that has operations and assets in the United States from which judgments can be satisfied there. Blocking statutes designed to protect European company secrets from the prying eyes of American discovery have similarly failed to prevent U.S. district judges from requiring European parties to American litigation to cooperate with American discovery procedures.

The most disappointing recent development in this area has been the failure of the delegates to the Hague Convention on Jurisdiction and Recognition and Enforcement of Judgments to come to agreement on principles and limits of international jurisdiction that are symmetrical on both sides of the Atlantic. Perhaps what we have learned in this dialogue will enable us to reach more common ground in the next round, whenever that may occur. An encouraging development is the adoption by UNIDROIT and the ALI of *Principles of Transnational Civil Procedure*, an effort by European and American academics and practitioners to identify principles for conduct of civil litigation that would be acceptable on both sides of the Atlantic.

## D. AMERICAN PUBLIC LAW AND THE MODERN
### DEMOCRATIC WORLD

A word should be said about the influence of American public law and legal institutions in the modern world. Many aspects of American democracy and its public legal order have been admired abroad since the times of de Tocqueville. Some of them, such as the written constitution and the notion of judicial elaboration of that constitution, have served as models for similar developments worldwide. Some of this emulation was voluntary as formerly colonial or even Soviet countries evolved into self-governing democracies. In some cases, the American constitutional model was promoted to former enemies emerging from post-war occupations.

It should be stressed again that American constitutionalism and much of American public law does not lend itself to easy adoption. America's peculiar form of federalism, largely a product of its own colonial history, is not susceptible to easy transplantation. With the possible exception of Switzerland, the United States is the most thoroughly federalized nation in the modern world in the sense that power is more deeply and fundamentally divided among state and federal governments than anywhere else. The result is tremendous complexity and overlap between jurisdictions and responsibilities of states and the federal government. Institutions and responsibilities of public law are fragmented and divided both horizontally and vertically. Because so many areas of public law are within the overlapping competencies of state and federal governments, in many important areas of public concern there is no unitary system with a clear set of policies and social priorities.

Take, for example, criminal law. The fifty states plus the federal government all have separate and complete systems of criminal justice. The same conduct can be punished under the law of one or more states and under federal law. There is some variation in criminal procedure (subject to constitutional minima) and considerable variation in criminal and penal policy among the states and the federal government. Some states have not had capital punishment for more than a century; others are killing hundreds of convicted persons each year. There is no wonder that this hotchpotch does not commend itself to easy study and emulation by other nations.

To be sure, there are some underlying themes of public law that have found widespread resonance abroad. The concept of judicial review of the constitutionality of legislative action is now embodied in the legal orders of several leading nations of the world, albeit in different institutional forms.

The institution of jury trial was developed in England but, in the last century, America became its leading proponent. Since jury trial was first praised by de Tocqueville in the 1830s, it continues to awaken interest abroad, at least in criminal cases. The nineteenth and twentieth centuries saw a number of experiments with jury trial in France, Japan, and other countries. Currently, Russia and Korea are experimenting with forms of jury trial as reforms to their criminal justice system. On the other hand, efforts of the American trial bar to export jury trial in civil cases have met with a cool reception.

Finally, in those areas where American public law has developed to manage and govern a modern economy, there has been a degree of influence based on the actual merits of the solutions reached. Examples include the influence of American federal legislation for regulation of financial markets and bankruptcy. As indicated previously, sometimes this influence has been intensified by the requirements of international financing or regulatory bodies such as the World Bank or the WTO, which have required American-style regulatory regimes as conditions to financings or membership.

One interesting example of U.S. influence on public law in Europe started with the adoption by the U.S. military government in Germany of anti-trust regulations in 1947. The German Parliament replaced these by a comprehensive anti-trust law in 1958, which was based in part on the American anti-trust legislation and reflected American anti-trust theory. The U.S. influence can be traced to the fact that some of the top jurists in the German Federal Cartel Office received some of their legal training in the United States. Currently, elements of American anti-trust law are once again under consideration as the European Union and its Member States consider whether private anti-trust remedies like those available in the United States should be expanded in Europe.

### E. AMERICA AND THE WORLD LANGUAGE OF LAW

The influence of American law and legal institutions throughout the world had been immeasurably furthered by the general acceptance of English as a world language. In recent years, English has also become the world language of law.

The intimate relationship between law and language is well known. All legal precepts are embedded in language traditions that give them meaning. Legal principles and terms are difficult to translate to persons not familiar with the language in which they were created. That is why comparative law scholars must be equipped with skills in multiple languages to properly understand and analyze the legal systems or norms that they are comparing.

The nearly universal knowledge and use of the English language makes American law and legal culture immediately accessible to practically anyone in the world who has a good secondary education. Not only academics and legal scholars but also ordinary lawyers, business people, and journalists can learn about American law in the language in which it is created. The huge secondary literature about American law is similarly accessible. So is the immense American popular culture involving the law, discussed in greater detail herein. For instance, when the American book, *A Civil Action*, was assigned for reading by a class on American civil justice at the University of Freiburg in 2001, the great majority of the class chose to read it in English rather than the easily available German translation.

The accessibility of American law and legal thinking to persons who use English as their second language is enhanced by the nature of American law as a law of practical outcomes rather than abstract principle. By and large, American common and statute law focuses more on desired policy outcomes in specific real-world circumstances than on abstract, logically coherent principles. Dialogue concerning these policy issues and outcomes does not require a knowledge of the many nuances of English language and rhetoric that might be required for discourse on abstract philosophical legal principles, where the exact meanings of words and terms would be more important. Its lack of theoretical structure makes American law more accessible to persons not imbued with the English language from birth.

This universality of English as a world second language means that jurists throughout the world can talk not only with Americans and other native speakers but also with each other about American law and legal culture. The commonality of English language enables American law to become a common element of discussion among world jurists in a way that no other law can be.

## F. AMERICAN LEGAL CULTURE ON THE WORLD SCENE

The influence of American law abroad is closely related to the spread of American popular and general culture throughout the world. Spurred by such interrelated factors as America's economic success in the last half of the twentieth century, the presence of substantial numbers of Americans in Europe during the Cold War, and the universality of the English language, American culture has had a profound effect – for good and for ill – on the general culture of the twentieth- and twenty-first-century world.

American media culture in particular has projected images of American life, including American law, in every land. Boys and girls, young men and women learn early from movies and television about American notions of the law and lawyers. At the turn of the twenty-first century, as many members of law classes in Freiburg, Germany, were aware of the American TV lawyer programs *Allie McBeal* and *LA Law* as were members of similar classes in Cambridge, Massachusetts. Young Europeans and East Asians are exposed to jury trial, (American) constitutional rights, and cross-examination at about the same time in their cultural development as are young Americans. The relative prominence of legal drama in American popular culture means that foreign consumers of this material are all the more likely to get a lot of it early.

One byproduct of this "soft-law" export is that foreigners may be coming to form their own images of lawyers and what they do partly in the American image. One would think that foreign-trained jurists might face such American practices as witness examination and cross-examination by lawyers, or argument to a jury, with some reluctance and difficulty. Whatever may have been the case in the past, in recent years, the experience in American skills training programs such as the Harvard Trial Advocacy Workshop makes clear that foreign jurists now have no difficulty whatsoever in adapting to the cultural role of the American lawyer. In the early years of the twenty-first century, foreign LLM students from East Asia as well as Europe have shown themselves to be indistinguishable from Americans in their ability to function in the hurly-burly American trial process.

This phenomenon of popular culture is complemented by the immense interest of foreign jurists in exposure to American legal education. Each year, American law schools provide post-graduate education to more than a thousand outstanding jurists from foreign lands in American as well as global law and legal doctrine. They come not only because of the attraction of the American economy and the lure of the fruits of free enterprise, they come also because American law schools offer instruction in English, a language that many peoples of the world understand and use, and because American law schools provide programs specifically designed for foreign jurists.

These young jurists return to their native lands with an appreciation of the positive aspects of American law and, hopefully, leave most of the negative features behind. Many become leaders in the bench, bar, and governmental administrations of their native countries. It is not surprising that their exposure to American law and legal thinking should inform their future careers in these capacities at least to some extent.

Sometimes the glitz of American popular culture or the mind-opening experiences of foreign LLM students will generate enthusiasm for particular features of institutions of American law and a desire to transplant those institutions abroad. This kind of enthusiasm resonates with the enthusiasm of most Americans for their own legal system so that there are, from time to time, efforts to introduce such individual features as American jury trial, contingency fees, and class actions in other parts of the world. The discipline of comparative law teaches, however, that piecemeal adoption of individual legal institutions without particular regard for the function of the system as a whole is not likely to be successful and may disturb fundamental systemic balances or cultural values.

For instance, the entrepreneurial lawyer, who works on contingent fees, is an important guarantor of access to the American system of civil justice. Introduction of such a figure into the German legal culture, however, might seriously undermine the institutional role of the lawyer as a professional organ of the system of justice and upset the systemic equilibrium founded on this concept.

For another example, one can look to recent developments in Korea. There, the recent upsurge in democratic government has engendered an interest in American-style jury trial as a means of introducing democratic values and legitimacy to the activities of the judicial branch of government. Past experience has shown that the jury is not easy to transplant. Any effort to do so requires reexamination and adaptation of a number of judicial and societal institutions. Jury trial procedures are based on a certain relationship of lawyer and judge. Adoption of such procedures may require reexamination of such fundamental issues as lawyer training and compensation and the status and work of judges in the justice system.

### G. AMERICA AND WORLD PUBLIC LAW

America's outward orientation with respect to its own institutions and rules of private law is not matched by a corresponding receptivity toward international law and supranational legal regimes governing all nations of the globe, including the United States. Many of America's friends around the globe are disappointed and concerned about the reluctance of the United States to recognize the applicability of international legal norms and to participate in various organs of world governance. The so-called hegemony of American law is perceived as all the more onerous because the United States steadfastly refuses to subject itself to international norms that virtually all other modern regimes have embraced. This tendency seems to have reached an extreme during the first years of the twenty-first century.

At the outset, it should be observed that America has historically been somewhat reluctant to embrace international treaties and alliances. In his departure speech, George Washington admonished the young nation to eschew foreign alliances. Throughout the nineteenth century, the Atlantic and Pacific Oceans seemed to obviate the need for the kinds of treaty alliances that maintained the balance of power in Europe at the time. America came into World War I very late and refused to participate in the League of Nations, despite President Wilson's key role in helping to found that organization. Americans' reluctance to entrust national interests to supranational institutions has deep roots.

World War II brought the United States out of its traditional isolation. By the end of that global conflict, it was clear that oceans were no barriers to modern weapons and that world security depended on strong and reliable multinational organizations such as the North Atlantic Treaty Organization (NATO) and the United Nations (UN). The Cold War, which arrayed two vast alliances against each other in a political and military standoff, confirmed the importance of international institutions to American interests. The United States entered into bilateral and multilateral treaties and organizations at a level of engagement that would have scarcely seemed imaginable a generation before.

American engagement with international law and legal institutions began to diminish after the disastrous experience in Vietnam. Although that was scarcely an exercise in international cooperation, the Vietnam debacle caused many Americans to look inward and concentrate on American culture and institutions, to try to recapture the good old American way, to reassure themselves that America was still the very best place in the world to be. Professor Detlev Vagts commented regretfully on this trend in 1988 at an international law conference in Thessaloniki, Greece, in the following terms:

> It has been since the disastrous venture in Vietnam and particularly during the presidency of Ronald Reagan that observers have begun to see signs of a new United States deviation from the general understanding of international law.

Professor Vagts cited increased American dissatisfaction with UN agencies as well as the American withdrawal from the jurisdiction of the International Court of Justice with respect to the Nicaragua controversy and noted that American international law scholars seemed at the time to be more concerned with defending the actions of the American government than addressing norms of universal applicability.[1]

The fall of the Wall and the removal of the Soviet Union as a serious contender for military world domination left the United States for the time being as the single strongest military power. The phenomenon of American exceptionalism has come into full bloom. United States political leadership currently seems reluctant to exercise America's current measure of economic and military power only within the framework of international institutions and alliances focused on global security, such as the UN. Instead, there has been an unseemly flexing of American military muscles and an unfortunate attitude of "America first" that has undermined the U.S. image in the world and has failed to support and promote global security through international cooperation. The ideas that every country except the United States should be subject to international war-crimes jurisdiction, or that the rest of the world can agree to restrict emissions but that the world's largest energy consumer will not, are as distasteful to many Americans as they are to people in the rest of the world.

History is full of examples of how relatively overweening economic and military power has brought a tendency to dominate rather than support, a tendency to believe in the importance of one's own interests rather than the common interest, a certain arrogance of power. Many Americans had hoped that America's

---

[1] Detlev Vagts, *Nationalism and International Lawyers; Centrifugal and Centripetal Forces in the International Legal System* (Thessaloniki Institute of Public International Law, 1992).

history, its fundamentally democratic form of government, its values of freedom and equality would have made us immune to this historical human failing. Many still hope that the lessons of history, international dialogue, and greater understanding of the interdependence of all citizens of the modern world will bring the American people quickly to a realization of the folly of any belief that America can carry on this way for long and to a mitigation of the consequences of what has happened so far.

Sad to say, it cannot be denied that America's recent actions have tended to undermine the influence of American institutions of public law in the world at large. American constitutionalism has been a beacon for the development of constitutional democracy throughout the world. Its delayed and insufficient response to the excesses of Guantánamo Bay and Iraq certainly diminish its light. The continued use of the death penalty in the United States undermines America's voice in human rights. Results of the 2000 presidential election make American electoral democracy somewhat suspect.

Present conditions pose an interesting dichotomy. Over the second half of the twentieth century, American influence on private law and legal culture and, to a lesser extent, national public law has been profound and is ongoing. At the same time, American engagement in international law and legal institutions is now seen as rather negative and in disrepute. Is the current situation tenable? Or is the world in a time of transition that will lead to a new role of the United States in the world legal order?

## H. AMERICA AND THE LEGAL WORLD OF THE FUTURE

What will be the ongoing influence of the United States on private, public, and international law in the world of the future? Although the outlook seems very uncertain, some predictions can be hazarded.

To the extent that influence on private law is based on economic power, such as cases in which investment banks insist that the law of New York apply to international financings, the influence of American law will continue to depend on relative economic power. To the extent that American investment banks continue as preeminent in the fields of corporate acquisitions, mergers, and major corporate financing on a worldwide basis, American law will continue to be exported in such transactions.

On the other hand, if and when economic players associated with some other legal culture obtain the economic power to specify the law that will apply, the law chosen by these players will gain in influence. This evolution will, of course, be affected by intrinsic merit of the respective rules and regimes. Some non-American investors or deal makers may be accustomed to and comfortable with American law based on the recent history. In the long run, choice of law will follow economic power.

It is difficult to imagine that the United States will maintain the degree of influence exercised over the last fifty years as a source of national public law. There are many functioning democracies in the world. There are many ways fundamental human rights can be recognized and safeguarded. America can no longer claim to be the foremost guardian of freedom and equality. American legal institutions are and will continue to be one among many choices for public-law solutions and institutions.

American law's influence will continue to be promoted by the use of English as an international language. Easy access to law in its original language facilitates comparison and adoption immeasurably. That factor cannot be denied and should not be underestimated.

American civil litigation will come reluctantly in line with the rest of the world. The American system of civil dispute resolution lies well outside the world mainstream in terms of complexity and expense. Too much of America's national resources are expended on making this highly privatized system work. American public civil justice will have to move more in the direction of the systems of civil justice in the civil law world in order to survive as a viable institution on the international stage as the world gets ever smaller and the world economy becomes more integrated. The developments in England, which reformed its civil justice system substantially in the direction of continental Europe at the end of the last century, may show us the way.

That is not to say that there will not be influences both ways. As we watch the actual use of jury trial diminish in the United States, Korea, and Russia, consider how forms of this institution can be introduced into their legal systems. Europeans skeptical about American-style entrepreneurial class actions are considering various forms of collective litigation to make civil justice remedies more accessible and efficient.

Scholars from Europe and the United States are developing principles of transnational civil procedure that embody both European and American elements. As we approach a unified world economy, differences among the civil justice systems that serve that economy will tend to diminish. This tendency has been discernable for some time now and will certainly continue. Disappointments such as the recent Hague impasse should be regarded as temporary setbacks rather than any indication of a divergent future.

Finally, it seems clear that American exceptionalism vis-à-vis international public law is a phenomenon of finite duration. The United States will not continue indefinitely as the world's predominant economic and military power. History has shown that no country has ever been able to maintain such a position for a long time. Maintaining a role of world economic and military leadership is exhausting. Inevitably, some other power or combination of powers will rise to challenge the hegemony. When it is clear that America's unilateral power will not protect American interests and guarantee its security, it seems highly likely that American leaders and the voters who elect them will see the value of international institutions and relationships that do.

The past challenges of World War II and the Cold War caused the United States to abandon go-it-alone policies in favor of membership in international alliances and organizations to recover and maintain world peace. It is already becoming clear that America's current adventure in unilateral foreign policy through war is much more expensive and difficult than ever imagined by our leaders. Current American overtures to Europe reflect more than a desire to have Europeans and Americans smile at each other again. It is also clear that challenges posed by the rise of China as an economic and potential military power, by the activities of regimes such as North Korea and Iran, and indeed by the entire imbroglio in the Middle East, can only be solved by concerted activity of the world's leading nations. No single nation, no matter how powerful at a particular time, can serve as policeman for the world.

It is to be hoped that the decline of America's comparative economic and political power will occur in such a manner as to preserve international order and spare current and future generations of American citizens the consequences of violent or precipitate readjustment. However, it seems inevitable that it will come and that as world relationships change, the value of international law, international legal organizations, and an international legal order will become more apparent to even isolationist America.

Throughout recorded history, various countries and civilizations have enjoyed times of preeminence when their economic, legal, and cultural institutions exercised great influence in the remainder of the then world and were sometimes seen as hegemonic. Ancient Rome, seventeenth-century Spain, eighteenth-century France, and nineteenth-century England spread culture, political thought, and law far beyond their traditional national borders. These influences have persisted and enriched the world long after the political and economic power that originally projected them had receded and dissipated. Perhaps the influence of American law and legal institutions on the global legal order will be seen in this light by the world to come.

# Index

Index

# Index

Inquisitorial principle, 168–169
Instructions to jurors, 219–220
Internal Revenue Code, 6
International commercial arbitration,
    protection from adjudicatory
    jurisdiction through, 246
International Court of Justice, 293
International law. *See also* World legal
    order and American law
    reluctance of US to accept, 291, 293
International Monetary Fund (IMF)
    and influence of American law
    on world legal order, 280–281
Interrogatories to jurors, 219
Interstate commerce, regulation of,
    108–116
    areas of state concern and, 112
    cigarette manufacturers, 114
    deference to courts, 113
    discrimination in favor of local
        commerce, 112
    early reluctance of Congress to exert
        power, 111–112
    *Gibbons v. Ogden*, 109–111, 146
    guns on school premises, 115–116
    health, state laws protecting,
        112–113
    *Lopez; United States v.*, 115–116
    New Deal legislation, 114–115
    overlapping federal and state
        regulation, 113–114
    overview, 109
    police powers of states and, 112–113
    recent limits on Congressional
        power, 115–116
    sensitivity to state interests, 115
    steamship monopolies, 109–111
    taxation and, 113
    UCC, reasons for refraining from
        adopting at federal level, 115,
        130–131
Iraq War, 284, 294
Isolationism of US and world legal
    order, 291–292

Jackson, Andrew, 154
Japan
    American jury trial system, influence
        of, 286
    German law, influence of, 276
Jefferson, Thomas, 108, 142, 154
"Judge-made" law, authority for, 37
Judges, 269–272
    election of state court judges, 270
    jury trials, role in, 224–226
    legal background of, 264
    Missouri Plan, 270
    qualifications of, 269–270
    selection of
        federal judges, 270
        political considerations in, 271
        state court judges, 270–271
        Supreme Court Justices, 270
    strengths and weaknesses of, 271–272
    tenure of, 271
Judicial branches
    federal courts (*See* Federal courts)
    state courts, 116–117 (*See also* State
        courts)
Judicial decisions
    advisory opinions, reluctance to issue,
        12
    common law
        authority for, as, 27
        importance in, 7
    detailed reasoning of opinions, 7
    dicta, 11
    facts of case, limited to, 159–160
    holdings, 11–12
    "judge-made" law, authority for, 37
    legislation, overruling through
        comparative law analysis, 10–11
        Constitutional matters, 11
        overview, 45
    organization of, 7
    particular case, effect on, 8–9
    publication of, 7
    *res judicata*, 13
    retroactive effect, 13

# Index

South Africa, expansiveness of
American jurisdiction in human
rights law and, 284
Sovereign immunity for prosecutors,
196
Specific performance
common law, at, 3
equity, at, 3
Standing, relaxation of requirements
for, 140
*Stare decisis*
Constitutional matters, power of
legislatures to override judicial
decisions, 11
courts bound by own decisions, 9–10
differing views regarding, 10
federalism, effect on, 10
hierarchical principle, 9
judicial innovation and, 36
judicial review constrained by, 159
legislation, applicability to
interpretation of, 15–16
legislatures overriding judicial
decisions
comparative law analysis, 10–11
Constitutional matters, 11
limits on, 11
multiple grounds, decisions based on,
12–13
overruling of precedent, America and
England contrasted, 36
overview, 9
power of judges, as limit on, 37
State bar associations, 266
State constitutions
criminal law, protections regarding,
192
English common law, reception of, 33
European civil codes compared, 5–6
jury trials in criminal law,
incorporation of, 200
retroactive application of statutes
under, 67
rise of, 5

state courts, authority of based in,
116
state legislatures, as foundation of, 5
State courts, 116–117
adjudicatory jurisdiction in, 232
appellate courts
scope of review, 117
structure, 117
choice of law in, 232
conflict of laws in, 231–232
criminal jurisdiction, 121, 189
domestic relations jurisdiction, 121
exclusive jurisdiction, 121
federal issues, determining, 120, 121
federal question jurisdiction, 122–123
judges, selection of, 270–271
jury trials in
criminal law, in, 200
overview, 117
private international law in, 231–232
recognition and enforcement of
foreign judgments in, 232, 237
removal of federal court actions to,
121
rules from other legal orders,
application of, 121, 122
state constitutions, authority of based
in, 116
structure of court systems, 117
ultimate review of issues, 121
State Department, promotion of
American legal institutions in
post-Soviet nations by, 281
State executive branches, 107
State legislatures
charitable immunity doctrine,
effect of legislative inaction on,
45–46
failure to overrule case law through
legislation as acceptance of
common law, 45
hierarchy of legislation, 14–15
judicial role in creating law, effect on,
6